Wild C...

PRAISE FOR *WEIRD LIKE US*

"An elegantly argued piece of cultural criticism. . . . Powers's personal-as-political argument, which has the potential to move bohemia from the garret to the townhouse . . . [is] refreshing and hopeful."—James Poniewozik, *New York Times*

"Ann Powers takes us on an intimate, thought-provoking, and surprising joyride through her own private bohemia—and America's."—Katha Pollitt

"There may be no truer test of Powers's ability to engage a reader than to say that . . . I kept finding myself forced to reconsider my own life. . . . [*Weird Like Us*] raises a central and compelling question: What are the parts of our youth that we ought to struggle to maintain, and what are the aspects of maturity that it behooves us to embrace?"—Ariel Swartley, *L.A. Weekly*

"Powers is a terrific storyteller . . . her determination to slow down and scrutinize the subject is refreshing and useful."—*Salon* Magazine

"Powers is a powerful thinker and a clean stylist."—*Cleveland Plain Dealer*

"Powers feels that the lives of people in their twenties are quite easy to make interesting . . . she gives those stories a weight, worth, and power."—*San Francisco Weekly*

"Powers tells us what all the slackers are up to now—busily nurturing an alleged counterculture so attractive it could become more norm than alt."—*Minneapolis Star-Tribune*

"Her book will make moral conservatives furious. . . . But the writer's intelligence and honesty make up for any and all of that, and the socially curious in all parties will want to read her book."—*Washington Times*

"Powers makes the crucial—and somewhat unprecedented—step of investigating this recent bohemia not for the quality or importance of its cultural output, but for the way its underground ideals shape the mundane concerns of daily life. . . . She forces us to ask how a way of life might be culled from lifestyle, character pulled from personality, knowledge shaped out of nonsense, and permanence negotiated within flux."—*In These Times*

"Ann Powers puts the Y to Gen X, and, using lived experience boldly, explodes complacencies and explores quieter rebellions, America's new frontiers. Heartfelt, engaged, fun, smart, brave, and honest."—Lynne Tillman

"Offering up an engaging, witty valentine to the improvised life and an equally impassioned rebuttal to the idea of the bohemian as a bongo-beating caricature, *Weird Like Us* is equal parts memoir and manifesto."—*Bitch* Magazine

weird like us

MY BOHEMIAN AMERICA

ANN POWERS

DA CAPO PRESS

AUTHOR'S NOTE

The people in this book created its stories by living them day to day. I lived through some, listened to others, and found the threads that, as I see it, connect them all. The events described herein are true, but in certain cases, names and identifying characteristics have been changed.

Designed by Karolina Harris

Cataloging-in-Publication data for this book is available from the Library of Congress.

This Da Capo paperback edition of *Weird Like Us* is an unabridged republication of the English-language edition first published in 2000. It is reprinted by arrangement with Simon & Schuster.

First Da Capo Press Edition 2001
ISBN 0–306–81024–7

Published by Da Capo Press
A Member of the Perseus Books Group
http://www.dacapopress.com

1 2 3 4 5 6 7 8 9—05 04 03 02 01

ACKNOWLEDGMENTS

■

This book grew out of a life shared with many inspiring people, and obviously it couldn't have been written without them. E. Blake Davis, Holly George-Warren, Nicola Ginzler, Rebecca Hensler, Tim Keck, Robert Lawrence, Ruby Montana, Laura Miller, Barbara O'Dair, Lynn Perko, Jonathan Poneman, Mark Pritchard, Carol Queen, Dan Savage and Terry, Jone Stebbins, Robert "Lou" Torregrossa, and Werner Werlwe all gave of their time and resources. Many other participants in this project are pseudonymous here, and I must thank them without divulging their real names. They granted me hours of interviews, connected me with new sources, and, most essentially, created the ways of life I explore throughout this book. Their stories are the ground of my ideas.

I began writing about modern-day bohemia at San Francisco's *SF Weekly* in the mid-1980s. I thank my colleagues there, particularly J. H. Tompkins, Cary Tennis, Andrew O'Hehir, and Pamela Gentile. Later, at *The Village Voice,* I began exploring some of this book's subject matter with the help of Richard Goldstein, Lisa Kennedy, Joe Levy, Andy Hsiao, Karen Cook, and Stacey D'Erasmo. Thanks to them for helping me take my thoughts beyond the chaotic stage.

My colleagues at *The New York Times,* particularly John Darnton and Jon Pareles, have been patient as I finished this manuscript. I am lucky to work with them. The floating gang of rock critics in New York City and beyond has inspired me constantly with new views of how popular culture informs emotion and ideology. Greil Marcus provided some small but crucial encouraging words as I worked on this book. Robert Christgau's introduction to his own excellent anthology, *Grown Up All Wrong,* helped me conceptualize the idea of sustainable youth. He and Carola Dibbell are friends and mentors, and both read the manuscript at various stages and gave important feedback. Katherine Dieckmann, Craig Marks, and René Steinke did the same, and are life-sustaining companions. Felice Ecker, Darcey Steinke, Josh Goldfein, and Yvonne Brown also made the world a more livable place during the years of completing this manuscript.

In San Francisco, Neil Hart and David Wasserman, John Farr and Anne Cox-Farr, and Barry Walters extended their hospitality and made it possible for me to work in comfort and peace. In Seattle that task fell mainly on my parents, John and Marian Powers. They have always loved and supported me, even when we have disagreed, and I hope they can see that my values come from the same root as theirs. My brother and sister-in-law, Patrick and Cindy Powers, have also given me important sustenance over the years. Seattle friends including Christopher Mascis and Stephanie Kurtz, Nora Carria and Joseph Bichsel, Greg Powers and Kathleen Gray, and Emily White and Rich Jensen kept my spirits up. And in New York, the interest and emotional nourishment provided by my adopted kin, Celia Lebenson, Nate and Wendy Weisbard, and Amy Weisbard Bloom and Mark Bloom, cannot be underestimated.

My agent, Sarah Lazin, has been unswayingly supportive of ideas that didn't always seem as if they would hang together in book form. She also provided important suggestions to help them get that way. My editors at Simon & Schuster, Mary Ann Naples and Dominick Anfuso, helped me see more sides of this story than I could have on my own. Carlene Bauer and Ana DeBevoise provided crucial insight, and Jolanta Benal did an excellent job of copy editing. I must also thank the participants in the e-mail poll that produced the book's title.

The reading room of the New York Public Library made an ideal setting for much of the research I conducted, and I was always happy when

I would run into my fellow radical scholar, L. A. Kauffman, there. I thank the helpful staff of the rare manuscripts room, who steered me through its outstanding lesbian and gay history collection. Also for the sex chapter, Mark Pritchard provided me with edifying copies of *Frighten the Horses*. On more general matters, the anthology *On Bohemia: The Code of the Self-Exiled*, edited by César and Marigay Graña, was my essential sourcebook. *Bohemian Paris: Culture, Politics, and the Boundaries of Bourgeois Life, 1830–1930*, by Jerrold Seigel, helped me see my historical context. The essays of Malcolm Cowley and Ellen Willis were just the most compelling of the many works on bohemia and its tangents that inspired me. Many other writers' words fed my brain, and I hope I've managed to give credit where credit is due.

Most of all, I must thank the two men who matter most to me in matters of the brain and heart. Nicholas Popovich is the best friend a girl could have; his influence shows on every page of this manuscript. Eric Weisbard is my partner in weirdness, my everyday editor, and my big, big love. This book was his idea, and I'm forever grateful for his astounding support and encouragement.

For Eric Weisbard

Contents

■

weird
like us

.

*Living by the rules is another way of hoping
the future will be like the past.*

—ADAM PHILLIPS

Become what you are.

—JULIANA HATFIELD

PREFACE TO THE
PAPERBACK EDITION

When this book was published in 2000, some readers had trouble with the title. Actually, they were bothered by its final word: us. In the age of the ascendant "I," we don't like "we"; it's too much of a risk for both its speaker and whomever it seeks to include. Readers can feel roped in by it, and chafe at its limits. And truly, the writer can abuse the community she imagines, imposing a vision that comes straight from her ego and insisting that what she sees must be shared—that's the royal "we," not the collective one.

I used the first person plural in *Weird Like Us* for two reasons. First, I wanted to acknowledge the fact that the stories here, though connected by my involvement, are elementally not mine. They belong to the friends and friendly passersby who created them, and who, in nearly a hundred interviews, realigned my memory with the gentle push of their own. Some crucial part of them is also possessed by strangers: the utopians and rogues of bohemia's history, and the contemporaries I've never met, following routes parallel to mine in other neighborhoods nearby and across the world.

The other reason I use "we" is purposefully arrogant. Especially in the opening pages of this book, I'm trying to inspire readers—you, dear reader—to admit to something. I want those who identify with these stories to recognize that the choices they make matter, that they are not alone in even these tiny decisions, and that each one has an impact.

Many observers of social change discount the influence of personal life and social consciousness on systems bigger than all of us: on capitalism, for example. The past few years have been particularly difficult for anyone suggesting that lifestyle choices can add up to anything beyond a shopping trend. The Internet-driven new economy caused an avalanche of wealth among the young, and the influence of bohemia has led to new paradigms of both work and play. But the money rolling down the slope has carried along with it old-fashioned vices like greed and self-indulgence. The new lofty ideas thrown about in those dot-com offices have often been obscured by the same old cravings.

Surprise! Rich people, new or not, still put themselves first. Consumerism turns passions into product. The 1960s counterculture opened up America's view of the underground beneath its feet, but did not overthrow the dominant culture that, after all, created it. The generations building new bohemias since then have rarely even tried to pretend that revolution is their aim.

This is not news, and in my opinion it's not an effective argument against the power of small gestures made in relative obscurity. The new economy did not kill "alternative" culture by absorbing it; it simply repeated the cycle of innovation and absorption that has made bohemia an engine of change for as long as artists and P. T. Barnum types have existed.

The dot-com phenomenon did cause some real turnabouts in the landscape described in this book, although I'm not certain that even these drastic physical shifts are permanent. Most crucially, San Francisco has become a much harder place for young seekers to flourish. Rents have skyrocketed, and the forbidding zones that attract urban pioneers have been colonized by venture capital–rich companies. Many of the people you'll meet here, established citizens of America's capitol of lifestyle inquiry, have either moved to cheaper climes or are contemplating that drift down Interstate Five to the inland neighborhoods of Los Angeles.

Even as I write, however, the storm of avarice beneficiaries called "the boom" seems to be passing. The stock market no longer offers speculators a quick fix, and real estate brokers are starting, in Manhattan at least, to waive their fees. Those young brainiacs at the dot-coms who put aside idealism in a frenzy to "monetize" now have to look beyond their own cubicles (or their spots in the unemployment line) and consider where they fit in a changing world. I'm already seeing signs that give me hope, including labor organizing at Amazon.com and collectives such as the Future of Music Coalition, a group inspired by the possibilities of music distribution on the Internet, challenging an entertainment industry that has thrived for decades on artists' exploitation.

Even more obvious is the growth in street politics that coalesced most strongly in the protests against the World Trade Organization, The International Monetary Fund, and the World Bank in Seattle and Washington, D.C., in 1999 and 2000. Pundits can dismiss today's young activists as mere rabble-rousers trying out slogans the way they sample music downloads on the Internet, but anyone with a line in to the grassroots left knows that these alliances are working for changes that can't be condensed within a thirty-second television spot. The causes tend to be local and viscerally inspiring—police and prison reform, anti–death penalty crusades, fights against sweatshop labor and for animal rights. There's no Viet Nam war to unite these protesters, and shouldn't everyone be glad for that? They are finding their way toward action on various fronts, and giving the counterculture a new sense of purpose. And many of these street fighters, young and old, came to their struggles through the usual bohemian routes: through music communities like the punk and hip hop scenes, or as an extension of their personal identities as weirdoes among the corporate drones.

The wheel is turning again, away from that moment when the protesting voices in a culture are incorporated and diffused. Bohemians are about to get pushed further toward the edge, and will eventually gain strength from that exclusion. The nation's new president, George W. Bush, shares blood with the Reagan–Bush dynasty, which fed the small rebellions recorded in this book. I'm not saying the "us" that I've tried to honor in these pages will ever be considered a powerful constituency by those who rule. But the dreams we've cultivated and the lessons we are still learning will continue to evolve and be renewed.

Ann Powers
February 2001
Brooklyn, New York

INTRODUCTION:
NEW DAY RISING

WE were walking along the boulevard when the fireworks started. They cracked and sparkled in the distance across Puget Sound, small violent signs of celebration. I waited for another detonation, this one inside my head: the two tiny pieces of paper Roger had slipped beneath my tongue, imprinted with burnt-orange phoenixes spreading their wings, had dissolved by now. "Do you think I took enough?" I asked him. He grinned at me loopily and said, "You can take more if you want." I could tell he was already useless for advice. While I tried to comprehend the drug's clock, my friends went elastic. Doug loudly recited one of his surrealist nonsense poems, shouting about figgy pudding and laughing like a dirty old man. Constance methodically jumped off the curb and then back up. Bernadette smiled her sphinx smile. A few steps ahead, Hank led us toward Discovery Park, bellowing a nineteenth-century patriotic tune he'd learned in his music history class. It was the Fourth of July, Seattle, 1980, the occasion of my first acid trip.

I was sixteen years old, about to enter my senior year at Blanchet Catholic High School, where I worked on the school newspaper and sang in the spring musical and wore perfectly coordinated hot-pink vintage outfits that made all the other students stare at me in the halls. I considered myself a poet. My pretensions bound me to my friends. The boys studied classical music at the university by day and played in a punk band by night. Constance made clothes and other art objects, mostly in shades of purple. Bernadette wrote anarchist essays and blank verse. We were nothing like the stoners who hung out in the parking lot during sixth period and lived up to the present-day image of the delinquent. Those kids hated us; one even sent me a death threat after I wrote something nasty in the paper about his favorite band, Rush. "You'd better watch it," he wrote. "And . . . YOU'RE FAT."

Imagination guarded me from regular assaults like that, and I worshiped at its shrines. My violet-colored bedroom walls were covered with posters I'd ripped off telephone poles, promoting local New Wave bands like the Heaters, the Girls, the Cowboys, and the Frazz, bands we girls would see whenever there was an all-ages show, even when it was at Shoreline Community College and we had to take an hour-long bus ride to get there. Then there were the bands the boys liked, too, artier punk groups like Audio Leter, Mental Mannequin, and Student Nurse. I first got drunk at a Student Nurse show at the Odd Fellows Hall; I downed several plastic cups full of vodka and De Kuyper Crème de Cacao and the bass player followed me into the girls' bathroom and kissed me until I vomited on his shoe. But the bass player was a nobody. Student Nurse's leader was a girl named Helene who, with her ducktail haircut, work shirt, and dungarees, looked like a guy from the 1950s and might have been what I had never seen before: a lesbian.

Sometimes Constance and I went to parties and people like Helene were there, although we were too shy, usually, to talk to them. It took us a while to get boyfriends, but it all worked out when Constance met Hank at one of his band's shows (he was painted gold from head to foot that night, and he played his horn just for her) and I got together with his best friend, the cello player Roger, at a Halloween party a few weeks later. Soon, the trumpeter Doug became enraptured by my lockermate, Bernadette, and we turned into a clique, which was new for us since we were all so used to going solo on the margins. We girls, especially, had been marked for exclusion young, because of our odd parents or habits, because we were chubby or adopted or brown-skinned or too smart for our own good. We struggled to fit in, then finally gave up. In whatever group deigned to admit us, we were the weirdest. Our other friends' mothers told us we were "so creative" and smiled, but we knew they really thought we might be a bad influence. Sometimes my more normal acquaintances treated me like a trick dog, as if my New Wave clothes were a clown costume and so when they laughed at me in front of my face I was expected to laugh, too.

On that summer holiday at the gray start of a mean decade, my friends and I sat in a circle beneath a shrub that looked like a giant snail and laughed with each other in love, not derision. It wouldn't stay like that forever—in a few years, divergent desires and ambitions splintered the group, and a few of us, including me, spun off like errant satellites. Others stayed entwined and became real family. We didn't know that would happen; all we knew, as the drug made the midnight world shine and the woods protected us from judgment, was that we understood each other. Everyone in the circle talked, babbled, exploded with deep revelations, sharing secret knowledge that the world outside refused. I turned to Roger beside me and started to tell him what I was realizing. It was then that I discovered that every one of us was actually carrying on a separate conversation, each stream of words its own crazy firework trail.

The LSD's buzzy light kept doing its trick of plucking profundity from the simplest passing thought, and my brain gleefully began to build a whole world—one where everyone babbled in their own stream until all the streams flowed into one big splashing whirlpool, sucking under every jock and prom queen who had ever cracked a joke about the freshman who spent lunch reading fantasy novels in the library, drowning them in the backwash of their own dumb power while my hot-pink friends and I rode high, masters of the chaotic waves. My favorite David Bowie song whispered in my ear. "Oh! You pretty things! Don't you know you're driving your mothers and fathers insane?" And everyone else, I hoped. Could the world stay tilted like this, always? Was there a place where the weirdos might actually win? The stars pulsed and I wished on every one to let me find it.

▪

LA VIE BOHÈME

I am now in the middle of a life spent exploring an elusive territory, a homeland hidden right in the middle of today's America. San Francisco and New York, where I have spent my adulthood, are its epicenters. But I've found it in all the places I've traveled in between: Austin, Minneapolis, Knoxville, Chicago—write in your town's name here. It's everywhere somebody opens a used-record shop, a laundromat-café, and a punk rock bar. Yet it's nowhere at all, at least according to the many fellow travelers I've met within its borders. They cast off their citizenship as soon as I assert mine.

"Bohemian?" said Amy, incredulous, as we slurped overpriced pasta in an East Village bistro. "I'd never call myself that." She's a veteran of Warhol's Factory scene who's lived in SoHo since the days when rents were cheap; she wears almost nothing but black, cares for seven cats and no man, spends her days watching films and her nights writing. She is not an average person. That doesn't matter.

"I'm not a bohemian. You're not a bohemian," insisted Evelyn over a pint at McHale's, a crusty old stagehands' bar near Times Square. Ev got married wearing a gorilla mask on the shores of Lake Michigan; she and her then-husband wrote their own marriage manifesto and didn't seek the sanction of the law. They published a little magazine focusing on feminism and postmodern ranting until the marriage soured; now she's writing a novel in her flat on East Fifth Street. She fits the profile, but that isn't the point.

"Of course you're a bohemian!" shouted Bob and Carola, who live with their daughter, Nina, just down Second Avenue from Evelyn in a chaotic, slightly remodeled co-op building, along with a bunch of pals who also contribute to *The Village Voice*. Sixties idealists, Bob and Carola want the tradition that changed their lives to carry their successors into the next century. But when pressed for evidence of my bohemian credentials, they hem and haw: Well, so far I'd avoided middle-class conventions like marriage and a decent-paying job. But so did my cousin, who's a waitress in Washington State.

"I don't even know what that word means," said Cathy in her Louisville Slugger drawl as we gazed down on the lights of the Central Park ice rink from the thirtieth-floor penthouse that belongs to the parents of a fortunate friend. "Not in the context of now." Cathy was born working class, and it wasn't French painting or Beat poetry that lifted her out of her circumstances—it was rock and roll. She became a teenage denizen of the Kentucky punk scene, hanging out like one of the boys with the bands that would soon become darlings of American indie rock. A scholarship took her to Princeton, where she fed her music habit as a college-radio deejay. But she soon got involved in AIDS activism, and after working for a few years in radical organizations in New York, decided that she'd be more effective with a law degree. So she went to Yale. "Now I go to parties in Williamsburg, and these painter boys tell me I can't be a bohemian, because I'm a lawyer. I live in Brooklyn, I'm working with poor women who have AIDS. And I'm not a bohemian because I don't spend my days drinking stale coffee in some loft."

The boys in Williamsburg, a warehouse district along Brooklyn's northern waterfront called the Newest Bohemia by *New York* magazine in the mid-1990s (that was before the art dealers took over and the real underground moved to Red Hook), may claim to understand what it means to be a bohemian in this era. But they're the only ones. The term, which arose to label Paris's café-dwelling rebels in the 1830s, was coined by Henri Murger in his 1849 story collection *Scènes de la Vie de Bohème,* and became ubiquitous at the turn of the century thanks to Puccini's opera, now seems worse than quaint; it seems decrepit. To lifestylers in San Francisco, still America's capital of pleasure and perception, Bohemia is nothing but a Mexican beer. To scroungers on the edges of New York's art-and-culture club, it's a gimmick trotted out occasionally on Broadway or in *Vogue* fashion spreads. And for everyone else living by their own code in the so-called alternative communities that survive in every urban center (and, increasingly, in suburbs and small towns, too)—indie rockers and hip-hop poetry slammers, queer activists and dreadlocked yoga jocks—bohemia is just what it sounds like: a country of dead kings and queens that's as far from here as Czechoslovakia.

So I declare bohemia disgustingly dead. I'm hardly the first to set this corpse out to rot; it has perished and revived countless times since the original garret-dwelling snobs decided that the other weirdos they knew were just fakes. "It seems to take shape, like a mirage, only in prospect or retrospect," wrote the journalist Orlo Williams about the Parisian prototype, which had turned into a cliché by the time he examined it in 1913. By then, the life cycle had been established in London, and Greenwich Village, and beyond: a few people drawn together by a dedication to the unprofitable and the uncommon—avant-garde art, progressive politics, the expansion of the senses, the perfection of a startling persona—settled in low-rent enclaves where they could afford to experiment. They wrote and painted, theorized, or simply acted out possibilities. The middle classes, from whose ranks most of these characters had fled, observed their innovations, scorning some and accepting others. The innovators then despaired, either because their visions were being ignored or because their secrets were getting out.

"Bohemianism does not consist in wearing long hair and unusual costume, eating unsavory foreign messes in dirty or disreputable restaurants, or drinking strange and wonderful drinks," wrote one defender, Edwin P. Irwin, at the turn of the century. Yet that's what most people saw—a lifestyle in the shallowest sense of the word, a fashion that repeated itself from the red waistcoat of Théophile Gautier to the flannel shirt of Kurt Cobain. Bohemians themselves rarely agree on what united them beyond these outward signs. Some idea of freedom endures, changing with each new perceived oppression, as the Romantics give way to the Impressionists, the communitarians argue with the anarchists, and the Velvet Underground makes fun of the Doors.

In every era, outsider elitism and the worship of individualism have worked against community spirit. Only traitors shared their ideas with the mainstream, but others, who hid, got stuck in their own romantic conceptions and became shabby old men who pestered young women in cafés. The tribal signs that had grown chic faded, as all trends do, and people began to be embarrassed that they'd ever adopted them. "I'm not a bohemian!" they started to exclaim.

It happened when the tour buses started rumbling into Greenwich Village in the 1920s, carrying out-of-towners eager to enter a real hashish den. It happened again with the Beats, as Jack Kerouac dissipated in a puddle of self-hatred and alcohol while his prose became the founding text for a thousand advertising campaigns. Anyone who has taken a tour of the dingy tie-dyed mall that is San Francisco's Haight-Ashbury district knows it happened to the hippies. From the postcard-selling salons of Montmartre to the grunge cafés of Seattle, bohemia has gone the way of all capitalist products, getting knocked off and marked down until it is nothing but yesterday's trash.

"Generation after generation, nothing changes in bohemia," the rock-and-roll writer Nik Cohn once wrote. The pattern repeats itself, and a new set of pretenders emerges to adjust its particulars. Lately, though, there has been a shift, subtle on the surface but momentous at its core. It started in the 1960s. The counterculture made lifestyle experiments mass phenomena, and forty years later there are Bob Dylan seminars at universities and New Age health spas at the mall. Some bohemian challenges have always been adopted in the mainstream, but the general refusal of conventionality remained a lonely choice. Now, however, this oppositional style has become another norm. "Think Different" is a slogan selling Apple computers, as free of the need for a context as Nike's "Just Do It."

Many of those cranky folks who refuse to call themselves bohemians view this merging of "us" and "them" as the stake that has stilled bohemia's undead heart. "There is no 'alternative,' ever," intoned Tom Frank, one of the ideologues of today's cultural underground, in an essay that helped him secure a book contract with a major publishing house. Young would-be bohemians lapped up his pronouncements. It was easier for them to refuse a legacy that had lost its shape than to figure out what its newest permutation might be.

Yet the loss of clear markers around bohemia actually creates an opportunity that only cowards could refuse, because the same boundaries have been loosed around conventional society. The mainstream has always been more myth than lived experience, and everyone struggles to adjust their imperfectly shaped circumstances to its mold. Bohemia is the countermyth, the other side of our shared story. "Bohemia grew up where the borders of bourgeois existence were murky and uncertain," writes the historian Jerrold Seigel. "It was a space within which newly liberated energies were continually thrown up against the barriers being erected to contain them, where social margins and frontiers were probed and tested."

At this moment in American history, those barriers have grown slack. We are in a state of confusion regarding the basic institutions that order our lives. Our nation is increasingly divided on matters of spirituality, ethics, and social roles. A population increasingly eager to embrace rather than stifle its diversity, with many languages, religions, and everyday customs, makes a uniform belief system seem not only impossible, but wrong. And the lingering countercultural ideal offers an expanded view of of self-reliance and personal responsibility, even as some of its adherents stumble into selfishness and greed.

We are on the verge of a morally richer society, in which old systems of judgment are giving way to more subtle and humane attitudes, yet a conservative backlash threatens to quell this evolution. The cultural right is organized against social progress, working hard in the streets and in the courtroom to calcify institutions, like marriage and the heterosexual nuclear family, that are nonetheless bursting with change. The general negative response to their efforts, evident at the voting booth and in poll after poll, indicates that most people do not agree with their views. Yet these champions of yesterday's oligarchies are the only ones willing to state a clear agenda. The average progressive seems unable to put her morals where her mouth is.

There are good reasons why people hesitate to speak on such matters. As left politics founder, with no overarching radical movement in sight and with liberalism moving ever rightward, setting aside public matters for private ones can seem like a cop-out. Many on the left feel that turning inward signals only laziness and narcissism. The bold cries for a new society that arose during the 1960s have been replaced by psychobabble and New Age spiritual dictums, frameworks for living that tend to be so individualistic, they end up utterly permeable. Liberal piety, currently demonized as political correctness, seems no better. Never mind that the contemporary left's biggest gains, those given shape within feminism and gay liberation, focused on bringing private matters into the public light, and seriously blurred the division between those two realms. Progressive thinkers now seem all too eager to castigate themselves for having focused on those achievements for so long.

Conventional political action does matter, and bohemian America has taken it up on many different fronts. Movements centered around the AIDS Coalition to Unleash Power (ACT-UP), Earth First!, People for the Ethical Treatment of Animals (PETA), Rock for Choice, Women's Health Action Mobilization (WHAM), women's clinic defense, and the struggle for free speech in the arts and on the Internet changed American activism in the 1990s. But there is a complementary layer of experience, which precedes these organized activities, supports them, and thrives independently of them. To haul out my favorite countercultural cliché, this is the level at which the personal becomes political. The more informal areas of our lives—the codes of behavior that we perfect over time, in our daily routines—set the stage for everything else, including how we vote and how we protest.

Academics and public intellectuals have grown adept at grafting the language of politics onto personal pleasures, staging endless debates about the real or symbolic resistance expressed through rave dancing or

Madonna songs. These efforts have greatly expanded our perspective on how popular culture shapes society. Yet progressive thinkers, ruminating upon leisure, or style, or the domestic sphere, often drown in their own apologies: *We're only talking about this stuff because it so perfectly fits with Marx, or Freud, and we can move past its actual substance and get to more serious matters fast.* The idea of developing a separate dialogue about the personal realm remains suspect. Such a discussion would be a moral debate, and if we were willing to engage in moral debates we would be doing what conservatives do. But deep down, we all know that our most intimate actions have effects. Conservatives recognize the power of acknowledging this reality; that's why they make such mighty use of religion, morality's historical resting place. Libertarians invoke morality when they speak of citizenship. Some spiritually minded liberals are negotiating the moral sphere, trying to get what they can out of ancient religious traditions while sidestepping their equally ancient failings, like sexism. Most of us, however, have lost the thread of this conversation, unable to take it into the secular realm, where we've all agreed to keep out of each other's worldviews.

To get our moorings, we can look to bohemia, the floating underground, which is really more a life path than a place. That its facade is out of fashion only makes it easier to get to what's inside. The bohemia that survives today is the one that escapes clichés, because it is not a show staged for others. It is a challenge undertaken in privacy, with the decision to engage coming after the infatuation with the sparkly sheen has worn off. From the sketch artists of Henri Murger's time to today's website iconoclasts, bohemians have preoccupied themselves with a challenge that outlasts the milieu's changing costumes and crazes—to confront and reinvigorate the premises of society, the definitions of kinship, labor, love, leisure, consumerism, and identity itself. It is time, now, for these serious matters to overshadow the flashy performances of the past.

An old-fashioned tour of bohemia would take you through its bars and cafés, art galleries and little theaters. But important as they remain for rest and relaxation, bohemia's essence never rested in those places. More important is what goes on out of plain sight, the huge decisions people make every day about how to form households, what kind of jobs to take and how to approach them, what money means and how to save or spend it, how sex can be more loving and friendship more durable. Chronicling these developments requires looking beyond the great artists and eccentrics who usually get all the attention, to the salt-of-the-earth voyagers who challenge the norm as a matter of course. Bohemia prospers now through the visions they forge and the communities they form more than through superstar displays of colorful character.

And so I declare "bohemia" resurrected, although it has lost that tarnished title and adopted a new group of aliases: slacker, genderfucker, riot grrrl, hip-hop nation, ecotopia, recombinant techno-revolution. Or it slips around anonymously, like some veteran of the federal Witness Protection Program, erasing its fingerprints. Throw out the old, ugly name, stained by the sour wine of exploitation. Don't even bother with a new one just yet. Concentrate on the breathing thing.

■

OUR INDIE WORLD

When I first discovered bohemia in high school, all I could see was its tarnished veneer, mostly at the points where it met the mainstream. Walt Whitman was required reading in my high school, and although the Beats hadn't made it onto my "Christian Themes in Literature" syllabus yet, J. D. Salinger had. The only hipster I ever saw was the pathetically leisure-suited character Reuben Kinkaid on *The Partridge Family.* Had I won the geographical lottery, and been born in an underground capital like Greenwich Village or North Beach, I might have been turned on by the poetry readings and happenings that never abated there. But I grew up in a mid-sized city blessed with the bare minimum of tools for cultural revolt. I looked in spots resembling the ones bohemia's dead heroes had written about, but came up short. At the Last Exit Coffeehouse, where I worked for a few clumsy months as a college freshman, I sought bohemians and found a lot of fading hippies, refugees from Bhagwan Shree Rajneesh's ashram down in Eugene, mentally unstable anarchists, and fellow arty young things like myself.

The scene at the Exit never drew me in. It was just too musty, too palpably over. I preferred a different kind of hangout, one I'd stumbled into a few years earlier. At fifteen I'd landed a job selling German sausages in the Food Circus at the Seattle Center. Constructed to serve the thousands of tourists marveling at the Space Needle during the 1962 World's Fair, the Center was an amusement park with all the trimmings:

carnies hawking chances at bursting a balloon, a rickety roller coaster and merry-go-round, and a lot of shady characters. My entry into its ranks of underpaid workers opened a gateway to mischievous adventure and a close view of the drifters and juvenile delinquents who slaved nearby at Yukon Jack's Fish and Chips or Orange Julius.

The Seattle Center hardly qualified as a bohemia, but it was the kind of netherworld that attracted the margin-walkers of the Plastic Age. Around the singing International Fountain, hippies sold fake Indian jewelry and jailbait couples quietly necked. Local bands played for free in the summer in front of the Horiuchi mural, near the Science Center, and my new friends and I checked them out between bumper car rides. For the first summer, I would give nearly anybody a chance to prove themselves unworthy of my company. Soon, though, I found myself drawn more and more frequently to the area's hub of artistic life. It wasn't some dingy bistro where philosophers opined. It was the Tower Records outlet across the street.

Elsewhere in America (mostly in New York), cooler kids hung out at illegal loft parties and discovered hip-hop and punk rock. I'd barely even heard of such forbidden gardens. Seattle wasn't the kind of nowhere town where dreamers prowl the cut-out bins at Wal-Mart, searching for anything remotely strange; but in the years before Microsoft, coffee, and grunge transformed it from an aerospace factory town into America's yuppie paradise, leisure offerings for youth didn't add up to much. Most of what was available came mass-marketed. Besides, I was a Catholic girl with a dad who'd fought in the Big One and a mom who stayed at home baking Toll House cookies in the afternoons. Folk mass and sewing lessons didn't exactly link me up to the underground.

So I took baby steps toward its shadow on the horizon. A guy named Michael who worked stocking Foreigner albums at Tower told me which New Wave records to buy. Reading the *Rocket,* the free local music paper I found in a rack near the door, I learned what movies played at the Neptune revival house: Fellini, *Don't Look Back, The Man Who Fell to Earth.* I heard about *The Rocky Horror Picture Show,* where boys in rubber dresses congregated to throw rice at the screen. My parents would not agree to let me go to that, but I did purchase a third-tier seat for the Hec Ed Pavilion when the Cars and Nick Gilder came to town. I wore a red wrap T-shirt and a checkered miniskirt to that show.

"Hot child in the city!" snarled Gilder, a silver-haired one-hit wonder, and though I couldn't really see him from my vantage point three hundred rows away, I felt he spoke for me. A guy came up to me that night and asked me if I wanted to take acid in his van. I declined the invitation, but I understood what it meant: I had finally arrived on the edge of having a future.

That future, as far as I could tell, was a gift from rock and roll. Without that music, so mysterious in its multiple languages of the boutique, the dancehall, and the alleyway, and yet so easily explored via radio and record store, I might have never learned how to make myself into a person. Forever, I would have remained the overweight outcast who published her poems in the Our Lady of Fatima grade-school newspaper but didn't have any friends. Unable to distinguish myself in any of the common jock–slut–cheerleader–science nerd ways, I would have grown up to become background.

Rock and roll showed me how to be something else. Its heroes were ugly by most people's standards; they looked greasy like Bruce Springsteen or wimpy like David Bowie or all bent out of shape like Mick Jagger. Nor were they considered proper "artists" by the arbiters of such matters. Even the roughneck paperback poets of the Beat Generation had played to an elite. But rock and roll, invented by entertainers as interested in money as in art and sold to teenagers who would rather dance than read, never could totally maintain its pretensions. Uncool kids like me could get to it too easily. So instead of trying to put boundaries around its oppositional world, rock and roll messed around with the modern world everybody lived in.

No rock spin-off did this more pointedly than punk, the bohemia that arose on rock and roll's edges once its center became big business in the 1970s. Taking names like Poly Styrene and Iggy Pop, punks declared themselves the mutant children of the plastic world. Earlier bohemias had promised an escape from middle-class tedium, the chance to transcend it through art; punk made art from the tedium itself. "I've got a TV eye, and it's trained on you," sang Iggy, who fathered the punk attitude practically by himself way back in the early '70s. The Clash sang about getting lost in the supermarket, and Chrissie Hynde of the Pretenders masqueraded as a diner waitress in her first music video. For a kid who worked in an amusement park and found hope in the aisles of a chain record store, punk's pilfering from the status quo made perfect sense. If I was going to help invent a new universe, I was going to have to do it with whatever junk I found lying around in the dumpster, at the thrift shop, in my own brain. Bohemia had always been a floating world, but punk showed how it could travel, like an oil slick, right on top of the regular one.

Not every modern-day bohemian owns a copy of the Clash's *London Calling*, but even those who move to the beat of hip-hop and disco can relate to rock and roll's code. This was something we inherited from the counterculture of the 1960s and adapted when that movement faltered. Disillusionment does haunt those of us who grew up in the age of punk; we've seen the failed attempts of our countercultural forebears to transform society or escape it, and witnessed that generation's horrible hangovers, such as the Jonestown massacre and the Symbionese Liberation Army fiasco. But for all our supposed cynicism, the communities we devised grew up practical and positive. Rejecting the counterculture's utopian fantasies left us to build alternatives that could survive within the confines of ordinary life. We think locally and act entrepreneurially. Kids like the ones I knew in those strangely named bands like Fred and Audio Leter, who wanted something different from what they could find at their local Tower, invested the cash to press their own records, make their own photocopied fanzines, put on their own shows. Then they'd go back to Tower and persuade some sympathetic shift manager to stock their stuff. These efforts coalesced into practices that went by names bluntly characterizing their hands-on approach: indie, for independent, and DIY, or do-it-yourself.

During the 1990s, the indie world changed my hometown from a zone barely on bohemia's map to one of its focal points. When I moved to San Francisco in the middle of the decade, I found the other essential element in the bohemia I came to love: the culture that was forming around radical gay rights activism. The AIDS Coalition to Unleash Power (ACT-UP) gave this scene its political soul, and the group's influence extended beyond the demos and rallies to affect the way people manifested their identities in art and in their regular lives. Taking on the pejorative "queer" as a badge of honor, the ACT-UP crowd worked the rock-and-roll trick of making their perceived strangeness first a confrontation, then a challenge. And like punks, queer bohemians took a DIY approach to the culture they inherited. The queer aesthetic also emphasized homemade reclamations of omnipresent popular culture—performances by female "drag kings" like Elvis Herselvis and political actions like kiss-ins staged at malls staked turf within the symbolic, and literal, heart of the mainstream.

Queer culture was subversively do-it-yourself in more private matters, too. Reacting against the conventions that had hardened over two decades of gay and lesbian liberation, from the rigid separatism of some radical lesbians to the Ken-doll beauty standards of Castro clones, self-styled queers insisted upon erotic self-rule. Queer leaders were often the outcasts of the gay and lesbian communities: not only drag queens and kings but fetishists, transsexuals, and, most crucially, people living with AIDS. (One legendary AIDS awareness publication was called *Diseased Pariah News*.) Bisexuals, too, claimed the right to express themselves, although some full-time queers regarded them suspiciously. Queer culture's expanded view of sexual identity stimulated groundbreaking inquiries into the nature and uses of desire, not only in heady academic and activist circles but informally, among friends, where new values form. Its influence is obvious on the general public, which is growing more comfortable with sexual diversity, and especially on today's youth, the first generation to include many openly gay, lesbian, and bisexual teens. When I was that age myself, I had no language to express the intense romantic feelings I sometimes had toward my female friends, the deep friendships I forged with young gay men, or even my unruly boy-craziness, which by straight standards was slutty. Discovering queerness, I immediately connected its new attitudes about gender, sexuality, and eroticism to the impulses within my own hungry body and soul.

This is where I started: at the intersection of two bohemias, punk and queer, that rejected and redefined the old name in order to refresh its subversive agenda. These scenes found their own ways of judging who belonged inside, and battles over propriety have threatened both at various times. Like most of my fellow travelers, I have occasionally experienced the ire of self-appointed guards who didn't consider my credentials up to snuff. I have felt uncool and incorrect. Such exclusionary moves are part of the process of self-definition, but the judgments that spark them are the source of my biggest doubts about bohemia's potential, since they threaten to force its insights back into the shadows. I believe that alternative America becomes stronger by willingly engaging with the mainstream. The moment everyone can see themselves as a little bit punk or queer, those safe havens for outsiders threaten to collapse. So does the intolerance that made those words insults in the first place.

■

OUTPOSTS OF PROGRESS

I'm getting a little evangelical here, and I know that isn't cool. Bohemia is supposed to just happen; its informality is nearly the only thing agreed upon by the contrarians who populate it. Most came to this life because the dictates of the larger society struck them as soul-threatening. They've developed a personal ethic that suits the contradictions of unstable reality instead of some calcified ideal. Rules are their enemies. People who want commandments can go to church or join the Revolutionary Communist Party.

This resistance to rigid standards has allowed bohemia to slip through history in many guises, leaving a trail of anecdotes and only a few rare attempts to examine what the stories add up to. Malcolm Cowley identified eight bohemian doctrines in his 1934 memoir of Greenwich Village, *Exile's Return*. Number one states that standardized society crushes the human spirit, and number two declares self-expression the primary purpose of life. Another reads, "Every law, convention or rule of art that prevents self-expression or the full enjoyment of the moment should be shattered and abolished." This is doctrine for the willfully unchurched.

Such openness deserves to be honored, not only because it has helped bohemia change with the times, but because it acknowledges the polyglot nature of modern life, especially in America. Respecting the full humanity of such a diverse population means admitting that no one way of being is *the* right one. Bohemia at the end of this century is as fractured as any other layer of society, and the outposts where I've dwelled do not represent the whole. Indie rock, for example, is a largely white and middle-class scene. It grew up in college towns, supported by students who could afford to spend hours volunteering at their campus radio station or writing for fanzines that paid them in promotional T-shirts. Some were on scholarships, and others worked night jobs to pay the rent, but many had the luxury of a parental cushion. And although some were Asian and Latino, only a few were black. The fascination with African-American culture that fueled rock and roll for so long, and that has returned to inspire today's youngest bohemians, only affected indie in small pockets, such as the New York scene dominated by the Beastie Boys. Indie fans were often hip-hop fans, too, but from a distance.

The hip-hop culture that emerged in sync with indie rock, and has overtaken it commercially and artistically, created its own bohemian edge. Afrocentric bookstores, Egyptology, and natural foods are a few of its details; cities like Atlanta and neighborhoods like Fort Greene in Brooklyn are its capitals. This compelling culture offers lessons to all, but belongs to the people who made it. The late 1980s saw the rise of identity politics on campuses and in activist circles, and this much-needed endeavor to redistribute power caused a certain separation of white, black, and brown people. In forming my own perspective, I have listened to the powerful representatives who have emerged from this realm, writers like Greg Tate, Sapphire, and Paul Beatty, filmmakers like Spike Lee and Julie Dash, and musicians like Erykah Badu and Lauryn Hill, and I hope my voice runs in harmonious counterpoint to theirs.

It certainly seems that this moment's baby bohemians, those teens and twentysomethings currently soaking in and rebelling against the legacy of my generation, believe that racial and ethnic influences can mix without any being erased. The interracial style of the coming century is not a revival of the White Negroism Norman Mailer described in the 1950s; the civil rights movement, which forms the basis of every young bohemian's understanding of race, rendered such simple appropriations forever suspect. Certainly there are white kids who adopt hip-hop style without knowing many black people. But there are also the Asian kids who have made thrash metal more than a white suburban phenomenon, the Latino rebels behind Rock en Español, and the increasingly integrated communities behind ska and extreme sports. Young people of all races are no longer as segregated as they once were, and their desire to find genuine commonalities is palpable in their everyday actions and expressions.

The diversity of these growing clans reflects what I experienced in San Francisco and New York, the two cities that provided my own moral education. The California enclave where I was lucky to spend my twenties is as famous for its smugness as for its golden bridge, but I challenge anyone who has felt its enchantments to demand humility from its citizens. San Francisco is the lifestyle capital of the world, and although that designation has justified much silliness, it also has resulted in a deeply considered approach to daily life, both public and private. The stories I have to share might have taken place in any city from Amsterdam to San Diego, but the fact that most unfolded in San Francisco connects them to a heritage worth embracing. New York exposed me to a different legacy, of transforming bohemian ways into the ideas and fashions that shape our culture at large. Living in Brooklyn now, I gaze outward and see many other cities and towns serving as bases for the same ventures my friends and I undertook. But I am glad I came of age in places where the journey was so well supported.

My narrative is indeed a coming-of-age tale in some ways, although I haven't abandoned any of the questions that preoccupied me over the past decade, and I don't expect to ever totally resolve them. My first impulse was to erect a generational wall around these testimonies, but over time I realized that my bohemia does not completely break with the past, nor will its influence cease in the future. To reclaim a bohemian history can only make alternative America more powerful. This chronicle is one chapter in a saga whose last page will never come, unless human beings lose their capacity to confront, investigate, and dare, to walk out to the frontiers of their own lives and survey the possibilities.

At the same time, I do think our moment offers unique challenges. Not least among them is the intense shadow cast by the countercultural generation. "We made the rules; you have to live with them," a baby boomer friend once told me, and although his arrogance made me flinch, I knew on one level he was right. The civil rights movement and its offspring, including feminism, gay liberation, and the youth movement, set major social changes in motion. My generation inherited those new paradigms—right up to the idea of identifying with a narrow age group. But as history has often borne out, the real work of a revolution comes after the bonfires die in the streets. What has seemed to some like apathy or despair at our relative irrelevance has really been a shift in perspective. Bohemians now tend to be less given to grand pronouncements than our immediate forebears, and more pragmatic about the effects of our choices. Our impact isn't always loud. But it is deep, as we refine and institute the ideals of our elders, and many innovations of our own, on the only level that really matters—not of dreams, but of unfolding experience. After all, in a democracy, living by rules means changing them to fit new circumstances.

My bohemia has produced its share of noteworthy artists and social movers. Like their less visible peers, they tend to focus on shaking up old stories and stale assumptions. David Foster Wallace explores the surreal corners of suburbia in his writing, while Mary Gaitskill strips bare the romanticism of urban hipness in hers. Visual artists like Rita Ackerman, Mike Kelly, and Marnie Weber distort images of innocence borrowed from toy stores and children's books to conjure the terror that sometimes lurks behind a perfect childhood. The independent film-maker Todd Haynes exposed the homoeroticism of rock in *Velvet Goldmine*. Comedians like Janeane Garofalo and Chris Rock are taking stand-up to obsessive new levels of self-awareness, while the music of Courtney Love, Beck, and the Beastie Boys is doing the same for pop. Joss Whedon, the originator of *Buffy the Vampire Slayer*, Kevin Williamson, who gave the world the *Scream* movies, and Trey Parker and Matt Stone, the iconoclasts behind *South Park,* are mischievously remaking teen and kiddie culture. Many pioneers of the computer industry and the Internet also come from this generation, sharing with its artists an earthy, sharp-witted approach.

The attitudes and fads of today's bohemia have traveled the usual route from subculture to mainstream fashion to cliché. From slackerism to the 1970s revival to "post-feminist" grrrl power, the parlance of so-called Generation X has been absorbed into everyday discussion, so much so that trendmongers are saying its moment has passed. In fact, this bohemia has simply done the work many others have done before, infiltrating and changing the mainstream it once rebuffed.

This process includes becoming the older generation to that new bunch of baby bohemians, who are ready to tear up the patches of ground we cultivated and plant arbors of their own. But the seeds remain. The young women who won't call themselves feminists, but enthuse about the sass of Missy Elliott and the strength of women athletes, are practicing a form of "girl power" that first gained shape within the indie rock rebellions of the early 1990s. The rave kids who experiment with drugs and seem obsessed with play are going one step beyond behavior that began in queer and punk clubs. The underground debutantes who embrace a trashy polyester look never would have gotten there if vintage culture hadn't paved the way. These precocious pacesetters will work new variations and grab new insights as they go through the process of declaring bohemia dead and raising it again.

No matter what happens on the surface of alternative culture, its profound work will continue in less ostentatious ways. What constitutes a family? What is the worth of work? What are the parameters of sensual pleasure, of love itself? It is the historical prerogative of bohemians to confront these questions with clear eyes and lots of discussion. And as conventions continue to self-destruct, the bohemian choice to live differently suddenly becomes essential for everyone. The average person may not see herself in the pierced and tattooed body and black leather pants of the stereotypical freak, but she may be surprised to discover that this wild creature's reinventions of kinship, the work ethic, consumerism, and even desire—matters that reveal the bohemian soul, not the costume—intersect with her own quandaries and solutions. If we who are working on those reconfigurations begin to reflect openly upon our choices, we can provide a moral vision that challenges the antiquated one that conservatives cling to and that most Americans seem eager to reject.

This is not a book of virtues. I would not presume to dictate the meanings of the stories I have to offer. I prefer to think of them as fables, with commentary and multiple-choice conclusions. Fables of the reconstruction, as R.E.M., an indie-born band named after the active dream state, called one of its albums. Fables for troublemakers. These tales are still being written, not only by the characters who shared them with me, but in different versions wherever a group gathers and decides to try to make its own conclusions. Such efforts often become most interesting at the point where certainties fade and things get a little dangerous. At other times, people do settle on customs that serve them well, although most never totally give up their questions. Whether or not they reach any resolution, be assured these bohemians (by whatever name) are committed to their task. People like us are often accused of running away—from responsibility, from society. We were running, it's true. This book is about the luminous corners where we stayed.

1

■

HOME FREE

I N 1984, a twenty-year-old punkette with two-toned hair and a plastic raincoat boarded an American Airlines jet and left home, in search of a fantasy that she wanted to make into a life. That nice Catholic kid gone haywire was me, fleeing toward a future as a poet, a rock star, a groupie, anything but the accounted-for accounting major my dad said I should be. My fantasy was the floating world where artists and other weirdos made their own rules, turning their lives in the city's twilight into one long experiment.

San Francisco was the logical place to touch ground, and I held a naive hope that its history would rub off on me. As soon as I checked in to the Geary Street YWCA, I hiked up to the faded cafés of North Beach. Nothing happened as I sat there with my lonely notebook. I tried my luck on Haight Street, past the head shops and the spaced-out huddling Deadheads, but I never met anyone there who offered me a useful revelation. Those neighborhoods' dreams were done, their shells transformed into theme parks. I soon tired of hucksters selling memories of Ginsberg or Garcia along with their bad manifestos and patchouli oil. I didn't want to be a Beat, or a hippie, or even a mohawked English-style punk like the ones who hung out in front of the Mabuhay Gardens. The costumes those characters wore seemed about as daring as Mickey Mouse.

I had to find the bohemia that was still forming, as I was. In the 1980s, that meant moving to the Mission District, a bilingual neighborhood where kids with fresh tattoos lived across the hall from Latin American political refugees. The Mission had the resources wage slaves and students need to survive: cheap rents, easy subway access, and taquerías that served giant two-dollar burritos. I found a room in a creaky fifth-floor walk-up on South Van Ness, next to Paco's Tacos, the cheapest stand in the neighborhood. It was only two blocks from the neighborhood's oldest café, predictably called La Bohème. But I soon realized that I could make more interesting connections by staying in.

The flat I'd moved into was an ordinary San Francisco group house, occupied by a rotating cast selected by its leaseholder, a girl my age named Sally Frederick. At first, it didn't seem that different from the dorm rooms and off-campus shacks I'd passed through in my year and a half of college in Seattle. But unlike the postadolescent drifters I'd known, Sally had made a commitment to the spot where she'd happened to land. She expected her roommates and the small circle of friends who spent most evenings in her living room to go beyond the coincidence of our meeting and become one another's lifelines. Our efforts at the domestic arts didn't amount to much beyond hanging up a few movie posters and occasionally throwing together a curry from a mix. But emotionally, Sally pushed us further. She encouraged us to invest in each other, to open up, and to answer each other's trust with a willingness to provide support. Her intensity turned off some people, and they fled, but those willing to match it entered a network of steadfast companions that survived individual conflicts and disenchantments.

Sally had some kind of magic with people; I attributed it to a natural grace that made everyone in her presence feel a bit more beautiful. Now I recognize that her charisma was intensified by her self-imposed mission. She was trying to make us into a family. Hard times had struck the one she'd been born into: her parents were divorced, and a brother had drowned in a boating accident when she was a teenager. Her impulse to reach out beyond her bloodline was personal. Yet it suited all of us. As I moved from her little clan into others I helped form over the next decade, I realized that this is one of the first tasks any would-be bohemian faces: to create a sense of home that lasts while your life changes, to cultivate a family spirit beyond the boundaries of the white picket fence.

Making "family" where you find it is also one of the hardest ambitions to fulfill. No matter how strong the impulse may be to reinvigorate tired customs with the juice of inspiration and personal experience, applying your bright new ways to the life you actually lead can be difficult and even painful. You can declare the nuclear family as antiquated as the corset, but that doesn't make it easier to explain to your mother why you've decided to celebrate the holidays with your housemates instead of flying home. She will be hurt, and those beloved roomies may succumb to their own pressures and abandon you anyway. You could invite them all home with you, except that Uncle Gene might go off on one of his tirades about the gays getting all the good real estate, or your activist pal Amber might try to coax your grandmother to explain why she's prolife.

Those fortunate enough to share beliefs as well as blood with relatives usually have more luck integrating their clans, but in the hardest and best of times—when you need money, when you have a baby, when someone dies—old-fashioned family usually takes precedence. Some of the reasons for this are legal, since the state dictates who can enter a hospital room or choose a funeral plot. Others are a matter of habit. Not to discount the genuine trust and love that flourishes in blood families; expanding the definition of family doesn't have to mean rejecting the people biologically joined to your existence, especially since they most likely rose to the occasion and nurtured you. The ultimate goal is to take no one for granted. Today, though, many people end up doing just the opposite. They push away siblings and parents in a fury over their inadequacies, yet they expect even less sustenance from their friends. As long as orthodox family structures continue to represent the "best way" for people to dole out emotional support, more and more people will fail to find ways to gain such nourishment at all.

The old edifice of the family unit is obviously decaying. The journal American Demographics reports that as the new century begins, over five million adults will live with other adults unrelated to them by blood or marriage. As the human life span increases, more elders are finding it necessary to share housing, with more than four hundred placement organizations matching up senior tenants with homeowners who have an extra room. Policymakers see this trend as an ideal option for the burgeoning population over age sixty-five, but as the rising cost of housing does battle with the average person's enduring desire to settle into a home, members of all age groups find life with roommates becoming permanent. Friends are raising children together, buying property together, nursing each other, and forming lasting ties.

Although two-thirds of the housing in this country was built for Mom-Dad-and-kids, with healthy-sized kitchens for home-cooked meals and a big living room for lounging, less than one-quarter of the population still lives out that particular family romance. "Family" is an idea in transition. It is being recast in every town and city by homesteaders like Vivian Segal, who has lived in the same group house on Steiner Street in San Francisco for over a decade. "In the eighties, there was the Reagan-Bush-Quayle return to family values, espousing family values that I don't necessarily agree with," said Vivian. "Here we were, living amongst all of our friends, whose family values were a lot stronger and more valuable to each other than the ones that were supposed to bring us back to some moral, beautiful, peaceful time in the fifties. We were nicer and kinder to each other than that model suggested. We weren't going back."

I know why Vivian puts so much stock in the family she helped invent; for several years in the mid-1980s, I lived within its sanctuary. After my first taste of reconstructed family life, I left South Van Ness and Sally, in hopes of conceiving one of these unusual clans myself. Steiner Street was one of two households my closest companions established as new citizens of the free state we were trying to make of our lives. I lived in the other flat, a mile away on Fulton Street. All told, about twelve people joined in the family activity. On any given night, the members of one household might be found in the living room of the other. Everyone gathered for holidays and casual Sunday dinners. Other roommates came and went, but their presence in our lives was a matter of chance. For us it was different—even though we'd moved into each other's rooms with an ease that, upon reflection, bordered on recklessness, over time our ever-changing fellowship became the rock in most of our lives.

My days on Fulton Street and Steiner Street taught me what family can be in an age when biological ties don't always hold, as the contingencies of life make "home" a concept as fluid as the speed limit. The households weren't always models of harmony and joy—there were bitter fights and deep misunderstandings, there was pot slamming, money mismanagement, and extended bouts of the silent treatment. We repeated many of the mistakes we'd made within our biological families. And we couldn't always figure out how our new bonds, our new values, could replace or renew those habitual ones. There was heartbreak. We could be careless. Yet the pain we put each other through was a part of the process, the first proof we'd had that you can't just career through life clinging only to yourself. We were young, and most of us felt that our own families hadn't given us enough understanding. What we didn't realize at first was how complicated giving to each other would turn out to be.

■

M Y   K I N

How to grow a new family tree: from the branches, backward. My brother, Patrick, shouted at me from across the table at his neighborhood brew pub three days after Christmas 1996, "Family is important! I know that now! Do you?" Patrick wanted to make sure that when my parents finally pass I'll still return for visits, and stay with him and his wife, Cindy, although I am allergic to their dog. Patrick worries about me, I know, and who can blame him? I left him behind when he was only fourteen, and headed south like a fugitive, running from kin who had never tried to hold me back anyway. Since that time I have run toward a lot of things, including back toward them. But in making that circle I missed the point when Patrick became his own man. I realized this at his wedding. Who were all these young men in tuxes, these former high-school teammates, Coast Guard comrades, college pals? They were Patrick's best friends, the surrogate family he'd made while I was busy making one of my own. As for me, who was I? His sister, and prized for that. But what I wanted to be, watching him grin and slap his buddies on the back, was his friend.

People tend to elevate blood family and resent it at the same time. Jokes about it have become rueful; for a special issue in the early 1990s, the literary journal *Granta* stole a Philip Larkin line that became a catchphrase for the wreckage of an institution: "They Fuck You Up."

Why do we cling to our families, then? Because we have no one else? That's just not true, in a world so overpopulated and hungry for love. Because we owe them something, like our lives? American ideology has long advertised that each of us gives birth to ourselves. Patrick fled, too, all the way to Antarctica, on a military icebreaker. When he came back, he says, he had a fight with my father that leveled the emotional playing field between them. We leave because it gives us a right to return. Otherwise, we fear, we'd just keep running in place.

I share Vivian Segal's conviction that loving your family means something only when it is a choice, and that given room to do so most of us will make that decision willingly. But it isn't always easy to clear that space. Family is the central given in our society, ostensibly uniting people of different classes, faiths, and political affinities under one welcoming paradigm. In fact, the simple truths of family life held up by moral conservatives are the kind formed in fear, to stave off changes that have already happened. In this nation of former immigrants and slaves, very few citizens can trace a clear line of ancestry. African Americans, forced centuries ago to reconstitute ties destroyed by slavery, and Asian or Latin Americans, who maintain broad support networks, the better to settle into a new homeland and native tongue, favor an extended-family model that is really more traditional than the smaller modern version of family. People of all ethnic backgrounds have similarly broadened their notions of kin to remedy the displacements of modern life, from serial marriage to the migratory nature of much modern employment. Yet conservatives refuse to see the potential in supporting a more fluid notion of family to better suit reality. Official discussion about "the crisis of the family" maintains the fallacy that so many people reject the nuclear cliché not because of its limits, but because of their own moral failure.

Most of the people I've known who live in unorthodox ways had good reasons for refusing to adjust to the conservatives' ideal. Maybe their parents were abusive. Maybe they grew up in one of those patched-together families middle-class truisms don't register. One of my San Francisco housemates, Edie Rice, spent her teen years on a religious commune with her mother. Another, Paul Coughlan, grew up gay in a strict Catholic home, feeling trapped because he could never tell the truth about himself. Others, like myself, felt loved by our parents yet were misfits, as uncomfortable in conventional family life as we were everywhere. Whatever the specifics, we all grew up to see ourselves as walking contradictions to the way things were supposed to be.

This is why the mind-set of contemporary bohemia is rooted in a critique of the family. Jerrold Seigel has called bohemia the reverse image of the bourgeoisie, arising "where the borders of bourgeois existence were murky and uncertain." Right now, no arena is so troubled as that old stereotype of home. "Are you my family?" people ask each other everywhere, and their answers often astonish and dismay them. To establish new standards, we need to examine the informal arrangements and uncelebrated ties people have cultivated outside the norm.

Bohemians from the denizens of Murger's Latin Quarter to the romantic experimenters of Bloomsbury have long taken an open view of intimacy. But it took many years for their experiments to overcome old tendencies. To learn the history of the Left Bank or Greenwich Village is to discover an endless string of husbands taking advantage of the labor of their wives, keeping mistresses on the side, leaving their children with no emotional or financial support, and ultimately claiming that the women who pampered them were as square as the parents they'd rejected. Veterans of those scenes, like the New Yorkers Joyce Johnson and Hettie Jones, have chronicled the downside of these masculine playgrounds. The women who lived there certainly had more freedom than their mothers, but they could not fully address the issue of family. A woman who tried would come to *represent* family—and thus be a threat. Simple freedom remained the cure-all, and no attempts to rethink the basic nature of family ties were sustained. This was the limitation of the genuine gains bohemians in earlier eras made in remaking family.

In the 1960s, the counterculture revitalized an older model, that of the commune, to set formal standards for its domestic ventures. The commune in America dates back to the earliest days of the nation. The Puritan settlement in New England was a commune; its residents shared resources, religious principles, a way of dress, and, as Thanksgiving memorializes, ritual feasts. In the early nineteenth century, religious revivalism and the promise of the frontier combined to inspire a burgeoning of communistic enterprises with such fanciful names as the Harmony Society, the Icarians, and the Separatists of Zoar. Countercultural hippies could relate to that idealism, but rarely approached their projects as rigorously as their religious forebears had. The stereotypical image of the commune as a ramshackle hippie farm overflowing with

unkempt, patchouli-burning, bean-sprout-tilling, hemp-smoking amateur New Age philosophers, all paying homage to some orange-clad
spiritual charlatan, stems from these ventures and lingers today. To
counter it, many formal communes have adopted a sleeker marketing
term (one that, like so much good design, originated in Denmark): cohousing. Cohousing groups consist of separate homes sharing certain
common spaces and some resources, rather like retirement communities
for young people, or what suburban planned communities might have
been, had everyone used the same rec room.

Communes and cohousing provide viable options for people willing
to take on a serious formal structure to order their home lives. Yet, as
the decline of the 1960s communal movement proved, few people want
to be so aggressively organized. One alternative, which emerged in the
wake of the feminist critique of the family in the 1970s, was the self-
conscious establishment of chosen families. Unlike communes, which
usually espoused an ideology based on either religious teachings or revolutionary politics, chosen families do not demand adherence to any belief system beyond the ethics of the group itself. Still, they are not merely
group marriages of convenience. The term "chosen family" arose to define a particular and very politicized effort by feminists and gay liberationists to adjust the notion of kinship to make room for them. "Love
makes a family—nothing more, nothing less," read one sign carried in
San Francisco's Gay Pride Day parades during the 1980s, when the sociologist Kath Weston did a study of these new intimate circles. No more
would gay men and women live in lonely bedsit rooms, rejected by their
parents and unable to form lasting ties with their sexual conquests. (No
more, in fact, would that trash-paperback narrative be acceptable as the
standard biography of a gay person's life.) In the 1970s, people began to
speak of the bonds they created through love affairs, friendships, and
shared neighborhoods as more than just simple friendship or temporary
comfort—this was family, as secure and comforting as any offered by
Straight Town, U.S.A.

Two elements combined to cement the notion of the gay family. The
first was the lesbian-feminist movement, which demanded a fundamental change in women's domestic role. The second was the flourishing of
San Francisco's Castro district, the first openly gay American neighborhood. "We had no role models. We had to find new ways to live," Castro habitué Randy Shilts told fellow journalist Frances FitzGerald in the

1970s. Unlike past gay districts or most bohemian enclaves, the Castro was not a shadow society but a proud and open one. Merely by appropriating the word "family" for themselves, gay men and women redefined it. Their example, more than any other, inspired gay *and* straight bohemians of the 1980s and 1990s to reenvision family.

Trial by fire made the example of the gay extended family all the more powerful. As the pleasuredome 1970s gave way to the battlefield 1980s, the ravages of AIDS forced people to prove their commitment to each other under the most painful conditions. My peers, somewhat younger than the Castro pioneers, live inside this epidemic, too; many have faced the same horrors and know what it means to really sustain each other. We all know stories of roommates who've been the only ones left to take care of young men and women who lay dying. It is ridiculous to suggest that those ties cannot be as tenacious as those that might be identified by a DNA sample. If AIDS could teach us anything, it was that the smallest, most intimate decisions can shape the rest of your life. Knowing that, we have set forth to reinvent home—the first step in reinventing the world.

Two thirtysomething women pals buy a brownstone together in Park Slope, Brooklyn, to defray costs; their collaboration in domesticity solidifies and last for years. A gay journalist and his best friend, a straight woman with her own business, pack up their separate histories and move from the East Coast to Seattle, making the proverbial journey of newlyweds, but with a difference. A black woman decides she wants to have a baby, and her white female lover agrees; the chilly option of a sperm bank hardly appeals, so they ask the lover's Peruvian green-card husband to act as dad—and he does, joining in as a full participant in this new rainbow clan. A bunch of Midwestern graduate students organize a Passover seder that lasts three times longer than any experienced in childhood, what with all the arguing over the Haggadah, and it feels that much more meaningful. In Miami, friends who've nursed too many AIDS-stricken loved ones rejoice when protease inhibitors save a companion from death. Five families in Vermont buy land together, calling their collective Rocks & Trees; each has a private lot, but the rolling green meadow connecting them is shared. A couple elopes to Reno, Nevada, bringing one person along for moral support—their roommate. In Los Angeles, a musician killed in a car crash receives his most personal memorial not from his family but from the dear friends who raise money to release an album of his work. Families are growing in many different forms, adding up to a new definition that can't forever be denied.

■

THE TERRARIUM

When you fall in love, you tell yourself the story as you go along; with kin, the plot precedes you, and you bend to its character. But there's another kind of love, whose story only reveals itself years after you thought it was over. Oh, yes, you say, that mattered more than I thought it did at the time. I slighted her; I lost him in the rush. This love usually comes between friends, with no declarations and no vows. It feels lucky at the time—simpatico—and, taken for granted, it often falls apart. But it teaches you its elements without even letting you know you're learning. Inside such a love is where my story continues, with a family that was a reverie, conjured up within a whimsical Eden where we named ourselves.

Fulton Street, in the Western Addition, 1984 to 1988: the ugliest building on the block, the color of cat food, with falling-apart window frames and the rumble of a laundromat below. Four bedrooms, three of them adjoined by doors that stayed open or shut depending on the friendliness of their changing occupants. A typically tiny San Francisco living room, stuffed with vinyl records and furniture dragged up from the curb; a kitchen, fitfully cleaned, with mice living in the stove. A long stairway leading up to a hallway where people tended to linger, smoking cigarettes and joints and talking on the phone, contemplating the cheap posters on the walls. One depicted the Lady of Shalott, set adrift by a passion that inflamed her mind; the girls in the house identified with her. The other was an advertisement for the latest album by the Violent Femmes, whose title could have been our motto: *The Blind Leading the Naked.*

Up those stairs came a revolving doorful of vagabonds, splitting a monthly rent of $700 for the privilege of laying down a futon in one of the flat's crumbling rooms. Nearly twenty people lived at Fulton Street during those four years, with more cameo appearances than *The Poseidon Adventure.* There were the sisters who first secured the lease, Humboldt County outdoorswomen who scented the kitchen with the turmeric of vegetarian stews. There was Tim, the surfer dude who might have scored with any of us if he'd ever washed, and Josh the Clown, an irritating Jewish juggler who eventually went off to train with Ringling Brothers in Florida, much to our joy. There was the leatherman and classical composer who crashed for a while on our couch, not telling any of us he was dying of AIDS. There was the English expatriate who once moved her entire blood family into the living room. There were countless other floor-crashers, Sunday afternoon beer-sharers, and happily forgotten one-night stands.

This wacky crew would have made a fabulous cast for a bad sitcom about San Francisco, but its members weren't what held Fulton Street together. A particular clique did that, six around-the-clock companions who traded shifts at a local record store and brought one another into the house as rooms opened up. We were just beginners, eighteen to twenty-seven years old, building a fort for shelter. Edie Rice and Isadora Jackson had escaped Sacramento together after high school, lived for six months in the San Francisco State dorms, and then found rooms at Fulton Street. Paul Coughlan was Edie's best pal, and he grabbed a spot to get away from a boyfriend eager to make him into the perfect husband. Lucy D'Amico signed on after she tired of the punk-rock flophouse down the road, where she'd become den mother to seven cute but inconsiderate musicians. David Sherbourne was a cartoonist from the Central Valley who had the manic personality of one of his pencil sketches; he shared my room during our two-year relationship. And there was me. I waited impatiently until the last of the Humboldt sisters vacated a spot, then took a tiny berth in the middle of the flat, although I spent most of my time in the convivial hall.

It was the mid-1980s, Reagan's American morning. We felt like we were living in an alien nation, where robotic yuppies ate twelve-dollar plates of mashed potatoes at ersatz-retro diners and neck-scrubbing Christians fought artists in the streets. The air buzzed with words, speeding toward us like bullets: virtue, morality, values. According to everyone around us, we could lay no claim to these terms; we were expected to follow in the deep footsteps of the countercultural baby boomers or to stay in our corners, despairing at the failure of their revolution. We felt like we had to start at the beginning. And so, like children, we shut the door behind us, pulled out our gameboard, and played the Game of Life.

Nearly a decade after the house broke up, we met in Paul's apartment for a reunion—all but David, who'd married a fellow comic poet a few years after he and I parted and now lived a frugal life in St. Paul. The rest of us were curious to see what we all had become. When we first stood together in Paul's Dolores Street hallway, everyone burst out laughing. "You look the same," said Edie to no one in particular. "I expected one of us to have changed." Everyone *had* changed, of course, just as much as we hadn't. Edie still kept her hair short like Audrey Hepburn's and exhibited the natural elegance of one who thinks before she speaks, but the nineteen-year-old adventuress who'd once run off with the circus was now thirty, living with a carpenter in San Rafael, and teaching nursery school. We'd all made similar stabs at the fundamentals, work and love. Isadora had fallen for a woman and was exploring what it meant to call herself a lesbian; Lucy had started her own business. Still, we were people who would recognize each other whenever we met.

We couldn't help but get nostalgic as we nudged each other's memories. Fulton Street had been the site of our mutual education, an antediluvian dominion where we put aside our origins and hatched ourselves anew. When we got there we already knew that the eccentric phase our parents hoped we were going through would last for the rest of our lives. But nothing had solidified yet. Working jobs that weren't careers, a few of us taking classes at State but skipping more than we showed up for, we pursued our real interests after hours. Primary among them was the creation of an environment that would stimulate the insights coming fast and furious.

"My world. My mind." That was how Isadora described Fulton Street. "I was isolated—didn't have a television, didn't really read the papers. I was just writing poetry, dancing, singing." Isadora had lined the walls of her big room with vintage dresses on coat racks, almost three hundred in all. I painted the bathroom pink and hung a poster Sally had brought back from Vatican City across from the toilet, so every time you peed you could learn the life story of a different pope. Every corner of the house became a place to create art, and we felt like we were living in a revolution of everyday life. The stereo rang with music: Gram Parsons, Nick Drake, the Roches, Alex Chilton. We spent a lot of time sitting around, singing along.

As we tried to figure out how to make a home, we lived by share and share alike. Goods were casually distributed and space easily occupied. Our living room floor became the spare bed, and if someone's smelly presence bothered a housemate, she kept silent: to speak would have been to violate Fulton Street's edict of unstinting generosity. The same went for me borrowing Isadora's go-go boots or Edie drinking my last beer. Normal roommates would have turned red in the face and yelled. But we floated past every possible conflict on a wave of devil-may-care. If anyone struggled, they did so in private. "That was a hard lesson for me," said Isadora. "I didn't have a lot growing up, and so when I got into collecting dresses and other vintage stuff, I got attached to all the things I had. But as soon as I started to feel any jealousy I'd think, 'I don't need to feel that.' "

Maybe Isadora kept her frustrations to herself because she sensed that it was useless to express them. By tacitly agreeing to live together in a kind of daydream, we didn't leave much room for acknowledging responsibility. "I remember a lot of dust bunnies in the hall," Isadora said with a laugh. "I remember washing dishes," added Lucy. "The water would sit in the sink for three days until I did." I also remember a few months where Paul paid Edie's rent, and a certain amount of bad feeling about who owned which leather jacket or how Isadora's special German shampoo had been used up when she'd barely touched it. (That was me, sis.) I remember worse things, too: months one of us would spend avoiding another, unable to voice anger or frustration or to admit having done something wrong.

"What I remember lacking from that period is the ability to create intimacy," Edie said, measuring her words. "Really talking about what my feelings were and laying it all on the table." She paused. "I don't think any of us could have done it any differently."

Paul listened to the rest of us respond to Edie, and then he interrupted. "It just redefines intimacy," he argued. "It's something else that we don't classify as intimate. But you wouldn't be here now if you didn't feel it then."

It must have troubled Paul to hear Edie announce that she'd always felt a distance among us at Fulton Street. For much of their time there, Paul and Edie had been our Siamese twins. They would lounge for hours on the Salvation Army couch, smoking, exchanging few words, seeming to communicate profundities within the language of glances. Then they'd disappear, off to see a French movie and drink a bottle of wine. I grew very jealous of Paul and Edie, because when I'd moved into the house I'd shared a strong friendship with each of them. Then things changed; I'd ask Edie to dinner and she'd suggest that Paul come along. They started buying milk and cheese and cigarettes together. They threw the rest of us over for the seductions of the pair bond.

What were Paul and Edie sharing, if not intimacy? To an outsider, they seemed so well matched. They were both gorgeous—Paul a cross between a jock and a Scorsese-movie second lead, Edie a waif from a Marguerite Duras novel—yet they remained aloof from their own allure, seemingly oblivious as half the world fell in love with them. Both teetered on the edge of the identities they could have fulfilled so easily: Paul hated Castro clones and disco-crazed stud muffins, Edie chafed against the role of Beautiful Girl. Graceful and demure, they could play at convention much more easily than the rest of us. Yet in many ways they stood the furthest outside, pushed there by the force of their refusal. Each understood the cost of the other's decision, how much easier it would have been to go the other way. Although they were not of the same sexual persuasion, their shared languor created a powerful erotic pull.

Paul and Edie also saw each other through serious trauma. They shared another friend, a composer named Larry, and they invited him into the house when he lost his apartment and was just starting to get sick with AIDS. Larry never admitted the nature of his illness, and Paul and Edie were the only ones among us who knew him well enough to understand it. Larry's cynicism and rage made me anxious; I tried to avoid him. After a couple of months he moved to his own sublet. Then he entered the hospital with tuberculosis, and died without overcoming his denial. Paul and Edie endured his silent passing together. "After that we hung out consistently, forever," Paul said.

They supported each other through lost jobs and botched romances. Edie fell hard for an aspiring performance artist and left Fulton Street to move in with him and his wife in a threesome. The experiment soon proved disastrous. Paul was there when it ended, leaving the rest of us to rent a Mission District flat with Edie. Years of relative harmony went by. Then Paul introduced Edie to his coworker Scott, a burly bicyclist who'd fancied her from afar. He thought Scott might make another interesting fling for her. Instead, Scott and Edie became a steady item. Paul was shocked. Edie, whose main form of exercise had been inhaling and exhaling Marlboro smoke, took up marathon cycling. Then she moved with Scott to San Rafael. Once, Paul made it to a party at their bungalow; he felt awkward amid the chardonnay-sipping couples who were now their friends. "It was so straight," he told me later, perplexity darkening his face.

Paul had preserved the memory of his sibling bond with Edie despite the emotional gulf that later separated them. When Edie suggested she hadn't felt the same, he was flummoxed. So was I. Were the formalities of kinship the only preservatives that really worked? Or was the problem that Paul and Edie had actually fallen into the habit of treating each other the way we often treat our families, assuming closeness instead of cultivating it, and thus preventing their intimacy from growing deep enough to last?

Group houses have no rules of alliance, no schedules regarding affection. Such organized love belonged in the commune. The ways in which we made Fulton Street a home were spontaneous, beginning with the simple act of throwing in our lot together, agreeing to be friends and companions as well as roommates. At a time when the counterculture's conventions felt as restrictive as the mainstream's, our attempts to forge a way of life satisfied neither institution's rulebook. "Agreeing within our household didn't mean being cloned into a particular mold," explained Paul. "Your door was different than mine, but it was on the same hallway, so it was okay."

A decade later, it's worth asking whether being on the same hallway was enough. Fellow feeling ultimately didn't hold Paul and Edie together, and theirs was not the only relationship that frayed. Lucy moved out soon after meeting a responsible punk rocker who eventually became her common-law husband. Isadora and a boyfriend took up residence with his pals on Nob Hill. I moved my romance into Fulton Street, subletting my room to David when I took a cross-country vacation one summer and staying there with him after that. No one ever protested any of these disruptions, although they altered our relationships profoundly. When I asked David to move in, I couldn't imagine anyone minding. He'd been hanging around for a year, a full player in the house's creative life, decorating the kitchen with his drawings and playing guitar in the Aphids, a short-lived folk band formed by Isadora and me. Yet not everyone thought he fit in so perfectly. As our reunion turned into a soul-baring session, Paul admitted that David's arrival, not just Edie's need for a roommate, motivated his departure from Fulton Street.

"When he just sort of started living with us, maybe I felt threatened or something, but it didn't jibe with me," Paul told me. "It was weird for me that someone's boyfriend had actually moved in. My attitude was, Come and go, but make sure they're out by nine o'clock in the morning." My violation of that code signaled the end of the Fulton Street Paul loved. "I knew the situation was going to break up and it was inevitable that we would part, but I didn't want it to happen this particular way," he said. "The balance is very fragile, and as soon as you add another element it can change."

Plenty of warm bodies had passed through Fulton Street, but I know why Paul felt differently about David. Sex was the one thing that could always come between us. The primacy of the couple remains so strong in our society that even those who consciously strive to challenge it usually fail. David and I certainly did.

Over the time that David and I lived there together, Fulton Street subtly changed for me. It became the site of that relationship. As its ups and downs played out, the other bonds I'd formed in the house receded. Eventually David and I broke up, and when we did I forfeited Fulton Street to him. I had to get away from the romance that had come to dominate my life and then grown sour. My former flatmates and I stayed friends, but having abandoned our daily invention of a nest, we drifted off toward new loves.

If we'd had rules, or at least a framework within which to discuss our conflicts and desires, Fulton Street might have lasted longer than three and a half years. Yet it would have been a different house, one that none of us would have wanted to live in. We were learning our first lessons there. Spending hours at the kitchen table listening to each other's woes and wishes, helping each other find jobs and clothes and boyfriends, singing along to *Elvis in Vegas* in the living room we'd furnished with unimaginably ratty couches: in these ways we taught each other family as an enterprise, a kind of skill. Long after Fulton Street, this capacity to make family wherever we choose to find it continues to play a major role in the way we all shape our lives.

Fulton Street, our seedbed: The night we gathered to reminisce and wonder, Paul presented me with a souvenir he'd kept on his dresser for years. It was a photograph of our old refrigerator, its door covered with scraps from our *vida loca*: poetry-reading schedules, a postcard reading "Sin Cruise," an ad for a local performance of a Beckett play, a beefcake shot of country hunk Dwight Yoakam, a Bible Guidance pinwheel, a magnet that could emboss your piece of toast with the words "Good Morning," a bottle opener, a scrap of David's writing, a photo of us girls dressed for a party in coordinated red and black, a plastic statue of St. Francis of Assisi, a ceramic swan. On the top of the fridge is a soup pot out of which tumbles an overgrown houseplant. It's as if the ivy is being nourished by the mulch of all our preoccupations, our passions, and our junk. I look at this photograph now, and I think that ivy, it was just like us.

■

THE MODEL HOME

At Fulton Street, we never looked at each other and said the word "family." Elsewhere, the term surfaced more clearly. Our sister house stood about a mile away, at the northern edge of the Fillmore District. Steiner Street was a newly remodeled top-floor flat with comforts the Fulton Street kids could barely dream of: a dishwasher and washer-dryer, stone-gray carpets that weren't even ratty, and a roomy kitchen spreading out around a giant white countertop, which we declared an Aztec altar and made the center of our weekly feasts. Not to mention reliable heat. "Steiner was where you would come when you got sick," recalled Martin Cunningham, one of the house's original residents. "Friends would come do laundry. It had a function in a lot of people's lives."

Steiner Street had an emotional function, too, for the gang of ten or so who called it a first or second home. Edie, Paul, and I were the crossover members who tied Steiner to Fulton Street. We spent virtually every holiday around the counter, celebrating Passover, Christmas, New Year's Eve, and everybody's birthday. We'd gather regularly for Sunday dinners, though our Sundays sometimes fell on other people's Wednesdays. The spare bedroom—what luxury to have a spare bedroom!—was always filled by one of us strays, and the living room couch often made a bed for another.

Unlike most of San Francisco's broken-down bohemian flats, this one actually resembled the well-built suburban environs we had either grown up in or learned to long for from TV. Its kitchen allowed certain residents to explore their culinary talents, and since Martin was making a small fortune as a waiter in a bustling restaurant, he stocked the living room with a VCR, a stereo, and a TV. Few of us had been given free rein among such middle-class comforts before. Steiner Street was our Model Home, our House Beautiful. But it also was the theater for some of the fiercest domestic battles I've seen.

Home was no board game here, not when you had people who'd stake their lives to determine home's definition. The dominant personalities at Steiner Street made pledges that intense. Martin, like his close friend Paul Coughlan, was unable to reconcile being gay with the prejudices of his Catholic kin; he came to Steiner Street convinced he'd never find the warmth and stability he craved, and when it blossomed he fought to preserve it. He found himself caught between two willful women: Mona Harvey, who invited him into the house and reigned over its first incarnation, and Vivian Segal, whom Martin brought in when Mona defected. The evolution of Mona and Vivian from intimates into enemies, and the battle over aesthetic and spiritual control that fueled it, demonstrated the quandaries that can arise when you build a family without a permit, outside the stipulated hierarchies of convention. When I began to approach each person who'd acted in this drama, to hear his or her account of the house I so admired (twelve years going, still counting), I discovered that there would be no happy reunion for Steiner Street. Instead, there would only be a winding and contradictory tale of betrayal and misunderstanding.

In its first two years, Steiner Street was Mona's realm and our university. She developed her art of living in the late 1970s, as a baby hippie in Arizona. Her European mom had taught Mona to crave fairly conventional "finer things": good food and wine, opera, the feel of silk on her skin. In Arizona, she added her own indulgences, among them high-grade marijuana and the collected works of Roxy Music. She learned how to build a realm of comfort wherever she went. "The idea of putting roots down had never occurred to me," recalled Martin, who was twenty-one and fresh off the plane from Seattle when he met Mona. "Then I moved into Steiner, and I'd come home from whatever I was doing, and she'd be lying around in her kimono, drinking chardonnay, feeding her cat raw tuna. And I'd think, Hmm, there's something to this."

Key to Mona's homemaking wizardry was the ability to ignore what didn't mesh with her sensibilities. Sometimes this included people. The first housemates she and Martin had at Steiner Street were a pair of jazz musicians who treated the place like a bachelor pad, leaving their take-out containers on the coffee table and practicing their instruments in their boxer shorts. They offended Mona greatly, and she regularly sent them cowering into their rooms with a few scathing remarks. Then, all peace restored to our little world, Mona, Martin, and any friends who were present would pop a bottle of California sparkling, kick off our shoes, and relax. Mona would discuss her latest readings in African art history; Martin would report on whatever interwaiter intrigue currently occupied his restaurant. An hour or two after midnight the conversation would lapse, and everyone would nod off toward slumber, watching for the fifteen hundredth time Mona's personal videotape of *Cat on a Hot Tin Roof.*

The Steiner Street crowd came no closer than their Fulton Street siblings to the paths that lead to the advertised definition of maturity. Our jobs paid under five dollars an hour; our dreams involved unprofitable passions such as poetry, music, and post-Marxist theory. Martin, Edie, and Paul had dropped out of college by the time Mona rented the flat, and Vivian and I spent most of our class time in the campus pub. We'd all dismayed our parents in one way or another. Sometimes, at somebody else's party or in line at the supermarket, Mona and I would happen on someone our age in a business suit or a maternity dress, and we'd feel like Richard Dreyfuss at the end of *Close Encounters of the Third Kind,* staring in fear and wonder at a being from a planet far, far away.

Normal people. Mona called them Body Snatchers. "Oh, dear, the Body Snatchers got her," she'd say, shaking her head when a wedding invitation from a long-lost friend arrived in the mail. In a sense, though, we were the ones doing the snatching, nabbing the enticements of a well-endowed American existence without accruing any of the spiritual costs. It's an old bohemian maneuver, this slipping past both bourgeois stagnation and working-class entrapment by living for the moment and not worrying about the rent. In the yuppie eighties we did this by grabbing as much luxury as possible at very little expense, through ingenuity, scamming, and the careful deployment of a few credit cards. Though for the most part we endured the "dedicated intentional poverty" the sociologist Lawrence Lipton identified as a bohemian prerogative in 1959, unlike Lipton's grubby painters we wanted more than a plate of beans and a crash pad. We got it, for a while.

Our first strategy was to discern which niceties deserved to be relished, and which were merely status symbols seducing those less clever than we. Clothes from Neiman Marcus and martinis at fancy bars were what society said pleasure should be. Baked beans might be ideal, if they came from Do City, the barbecue joint Mona loved to frequent on Thursdays around two A.M. Jack Daniel's at the bowling alley could be exquisite, especially when sipped from a vintage silver flask. We could will glamour into being. Travel? We took our vacations every sunny day, driving down to Ocean Beach and drinking Bud Talls on the hood of Mona's car. Public acknowledgment? We got our kicks from the strange looks we got fingering the merchandise in expensive stores. The legendary bohemian Joe Gould once said that being a bohemian entailed making a spectacle of yourself; we considered everyone else the spectacle, and ourselves their most vocal critics.

Mona showed us how to feel deserving, something that didn't come easily to this bunch of former high-school outcasts. Foremost among what we learned to deserve was family, with all the trimmings. That meant Christmases with HoneyBaked ham and rum eggnog and shiny red-wrapped presents under the tree—and no more relatives' probes about our love lives and our bank accounts. "The very first Christmas I spent away," Martin recalled, "you and I opened gifts, and then we picked up Mona and went drinking in North Beach, then on to midnight mass at Saints Peter and Paul. Afterwards, we drove around the Presidio singing Peter, Paul and Mary songs." He smiled. "In the last twelve years, that was the only time I've ever wanted to go to mass." The kinship we created at Steiner Street inspired every one of us to take more care, to recognize why, of all the people in the world, we'd settled on each other.

I asked Mona how she knew when a friend could be family. "There's a sense of 'This is right and you fit,' " she said matter-of-factly. The chance to fit was a big attraction at Steiner Street, and those who did were honored and loved. But this system of judgment is also what ended up causing so much trouble in the house. Unlike Fulton Street, where our casual camaraderie allowed anyone a fair chance to come in and play, Steiner Street thrived on exclusivity. Our disdainful horror of the Body Snatchers was nothing new: in the 1920s, our bohemian forebears had called the dull masses Babbitts; in the 1950s, the Beats named them squares. But for us the lines between cool and not cool blurred. The obvious ways to distinguish a cool person—through his or her artistic pursuits, sexual adventurism, political radicalism, or street knowledge—didn't really work after the counterculture's emergence, since most middle-class people dabbled a little bit in one or two of these areas. An investment banker could be a foreign-film buff who donated to Greenpeace. An artist, for that matter, might be a sexist, homophobic asshole. It wasn't always easy to tell the true members of the tribe from the impostors. So bohemian clans like ours developed their own codes, secret handshakes that let them know whom to admit.

Mona was the main arbiter of Steiner Street's code. If a person didn't have that quality of cool, if she was too earnest, fearful, or prudish, or just not savvy enough, Mona reckoned that person didn't belong. She considered herself frank and antihypocritical, and her evaluations often hit the mark. But after a while, each of us found her snobbery directed at someone we really cared for. My boyfriend David was one target. Before I met him, Mona and I were as bonded as Paul and Edie, shopping, cooking, and eating together, closing bars and sneaking into movies, sometimes even sharing a bed. We were lovers without the sex. In most things, I was Mona's protégé, too, six years younger and eager to master her vocabulary of self-satisfaction. To be accepted by one so imperious made me feel golden.

David, however, was a choice Mona could not approve of. Perhaps she was jealous of the time I gave him, or of the influence he started having on me as we pursued our mutual interests in writing and music. She insists she was never that mean to him, but Mona tends to have a selective memory, and David was a proud guy who probably never let her in on his anger. One afternoon he stormed into Fulton Street after enduring an extra-nasty round of her insults. Broken down and furious, he demanded that I sever my alliance with his newfound foe. After that I began distancing myself from her in that careful way that begins with icy politeness and ends in phone calls never returned. She let me go, maybe because she recognized that the aspects of family that had crept into our friendship—the need to control and the desire to rebel—were not the ones she'd hoped to cultivate. Or maybe she was just tired of dealing with her bratty little sister.

Others at Fulton Street began to chafe against Mona's opinions. "She would say the meanest things about the people I liked the best. The most cutting, horrible things," remembered Vivian. "When it finally dawned on me how degrading it was, I didn't want anything to do with her." Welcome guidance had evolved into censure. Vivian stopped talking to Mona not long after I did. When Mona left San Francisco for graduate school a few months later, we barely said good-bye.

Martin, always our steadfast brother, held the house together. Eventually, he found himself alone and uncertain. "All my roommates moved out at once," he recalled. "So I just kind of rebuilt the house." His first move was to ask Vivian, who had been crashing in the spare bedroom as she plotted a cross-country move that never materialized, to officially move in. At first she planned to stay for only a few months, but as time went by she became Steiner Street's new governing force.

Vivian's sense of style was as exacting as Mona's, her desire to form family just as strong. But she had different motivations. Mona had developed a knack for portable homemaking, and it continued to serve her as she traveled up and down the coast after leaving Steiner Street, finally returning to her hippie roots in the rural Midwest. Vivian felt suspicious of Mona's wanderlust. When Vivian emerged as Steiner Street's new cook and coordinator, her roast chicken replacing Mona's brie and pâté, what she wanted was to make this household last.

Vivian's investment in the house was personal—her parents had died when she was in high school, and she felt she had no home, not even one to reject—and political. Like me, she came of age in the glory days of women's studies and heard truth in Shulamith Firestone's feminist description of the "perfect family" as a noose slowly strangling womankind. Vivian's hope for home was a hope for a social alternative, constructed quietly, without any rulemaking or ideological fuss. This was revolution as common practice—an attempt, on a manageable level, to realize the possibilities feminism had revealed. Her pragmatic approach meshed with Martin's sense of gay politics as lived experience. For both Vivian and Martin, acknowledging that the most spectacular battles in sexual liberation had already been fought in the 1970s meant neither accepting loss nor assuming victory. For them—for all of us—liberation became a matter of daily stealth attacks on values and institutions that were crumbling anyway. Steiner Street was one place where we could enact our covert, radical plans.

With Vivian and Martin in charge, Steiner Street more closely resembled the sibling environment of Fulton Street. Two new roommates moved in: Dionne Jackson, who had left her Oakland neighborhood and found work behind the costume jewelry counter at Macy's, and Ben Hart, who toiled in a cubicle at IBM by day and spent his evenings in the rock clubs of the Lower Haight. The four housemates shared a profound lack of interest in wearing the marks of their various "alternative lifestyles" on their sleeves. Steiner Street became a shelter for each of them, not only from the pressures of the straight world but also from the presumptions of communities—feminist, gay, black, punk—whose uniforms they rejected. "You say we were living an alternative lifestyle," said Dionne recently. "But I think my life's the norm. The freaks are everyone else."

The reassurance the Steiner Street foursome gave one another didn't stop them from struggling. They fought, and many of their fights came straight from the dysfunctional-family handbook. First, there was the matter of Mona's legacy. When Vivian moved in, she strove to wipe every corner free of her former mentor's scent. As far as she was concerned, Mona's controlling presence had to be eradicated if the house was to harbor a newer, healthier family life. Martin felt differently. A few months after Vivian moved in, he invited Mona to return for a few days. It was the winter holiday season. A bloody row ensued. "It was like Mom and Dad were having a huge, major fight," Dionne remembered. "Vivian was at the stove, and Marty came in, and he started slamming pots around. He was pissed."

"I didn't slam any pots," Martin insisted. "But I did blow up at her." He paused, shaking his head at the memory. "I've had very few major breakoffs with people," he continued. "The notion of washing your hands of someone was foreign to me. I just wanted us to have Christmas, like we'd done so many times before." Mona was family, Martin reasoned, and so despite her faults she should be welcomed back. But for Vivian, one of the privileges of choosing family was the chance to stay free of those who'd hurt you. Her new family had to live up to the standards that biological kin so often failed, including mutual respect and careful kindness. Mona had been abusive, Vivian felt, and just as an abusive parent or sibling ought to lose her right to kinship, so should Mona. This was the young feminist, who valued her right to choose, in bitter conflict with the young gay man, who relied on his community to survive in a society that had no place for him.

After Christmas, Mona left San Francisco for the last time, and these struggles sank back under the surface. The foursome reigned at Steiner Street for three joyful years. Every night, Vivian and Dionne would share vodka tonics and talk about their day; every month, there'd be a party celebrating whatever. Members of the household's outer circle still spent many nights on the couch or in the spare room. As long as no major differences arose, we thrived.

Then one of life's common crises started to eat at our easy camaraderie. Dionne lost her job. She'd already messed up on the gas bill a few times, and Martin had nagged her relentlessly until she finally settled the account. But with no steady income, she gradually became the Roommate from Hell, the kind everyone has confronted at one point or another, whose mere presence becomes an overweening burden. She spent more and more time in her room, letting the daytime soaps bleed into the nighttime sitcoms. Dishes disappeared from the kitchen and piled up just inside her door. Her friendship with Vivian evaporated as Vivian became frustrated with her messiness and lethargy. Vivian and Martin took a step they'd always hoped to avoid: they drew up a chores schedule. Dionne ignored it, and Ben, who had those problematic bachelor-pad tendencies, considered her refusal permission for him to slack, too. "I had no other home base, but they weren't going to do anything to make this into one," Vivian remarked. Her shouting matches with Ben escalated until he gave notice. Then the worst happened for Vivian—Martin, her only ally, was admitted to graduate school on the East Coast and decided to go.

Reflecting on Steiner Street in our recent conversation, Vivian made a statement that shocked me as much as Edie's words about Fulton Street had shocked Paul: "I don't think Steiner Street was a home for me until Dionne moved out." When I repeated this to her former housemates they were shaken, dismayed. "Those were some of the happiest years of my life!" cried Ben. All Martin could manage was a desultory "It's weird." As I dug into the household's history, though, I realized that Vivian's view wasn't so weird after all. At every point, she'd been the one urging more clarity and commitment. For a few years she coasted on everyone's goodwill and her own domestic gifts. But Martin had been the only one to actively join her in shaping the nature of this home, and although she loved him dearly, Vivian didn't share his feeling that the closeness born of time should transcend friends' changing attitudes. Vivian wanted consistency. She started with a set of convictions: that a household should be casual but well kept, its resident family open but cautious about newcomers, independent but active in each other's lives, individual but fundamentally tied by a few evident beliefs. She has played out those convictions at Steiner Street.

But family isn't just an idea, and Vivian knows that. She needed at least one full partner to realize her ideal. Martin's random replacement turned out to be her match. Elise Tremont hardly seemed a likely candidate for an alternative lifestyle when she showed up on a lead from a roommate referral agency. She projected the hearty aura of a former sorority girl, worked in advertising, and spent her nights in the yuppie bars of Union Street. But she also had survived an often-divided family of stepsiblings and Dad's New Wives, and her hunger for home matched Vivian's. The two women learned to like each other more and more. They finally kicked Dionne out a year and a half into her slump, and approached Steiner Street as a clean slate.

Elise and Vivian wrote lengthy statements of purpose about the house and posted them at Roommate Referral; they put prospective roommates through several interviews. "The main thing we'd always expressed was that this was our home and we wanted someone else who wanted a home," said Vivian. "It could be in varying degrees. Elise and I will make dinner together often, share some food, or not share. There's sort of a fluidity about it. But if you were going to be here it wasn't a transient situation. It wasn't about staying in your room and watching your TV."

They never found anyone willing and able to match their commitment. Five years rolled by and a procession of roommates passed through Steiner Street, some staying only a few months. Vivian and Elise made their home anyway, and a new extended family formed around them, including some refugees from the old one and others whom I've never met. I'd drifted away from Steiner Street after Martin's departure, having begun my immersion in the writing life that would eventually lead me to follow him east. My interests didn't seem to fit into the conversations at Steiner Street anymore. Busy with other things, I hardly noticed as my old home drifted beyond me. When I returned half a decade after I'd left San Francisco, I felt more like a distant relative than a sibling.

The house was in a nervous state at that point, as Vivian and Elise faced an unpredictable situation. Two years earlier, Vivian had begun a romance with Miguel Almovar, a waiter at the restaurant she now manages, where Martin had long ago secured her a job. This love match had its complications. At twenty-five, Miguel was nearly a decade younger than Vivian; he was also Guatemalan, with no legal papers. When a fender-bender alerted local officials to his illegal status, Miguel and Vivian eloped to Reno to prevent his deportation. Elise went along on their honeymoonless wedding trip. "I told her I wouldn't go without her," Vivian said.

In the White Lace and Promises Wedding Chapel on that cloudless Nevada morning, two partnerships faced each other and sought a way to become one whole. I wonder what it was like for Elise to stand there and watch her primary companion of the last five years pledge herself to someone else. Maybe she felt jealous; maybe it felt inevitable. She and Vivian weren't a couple. They weren't even sisters, really; in the beginning, it had seemed impossible that they would even be friends. They were roommates. Marriage, the institution that wins every time in the scissors-paper-rock game of emotional fidelity, surely would change everything.

Miguel kept his room in a nearby boardinghouse for a while, but everyone knew that there was enough space for him at Steiner Street. "We talked about it a lot," said Elise. "I was hesitant; it's a completely different dynamic living with a couple. With independent people it's separate principalities in one kingdom. To be honest, there had been other times when I'd asked if we would consider a friend of mine moving in, and Vivian had said she'd rather have things all on even ground, and I understood that. But I didn't want to look for another roommate. I'd done that for too many years." In October 1997, Miguel became the fourteenth official resident of Steiner Street.

The new arrangement had been in place for only two months when I sat with Elise and Vivian in their living room. It seemed remarkably comfortable. Shortly after we began talking, Miguel arrived, exhausted from work. He flopped down on the couch between the two women and stayed there, absorbing the history of the house that was now his home, massaging Elise's foot as he leaned against his wife's shoulder. Yet for all their warmth, this threesome remained uncertain of its future. "When this setup dissolves, it's going to be a major thing. Whatever happens, it's not going to be easy," muttered Elise. Vivian quickly dismissed the thought: "I can honestly say I haven't conceptualized that. I can't imagine it," she said with a quick shake of her blond curls. A dew of anxiety settled on the room. It was impossible to know whose fears and fantasies would prove true.

For now, though, Steiner Street endures. Some of the chosen family that formed there still gathers around its kitchen counter to sip red wine and eat Vivian's cooking on birthdays and holidays; others have been lost to time and carelessness, pride and misunderstanding. It's strange to feel disowned by people who only ever owned you because you let them. Kinship beyond blood can be just as cruel as the biological kind. After visiting a few years ago, Martin vowed he wouldn't stay with Vivian again. "She acted like I was a guest rather than somebody who belonged there," he explained. "Going back there and being treated that way was kind of a slap in the face." Vivian failed Martin, and her own ideal, in that harsh moment; in a world that makes us earn our love, one of family's often unrealized gifts is a chance to just be.

No one in this story actually has realized the dream of a perfect family. It doesn't exist, not in the Bible Belt and not in bohemia. At Fulton Street and Steiner Street, we chose each other hungrily, so determined were we to belong to something, somewhere. Then most of us fled, just as we'd sneaked away from the homes we'd inherited, capriciously seeking another adventure. Our youth was not the only reason we didn't always recognize the rare beauty of our closeness. We didn't have a way to describe it, not to each other, not to the world. So we let it take its own course.

"When I started out, I didn't have any idea that I was going to have some alternative lifestyle," Vivian said. "But I can safely say now that I am committed to those ideas. I can't say what my alternative lifestyle's going to be in ten years, but I can say pretty surely that I don't have any idea that it wouldn't be alternative. Whatever that can encompass." The family Vivian began with bears little relation to the one she claims now. Her ideas have changed, too; her sense of lineage has refined and expanded. But finally, twelve years and a thousand stories in, Vivian can call Steiner Street home.

■

Settling

"It's a phase," Mother says. "You'll meet some nice man and settle down." The parent within each person tells her which passages of her life have meaning and which merely serve as intermezzos, the entertainment between the acts of the real drama. We were growing up at Fulton Street, at Steiner Street; not as young as you'd think, not simply college kids reliving summer camp in dorm rooms, but still coming of age. We needed to stick together because we didn't have much money. Our requirements for enjoying life were minimal: macaroni and cheese, beer, music, occasional sex. If we played around with caviar and fine wine, if Martin bought opera pumps on credit at Macy's, it was only an extended bout of dress-up. And if we tried on new varieties of passion, of faith and trust in each other, that was dress-up, too.

This is what I hear when I speak to myself coolly, in the customary language of the adult. I did meet a nice man; I've lived with him and no one else for over a decade now. We buy furniture together and pay the mortgage on time. And I'm back in close contact with my blood family, trading phone calls every week or so, spending Christmases around Aunt Joyce's tree. You would think that all the love I spilled on the ramshackle floors of San Francisco rewarded me with nothing but a few good stories about an iconoclastic past. But look deeper. Let me tell you what I didn't know before I arrived in San Francisco. I didn't know that my life would never be like the photo albums piled up in my parents' basement den, its high points framed in the usual ways, by wedding cards and birth announcements, retirement parties and funerals. I threw myself out of that orbit, and I knew that meant something would change, but I still felt as if I should be waiting for something. Fulton Street and Steiner Street taught me not to wait. My friends helped me realize that all you really have is the love right in front of you, and that sometimes this love will remain a secret to everybody else, even when you don't hesitate to show it. In those homes, I learned bohemia's first precept: being radical often just means making it up as you go along.

Expanding your sense of family is the first step in developing this mind-set. You have to be able to adopt like-minded people as your own; otherwise, all your small, solitary acts of subversion can feel like shadowboxing in an empty lot. Everyone who lived at Fulton Street and

Steiner Street carried what they gleaned into their subsequent endeavors. Some coupled up, as I did, but sustained strong networks that enriched and offered rest from that pair bond. Others moved into different group houses, or, like Ben and Dionne, found themselves sharing a coat closet one more time. Those two rent a sprawling duplex on Potrero Hill. "What can I say? We know each other's history," Ben explains with a shrug.

My old singing partner from Fulton Street, Isadora, lives with her lover, Crystal, in an urban commune in San Diego. They're pursuing a 1990s version of the 1960s dream, with free love and shared resources the order of the day. Before moving south, they spent several years in an all-female house in the Upper Haight. Last summer, Isadora took me to breakfast with Crystal and their old flatmate Marina, who still lives at that Oak Street address, with another bunch of surrogate sisters as housemates. The trio recalled how they'd evolved a quotidian code similar to Vivian's, with specific goals regarding community, creativity, and nurture. Oak Street sounded like Fulton Street, with a little more organization and a TV. "People called our house 774-Coffeehouse," Marina laughed. "In the winter we'd just sit around the kitchen table drinking espresso. We'd always have a token boy over. On Wednesdays we'd watch *Beverly Hills 90210*. We'd never leave; we didn't need to."

Marina reckons group living will be in her future for a long time. "I want to have children, but my vision has always been that I'd raise them in a home with women," she said. Marina's words echo those of many women I've known, who have little faith in the durability of monogamous relationships but don't want their lives outside marriage to limit their domestic choices. These women, along with some enlightened men, are forming systems of mutual support that can accommodate the needs of children as well as their own changing concerns as they grow older. "It's not even that I necessarily want that. It's just how I've thought it would be," Marina concludes.

Paul, who hosted the Fulton Street reunion, sometimes thinks about children too. He doesn't have a steady romantic partner, but he does have a mom in mind—Gina Ellis, the companion who shares his comfy garden apartment. Paul met Gina when he was still living with Edie, and moved in with her after Edie moved on to Marin. Over six years, he and his new better half have developed an uncommon common-law marriage.

"Once I was at this barbecue, and Paul introduced me to some friends of his," laughed Gina as we sat on the couch she and Paul had purchased together. "And I said, Hi, I'm Gina, and I'd like you to meet my husband"—she gestured toward an imaginary figure beside her—"and my boyfriend"—another wave toward a different dream man—"and the man I live with." She smiled at Paul. "It really confused them. That was fun."

When Gina met Paul, she was involved with a merchant seaman whom she still sees when he's in port. In 1995 she married a German émigré, an old friend of Paul's, so he could get his green card. But her closest and most enduring bond remains with Paul, who describes their connection as the slow refinement of an intuitive understanding.

As a straight woman who's lived her whole life in San Francisco, Gina is comfortable with exploring the parameters of emotional and erotic exchange. I have known the same delicious sense of freedom. It comes from belonging to a community whose erotic charge goes in all directions, where men and women can be close in ways that are never sexual, and it's not assumed that the woman is either the possession of one lucky sod, fair prey for every other guy, an undesirable loser, or a bitch. Gina, who married and divorced at a young age, grants the icons of heterosexual domesticity little power.

Paul expresses the same lack of interest in the images of fulfillment that mainstream gay culture promotes. He's always chafed at the roles gay men have adopted for themselves, whether Castro clone or ACT-UP/Queer Nation queen; during the late eighties, when everyone in town seemed to be one or the other, he even doubted whether he could call himself gay. "Part of me would like to find the perfect gay lover and set up house," he said, exchanging glances with Gina. "But I've been offered that, and at some point decided to back away from it. If I do decide to have children, I'd like to do it in some kind of alternative family, three parents in a home or something. Which you can certainly do in this city. People we know are doing it."

Sometimes strangers get confused about Paul and Gina's liaison. "One of the new guys at work spoke to you on the phone, and thought you were a man and you were my lover," Paul told Gina at one point in our conversation. "I was like, No, that's my straight female roommate." But friends and close acquaintances consider the relationship exceedingly normal. The pair agrees that this very likely would not be the case were they to move outside San Francisco. Their form of wedlock isn't recognized in most states. But that doesn't matter; neither wants to roam. With both of them nearing forty, Paul and Gina are considering really settling down, buying a sweet little house, having a kid.

"Paul is my candidate to raise a child," explained Gina. "You want that person to be passing on some decent virtues and traits. Frankly, I have not met a lot of men in my life who have grown up enough—what kind of fathers would they be? And Paul's sexuality has nothing to do with my belief that [he] would be a good father. I know plenty of immature gay men too. And I'm sure there are plenty of mature heterosexual men out there. I just don't know them."

She laughed again, her quick chuckle, then gave her unexpected mate a serious look. "I can see living with Paul, into the future," she said. "I don't know, it's very strange because that's usually a judgment reserved for your lover. That I see a future with him. That he's not just what I'm doing until I marry a man and he takes me to the suburbs and we have children. But that is not what I'm waiting for."

It was late in the conversation my friends and I had staged in the kitchens and living rooms we've made home. I worried that we would face each other blankly, our connections broken like so many interrupted phone lines. But the warmth returned with little effort. Whatever else we shared now (some a lot, some very little), we all preserved a belief in the legitimacy of our shared heritage. This is not to say everyone agreed on what that heritage was.

One summer evening, Martin and I were driving up the Oregon freeway, away from a visit with a vacationing Mona, whom I'd barely seen since our uncomfortable parting ten years ago. "See," Martin began, in that tone of voice that says he's ready for an argument, "I just don't see how you can use the word 'family.' You don't even talk to half these people anymore." Martin has always been the one to hold the flying spokes of our wheel together, making phone calls and writing letters, forgiving small unkindnesses to preserve the larger bond. His accusation made me itch. Maybe I was lying to myself, assembling a fake ideal from a bunch of scraps. Maybe the need to belong was the only thing I'd really managed to cultivate.

I didn't want to fight about family values with Martin. I'd let him down plenty over the years; all of us could be as petty as we ever were magnanimous. But we had taken on something basic together, and the challenge had carried through the rest of our lives. Sometimes it led us to preserve our relationships over decades. That was the case with Martin and me, Paul and Gina, Vivian and Elise. It also made us ready to build fellowship whenever the chance arises, to fight the meanings of family that turn people against each other and develop the ones that unite. Our family history deserved to be shared and scrutinized, its holes poked at and its links to the future traced. If we denied its existence, though, it could easily wind up buried in an unmarked grave, alongside history's other bastard lines.

"Maybe what we did was just a step," I said. "It still deserves to be noticed."

"I can understand that," Martin replied. "We made something together, a real thing. Maybe you want to turn family into something you do instead of something that happens to you."

"Family as a verb," I said.

"That's one way to think about it," said Martin.

Organically grown communes, marriage without ceremony, the politics of domesticity dismantled with the tools of daily life—the dust of a whole epoch of utopian community-building gathers in the corners of bohemian America's group houses and shared apartments. I never wanted to live on a hippie farm in icy Vermont, but I can hear an echo of myself in a passage by the founder of Liberation News Service, Ray Mungo, who did just that: "The life of the community, the families building their new nation, is the only life on the planet now." He wrote these optimistic, solipsistic phrases in 1970, explaining why he'd abandoned an active career in New York for the isolation of goat-raising and pickle-making up north. Mungo's commune failed, like most, and life barreled on, offering up more and more images of counterculture paradise gone bad: the Manson Family figuratively carving the marks of their clan allegiance into the sprawled body of Sharon Tate; Patty Hearst trading in one brainwashed self for another at the klutzy, brutal hands of the Symbionese Liberation Army. These perversions of filial commitment seemed like the inevitable spinout of a bunch of pie-eyed kids who broke off from their nuclear households only to become as helpless as children in the grip of new patriarchs. For those of us who followed, family could seem like a poisoned structure, stifling in its original version and murderous when employed as ideology.

So what do I hear in Ray Mungo's words? I hear one man's realization that for all the work that can be done in the world outside the home, the home must change or nothing else will stick. Alternative families have emerged from Mungo's incomplete revolution, and from many others. These new clans are not simply accidental formations; they represent self-conscious choices to remake society from within its most personal sphere. Today, with fewer and fewer people even trying to live up to the nuclear fantasy, chosen families stand on another cutting edge of the status quo; once again, bohemians mark out what later becomes the norm. Many of us have done so without giving our radical actions proper names. Whether or not we see these choices as political, they form the center of our own experience and connect us across the gaps of taste, identity, and circumstance. It's like Ray Mungo said—a new nation of families, not the only life on the planet, but the life that centers our orbit nonetheless.

2

THE LONG (SEXUAL) REVOLUTION

IMAGINE yourself in the pages of a pulp fiction. Walking down a city street, you run into an old friend, someone who dropped off the face of your earth years ago. She's looking fine in elegant clothes—cashmere and high heels. Time for coffee? She says sure. Soon you're laughing and talking like old times about the lovers each of you dumped, the roommate who made it in real estate, the old coworker who's raising her kid on her own. Your friend wants to know all the details about you now, and you don't hesitate. You want to know, too. . . . She lowers her eyes. And says, I'm a sex worker. I massage men for money, feel them up until they come.

What is the proper response at such a moment? Stunned silence? A horrified look? Fingernails to mouth, eyebrows raised, like the girl on the cover of a trashy paperback who's just learned a terrible secret? In the movies, when a woman reveals she's fallen into such a state, her discoverer usually either turns away in shame or slaps her. Not a lot of conversation follows the shock.

When Isadora told me she was working in the sex trade, the thought did flicker through my mind: if we were living in any other place and time, I would have been horrified. Instead, I was . . . "delighted" is too strong a word, but certainly intrigued. And not surprised. Isadora had always been the mistress of herself, abiding by no one's preconceptions. Her mellow attitude about sex flows out of her general philosophy of following the moment. Once, when she'd sublet her Fulton Street room for a few months and headed off to Germany, word came back that, having been dumped after a short fling by a musician playing a Cologne jazz club, she expeditiously accepted the advances of the club's owner, a former ballet dancer. The two engaged in strenuous workouts both artistic and sensual, until Isadora started to miss California. He begged her to stay, but she left with no regrets.

Years of monogamy with a puppyish boy her age followed, but Isadora never stopped exploring her considerable talents for bodily pleasure. She was instinctively exhibitionistic, always flashing the crowd at parties or wearing negligees to work. She never hesitated to be physical with her friends; she especially loved taking Ecstasy, the drug that gave us all permission to stroke and cuddle each other without provoking anyone's jealousy. A while after she and her boyfriend parted ways, she met a wild girl named Crystal at a rave South of Market and discovered the other half of her sexual self. The new girlfriend was a speed freak, and the first thing Isadora did was straighten her out, get her eating vegan and sleeping regularly. In return, Crystal taught Isadora some things she knew—about sex, and about making home movies for erotic kicks and potential profit. When the pair moved to San Diego after a sojourn at a desert yoga commune, they needed money but they didn't want to work much. Lingerie massage and video work fit their employment profile.

Isadora told me these things when I first contacted her, not wasting breath to explain or qualify. When she brought up her new life to the Fulton Street crowd sitting around Paul's living room some months later, not everyone got it right away.

" 'Massage escort,' " repeated Edie. "Is that like going out on a date?"

"Sort of," Isadora answered. "These guys, older guys usually, will call up and say they want a date, so who knows what they're really expecting? But basically they get a massage and you model some lingerie and they'll jack off, or you pretend to masturbate. Or you do masturbate. There's a sexual interaction, but not intercourse. You can touch, but you don't have sex with a person. Though you are, from across the room."

"So what if he wants to get physical?" Edie pressed. "How do you keep your distance?"

Isadora had her answer ready. "I give people a lot of connection. They're not themselves anymore, but they are, because they're releasing their inner child or whatever. They're playing. They wanna have a good time."

"Do they gross you out, the guys?" I just had to ask.

"They're pretty gross." Isadora laughed. "But they're people."

Edie crinkled her nose as she reached for her wine. "There's definitely a jump from not having a moral issue about this stuff, to actually being involved in it." She wasn't quite ready to leap. But she was trying to not judge her friend.

At this point, Paul decided to share a story, an argument for Isadora's point of view. "Well," he began, winding up, "my friend is an acupressurist. And she's also a lap dancer. What she does is, she finds a physical connection, she needs that. That connection is sexual and it's healing. And it gets her through whatever she has to do."

"I really feel like my dance and my yoga have led me to this place," enthused Isadora. "I can understand body language, I can understand movement and the chakras. Sexual energy is one of the highest energy forms on this planet. It's very creative."

"And the guys get that," Edie remarked, raising her eyebrow.

"Oh yeah!" Isadora said. "Some guys, I'll start massaging them and they're lying on their stomachs and they're so tight and nervous and fed up with the world. Some of these guys have never had a massage before in their lives. They don't know the healing of touch. And they just start to open up and by the time I leave they're like, Aaaahhhh! I've seen people open up like that. It's amazing."

"Do you feel like these men would want to have dinner with you?" Edie asked.

"No, or have me be their girlfriend," Isadora said. That was fine with her; it was better. "It's like a play interaction, so they can figure out what they believe and what women are, and redefine themselves."

As our talk wandered on to different subjects, I thought, This is hardly a normal conversation. But it wasn't the first time I'd been part of such a circle, struggling to determine right and wrong, safe and dangerous, on new terms. Edie felt nervous about the risks Isadora was taking with her body and her heart, but she had no worries about her soul. Moral judgments would have been silly coming from a woman who herself had once lived in a three-way relationship with a married couple. We had all roamed down such crooked alleys at one point or another, if only as enthusiastic sluts cruising San Francisco's parties and bars. Most of us had known women who'd made a little extra cash by stripping at the Market Street Cinema or doing phone sex—such jobs were an integral part of the city's student-cum-slacker life in the 1980s, in the same league as bartender gigs. Instead of hiding their occupations, those sex workers—no one called them prostitutes anymore, although a few of the more audacious ones proudly reclaimed "hooker" or "whore"— played a key role in defining our moment in San Francisco's gloriously profligate history.

This is how the sexual revolution has kept moving through the past few decades, as fundamentalist Christians like Pat Robertson and extreme "feminists" like Andrea Dworkin—and the vast array of nervous opinion-shapers between them—did their best to suffocate it. Isadora's explanations seemed to reflect the work of feminist and queer intellectuals who emerged during the same era, but she hadn't read those books. Her conclusions came from the street-level lingo of the drag queens who hung out at Club Uranus and the pierced people of Club Fuck!, who considered their night lives performance art and an educational tool. They came from shopping at the feminist sex-toy store Good Vibrations and flipping through the lesbian porn and radical philosophy in magazines like *On Our Backs*. Long before Isadora met Crystal and headed down her new path, she couldn't help but trip over sexual adventurism everywhere she turned.

The magazines, stores, and ongoing events that still typify San Francisco erotica were informed by the famous sexual revolution our generation supposedly missed. As with so many fundamentals of bohemian life, we had to remake that revolution for ourselves. The idea of sexual liberation came down to us as a worn delusion—a vague tangle of mostly heterosexual bodies whose turn-ons turned off their brains. The romantics Gay Talese described in his best-seller *Thy Neighbor's Wife* had been made into jokes or demons by Hollywood. The swinger lifestyle was trashed completely by the movie *Looking for Mr. Goodbar* in 1977, when Isadora was still a virgin. The gay sexual underground received similar treatment in 1980's *Cruising*. By the mid-1980s, America had once again adopted a conservative sexual outlook. We'd come to Sin City to ascertain the shape of our bliss, only to discover we were living in a moment when we weren't supposed to even want it.

That didn't stop us from stumbling along, grabbing for love and other people's nerve endings. Some people I know never stopped the slide; they just keep reaching out and hoping pleasure would produce its own meaning. Others ended up running toward the wedding-cake scenarios they'd sworn they would never accept. Myself, I'd grown tired of frustrated free love and settled into a long, monogamous relationship. But the way I think about sexuality has grown ever more radical, more "perverted," as the world around me continues to transform sex in seemingly infinite ways.

■

PERVERTS UNITED

When I first found out there was a war going on about sex in America, it was 1981, near the end of the fall semester in my first women's studies class. I was informed by some women who brought in pictures from the front. Before that, I'd assumed there were just two opposing factions: the religious, who hated sex along with rock and roll and everything else I liked; and those lucky enough to be born without guilt, who did what they enjoyed and kept it mostly to themselves. I knew that skirmishes occasionally erupted between these two domains, and that certain key victories for the side I favored, such as the right to an abortion, were fresh. But it seemed to me that a détente had been reached, and that even nice lapsed Catholic girls like me could proceed with an average, active sex life.

Then a couple of activists from Women Against Pornography showed up to class with their slide show. They had come to show us newborn feminists the hatred male-dominated society felt for us, as manifested in the dark mirror of mass-produced sexual imagery. I remember their presentation's glum melodrama, the way each projected image of a woman bound or bent over like a dog gave way to one harsher, as the speakers intoned platitudes about dehumanization and violence, climaxing with their motto: "Pornography is the theory, rape is the practice." The mood mixed a horror movie's sense of building disaster with a docudrama's confident disclosure: *This is right in front of your eyes. Now you can't deny it.*

Young as I was, and itching for a fight, I was ready to sign up for WAP's antiporn army. Except for one thing. One of the slide show's featured images came from the promotional campaign for a Rolling Stones album: a billboard-sized rock babe wearing a ripped dress and a few purple bruises, proclaiming, "I'm Black and Blue from the Rolling Stones—and I Love It!" A protest that won the removal of this billboard from a Los Angeles boulevard had propelled WAP into existence in 1976. Now, I could see dissing Mick and Keith—they were old fogies, I preferred punk, and besides, the billboard was gross in that outdated slimy-rock-star way. But I could easily imagine WAP's condemnation of the Stones extending toward certain rock-and-roll artifacts I treasured. The Sex Pistols, for example, advertised themselves with posters of Queen Elizabeth with a safety pin through her lip. The Cars favored sleek Varga girls in fetish-worthy heels. I actually owned a pair of those shoes, gray spikes so high I couldn't wear them out of the house; they'd been the pièce de résistance of my eighteenth-birthday party outfit.

Then there was *The Rocky Horror Picture Show,* the movie that symbolized underground fun, attracting hordes of boys in nurses' outfits and girls in bondage gear to the Neptune Theater every Friday at midnight. In Seattle, lining up for *Rocky Horror* was one of the ways weird kids trapped between high school and the legal drinking age could meet. Would WAP keep us from it because its diabolical hero, Dr. Frank N. Furter, was a drag queen parody of the Marquis de Sade, who forced his degenerate fantasies on everyone he met? "It's a comedy!" fans would scream; but WAP's soldiers, rather like our parents, didn't have much of a sense of humor. They didn't have very good musical taste either, favoring lame folkie strumming to the growling independence of rockers like the leather-clad Pretenders leader, Chrissie Hynde, who'd included not one but three songs about loving rough sex on the band's debut album that year. On its back cover, Chrissie, in black jeans, a red leather jacket, and boots, bent to fasten her bass player (and ex-lover) Pete Farndon's boot.

Playing with sexual deviance allowed punks to distinguish themselves from worn arena rockers who generally stuck to conventional, straight portrayals of the music's call to orgy. The Stones had been bolder in the past, dressing in drag and flirting with bisexuality, but the babes they preferred during the 1970s were model-perfect and soft as bunnies. Punk divas were different. They were scary in their ripped fishnets and metal-studded belts, their kohl-smeared eyes promising that any man aiming to land them was in for a wrestling match.

Some observers, like the historian Jon Savage, have said that punks of both genders feared sex, and so they made themselves as ugly as possible. That was true of many people, including head Sex Pistol Johnny Rotten, who was so shy about his body that when he stayed at friends' houses, he'd take his trousers off under the covers. But the rebels and outcasts attracted to the scene were also fighting erotic banality. The glam world of David Bowie made sex polymorphous in the early 1970s, and disco had Grace Jones and the Dionysian rites of the gay after-hours clubs. But mainstream rock and pop at mid-decade took their cues from the simplistic feel-good vibe of the mass-marketed sexual revolution, which transformed sex into a fashionable physical exercise, like roller skating. Punk made sex risky again by emphasizing the elements that that fantasy repressed: its violence, its stickiness, the forbidding places it could go. Then, through humor and boldness, it made the nastiness fun.

This attitude seemed right to me and my few punk friends in those teenage years. Hippie idealism disgusted us, and we thought the 1970s sexual revolution was just another manifestation of it. We belonged to the era of sexual disease. One of the guys I served refills to at the Last Exit Coffeehouse was an orange-clad follower of the Bhagwan Shree Rajneesh who ate mayonnaise straight out of the packet and never washed his hair. One night at a party, he cornered me and pulled out a sheaf of explicit love poems he'd written to Bhagwan, insisting that I listen while he recited them. Minutes before, I had found out from an ex-boyfriend with whom I'd just had a brief, conciliatory fling that he'd very recently slept unprotected with a girl known to have herpes. I was not in the mood to hear any free-love crap. Instead, I grabbed my best friend, Martin, and headed for the Neptune Theater, where I enjoyed hearing the guys shudder when the geisha in *In the Realm of the Senses* cut her lover's dick off.

As I struggled to reconcile my enjoyment of punk with my fervent belief in feminism, a group of lesbians in my future hometown were taking a similar contradiction public and making it political. In 1981, as WAP brought its judgments to college campuses across the country, the feminist group Samois published *Coming to Power,* a book of essays, fiction, and poetry exploring positive views of sadomasochism. Their views had already been getting Samois members into trouble. When they tried to distribute the group's first informational pamphlet in 1979, nearly every women's bookstore in the Bay Area refused to carry it. Feminist magazines and journals refused to run the group's advertisements. The Women's Building denied them space for their meetings. Mainstream homosexual activists put up their own roadblocks: when Samois members tried to march on San Francisco's annual Gay Pride Day, parade officials harassed them so relentlessly that they ultimately gave up.

Samois posed a threat to the more traditional membership of these supposedly radical movements not only because its women practiced an extreme form of sex, but because they dared to come out and discuss it. "I have always wanted freedom to be as queer, as perverted, on the street and on the job as I am in my dungeon," wrote Pat Califia, one of the most eloquent theorists to emerge from Samois, in *Coming to Power*. Her choice of words anticipated an epoch during which gay politics, and sexual politics in general, would find strength in insurgency: the historical chapter defined by ACT-UP and Queer Nation's street activism. Although the main desire of Samois members was simple tolerance for their actions, and although many of their writings included a disclaimer to the effect that "We know this isn't for everybody," their rhetoric couldn't help but drift toward advocacy. Feminism had taught these women to deconstruct their desires, and in doing so they found good reasons for the sadomasochistic practice of making explicit the power games involved in sex.

"When feminists argue about SM, there is more at stake than sexual practice," wrote Gayle Rubin in her *Coming to Power* essay. "Some women are arguing for the logical coherence of their political beliefs. Others of us are arguing that political theory about sex is due for a major overhaul." Intellectuals such as Rubin saw Samois's brazen stance as a challenge. In the light of Samois's examinations, even the tamest heterosexual act was revealed as a series of negotiations and power exchanges. It's often been pointed out that the conclusions Samois members reached about the sometimes abusive and violent origins of lust weren't that different from those expounded by their enemies in Women Against Pornography. The key distinction was that while antipornography activists like Andrea Dworkin saw overtones of dominance and submission as grounds for recoiling from sex altogether, the women of Samois found in those impulses a reason to go deeper, down whatever shadowy road their hearts and their pussies led them.

They were not alone in taking those forbidden steps. Gay liberation itself had begun with a drag queen riot—the famous defense of New York City's Stonewall Inn bar against a police raid in 1969. Leathermen had long been accustomed to being branded sexual criminals—in fact, their style fetishized their outlaw status—but as sexual liberation progressed, some found themselves wanting understanding as well as tolerance. Groups like the Street Transvestites Action Revolutionaries, who held sit-ins and bake sales back in 1970, and the Gay Male S/M Activists, who did much to promote safe sex as the AIDS epidemic swelled in the 1980s, saw the politics in perversity. Pat Califia had her male counterpart in John Preston, a juicy pornographer who upheld the leather ethic in essays read by both practitioners and skeptical assimilationists.

Puritan feminists were also challenged by sex workers, who organized unions in New York and San Francisco and rallied behind charismatic leaders like Margo St. James. At the same time, academic feminists who recalled that the movement's early mandate was to liberate women sexually, not repress them, were becoming disgusted with the growing public delusion that Dworkin and her like were ruling their ranks. A group of such women organized a groundbreaking conference on the politics of sexuality at Barnard College in 1982; the resulting anthology, *Pleasure and Danger* (published in 1984), and 1983's similarly themed *Powers of Desire,* edited by Ann Snitow, Christine Stansell, and Sharon Thompson, helped stem the antisex tide in women's studies departments throughout the 1980s.

But there was something unique about the wave of activity that overtook the Bay Area in Samois's wake, just when both mainstream America and feminism were supposed to be in retreat from such experiments. San Francisco had always been on the cutting edge of debauchery, and it again became the laboratory for new models of intimate exchange. The gay community's rule over the Castro, and the presence of a large lesbian population in the East Bay, meant that anything that challenged the city's norms had to be several steps beyond the usual dare. There's something erotic about the very architecture of this pink-and-flesh-colored city. Plenty of explorers come to San Francisco simply to immerse themselves in the glow.

The town buzzed with hungry boys and girls, like Susie Bright, a teenage socialist who had passed through radical circles from Los Angeles to Detroit before landing in the Bay Area in 1981. Now a bohemian star also known as Susie Sexpert, in the 1980s Susie was the most influential editor of the lesbian porn magazine *On Our Backs*. This publication was born to provoke—its founders, Debi Sundahl and Nan Kinney, chose its name as a slap at the notoriously sex-wary feminist journal *Off Our Backs*. Under Bright's guidance, *On Our Backs* became the source of information and hot fantasy material for women curious about edge-walking lesbian sex. Unlike Samois, which you had to join, or the sex-toy store Good Vibrations, where you had to go, *On Our Backs* was a key that could be turned in private. Many women, including me, saw their first pictures of real lesbian sex—as opposed to the airbrushed Barbie-on-Barbie stuff available in men's publications—within its pages. Publisher Sundahl was a stripper, and her frustration at the available products on the sex market was one main reason she and Kinney founded the magazine. (They also produced the first lesbian videos made for women to enjoy, under the rubric Fatale Productions.) The politically minded Bright made sure that along with such features as the "Bull Dyker of the Month" centerfold there was plenty of educational content expanding people's sense of sexual possibilities. Vaginal fisting, butch-femme role-playing, body piercing, and female-to-male transsexualism were just a few of the taboo subjects the magazine delved into early and often.

Nationally, the AIDS crisis was sparking a new political energy among young gay men and their allies, spearheaded by the rowdy, stylish vanguard of ACT-UP and Queer Nation. In San Francisco, ACT-UP's insurgent forces arose from the bubbling cauldron of sexual inquiry stirred by Susie Bright and her friends. Queer politics there did not shy away from sexuality, as it sometimes did in other places where social identity was prioritized over sensual or emotional desire. The image of queer activists as a rebel army uniformed in slogan T-shirts and black jeans, its playfulness squelched by urgent anger, played well in New York. But it had a harder time holding in a town where half the people at meetings wore dog collars or drag. The pull of the carnival was just too strong.

Queer activism grew even more theatrical when a new cause asserted itself in the late 1980s. That's when Jesse Helms, the Reverend Donald

Wildmon, and other patriarchs of the Christian right took it upon themselves to cleanse the earth by cutting off the funding of a few controversial artists, most of whom worked in the medium of their own bodies. Artists like Robert Mapplethorpe and Karen Finley, whose controversial work led to court battles over decency, became causes célèbres. Although anticensorship activists argued that this struggle was about artistic expression, not sex, the content of most of these artists' work was explicitly sexual. Under fire, their work drew curious bohemians into the sex radicals' camp, and the anticensorship battle became a form of sex education, exposing large new audiences to all varieties of dramatic body play. From New York–based "postporn modernist" Annie Sprinkle, who offered fans a chance to gaze into her speculum-widened vagina, to Los Angeles's "supermasochist" Bob Flanagan, who connected his experience of cystic fibrosis with the tests of endurance he gave himself (most famously, nailing his penis to a board), avatars of sex were the on-the-ground practitioners of the anticensorship movement's ideology.

Everywhere else in America, a new conservatism was rising—or so the magazines said, though enough fellow travelers passed through the Bay Area's nightclubs and performance spaces to make us suspect all that nesting was a myth. AIDS was supposed to shut people down, but in fact it opened many to a whole new range of activities beyond the exchange of bodily fluids. Some of my friends were exploring them. Others played voyeur and came away with new ideas. So the flow continued, and does to this day.

Sometimes it gets a little silly, all this theatrical, rubber-clad tumescence. Certain players are less conscientious than they claim to be. Like religion and real estate, sex is a basic that can overtake people's lives, limit their communities, narrow their sights. Even masters of the erotic arts would certainly agree that sex isn't everything. But considering the powerful role desire plays in human relationships, sexual or not, and the teasing omnipresence of innuendo in every cultural corner, it is amazing how hesitant many people remain when it comes to understanding eroticism and integrating it into their lives. What I've learned from the perverts I've known is that you need skills to do that—skills that are not a given, even if you think what you're doing is perfectly natural.

■

L E S S O N S   I N   L O V E

I always knew my mother was wrong on matters of what her generation called "oomph." Wait—it's not fair of me to be so flip. In truth, I have no idea what Mom's views were on the stuff below the belt; we did not talk about such matters in our clean Catholic household. When it came time to tell me the facts of life, my parents sat me down on the living room couch, put on a record album entitled *The Joy of Sex for Young Christians,* and left the room. I remember some juicy stuff about petting ("Don't do it, kids!") on disc 2, side 2, but the biological stuff bored me, and as far as the crucial facts went, like everyone else in my seventh-grade class I'd already learned them from reading Judy Blume. My curiosity had also led me to dig out copies of *Playboy* and trashy paperbacks whenever I happened to be in a non-Catholic neighbor's house. I got one major lesson the afternoon I found Jackie Susann's *Once Is Not Enough* while babysitting the Golick kids up the street. "Does your mother know you're reading that?" Mr. Golick said when he found me rubber-cemented to the page on which Linda gives January instructions in oral pleasure. "Sure," I said. Being a fairly free thinker, he sent me home without calling my folks.

That was sex for me, an average '70s kid in a Christian home: the most accessible forbidden zone, easy to get a peek at in books and pop songs and movie trailers, but very rarely mentioned in real life. Dad sometimes joked about the Little Black Book he used to keep in his San Francisco bachelor days, but he never displayed anything but the most proper affection toward his wife in his children's presence. When my parents did acknowledge that sex existed, I rolled my eyes and tried to cover my embarrassment with just enough bravado to close the matter without making them think I knew more than they did. Which, at that point, was what I was beginning to suspect.

It wasn't as if I spent my weekends playing body games in some boy's basement. An ugly kid, too fat and too bright, I got no play from the grade-school studs. But the stuff that had begun to save me from my lonesome misery—those books, movies, and most of all, rock music—ran on carnal energy. I knew what Chaka Khan meant when she moaned, "Tell me that you like it," and I knew that even my doe-eyed prince, Paul McCartney, sometimes traded in his sentimental poetry for proposals like "Why don't we do it in the road?" Early on, sex got all tied up in my mind with freedom and transformation, the gifts that music had given girls like Chaka and boys like Paul. How could I fear it? No, I craved it. I waited for the day I could feel its power in me. And when that day came, later than it did for many girls, I was exceedingly lucky. I'd met a boy unselfish enough to stick with heavy petting until I was ready to go all the way. There was a women's clinic I could go to to find out about birth control, and the smudge of guilt that inevitably stuck in my nun-schooled head mutated into fanatical vigilance. And so I escaped the abortionist's table, where many of my friends (whose guilt took the opposite road, into denial) spent some painful time.

Eventually I ditched the boyfriend, headed south, and ventured onto the high seas of Aphrodisia. Anyone hearing tell of my love life during my first years in San Francisco would be justified in calling me a pirate. I always had someone in my sights. The Australian surfer, the Irish housepainter, the artist in his North Beach loft; the teenage bass player, the thirty-year-old classical guitarist, the Puerto Rican boxer with the scar across his cheek—they were all fair game to me, lured up to my Santería candle–lit room, into my magical four-foot-high bed. I'd read the fortunes of my conquests and pour them red wine, and make sure they made me come before they did. In those days, I carried my diaphragm in a purple Crown Royal bag, like a gun with its safety always pulled.

Yet as free as I felt then, as much like a marauder, my brain remained caught in an invisible trap. I couldn't see the snare because it actually contained me in those moments of bodily joy: the giant idea of meaningful sex, sometimes called romance, or misidentified as love. If I wanted a man to share my bed, I thought, I must want him to be there for breakfast and lunch and dinner, to call me his girlfriend and stop dogging after anyone else. I justified my promiscuity as the search for Mr. Right. Countless times, I convinced myself that some schmuck was my spiritual brother and intellectual peer, just because he looked pretty in his Levi's. The differences between us, which were usually considerable, I would simply ignore. I became a heartbreak kid, constantly wondering why the phone didn't ring after such good sex, feeling rejected despite the fact that I could attract more men than I even wanted. "I'm always alone!" I'd wail to Martin, who would just shake his head. "Please," he'd scoff.

"You're never without a boyfriend." The cognitive dissonance was deafening.

During the 1970s sexual revolution, women often reported that they were not satisfied with their random encounters. Men felt lonely, too. Why? Because the acceptable image of heterosexual sex ultimately devalued its pleasures outside monogamous, marriage-style relationships. Very few people bothered to consider how satisfying emotional connections might be forged within relationships that didn't play by those rules. Not that doing so would be easy; the utopian experiments of 1970s swingers and love-communists usually failed, partly because the players grew tired of the social stigma that greeted their experiments, but also because it takes almost superhuman energy to fight the norms embedded in our psyches.

The funny thing about norms is, not that many people strictly abide by them. Yet instead of questioning the rules, most folks condemn their own actions as insignificant or wrong whenever they don't fit. That's what I did in my pirate days, thinking that even the encounters that gave me the most delight were fiascoes when their natural limits set in. And the men who disappointed me were also getting screwed, suffering serious confusion and psychic harm at letting down someone whom they genuinely liked, even sometimes loved, because they couldn't fit into my mold.

When I was twenty-one, I met a guy named Jed. He worked as a sales rep for a record label, a job that often put him in Planet Records, where I worked, checking the bins. He'd dated one friend of mine for a long time, and when I ran into him he was casually pursuing another. One night, he needed an escort for a concert, and I was free; we ended up back in my room, surprising ourselves. We kept sleeping together for about nine months. The sex was, as they say, incredible. Maybe it was because of the similar shape of our flesh (we were once mistaken for sister and brother). Maybe it was the coke his dealer friend kept feeding us. Sometimes I've thought that because we had so much trouble communicating any other way, our bodies spoke with extra intensity. Anyway, the great sex finally stopped mattering. We made it stop. Both of us thought something must be wrong; we moved toward each other on an oil spill of confusion, sliding so close and then away, unable to navigate. I remember the last night he stayed over, the night he dumped me. "It's just lust," he kept saying, as if to forgive himself.

I wonder what would have happened if I could have recognized Jed for what he really was—not a savior or a soulmate, but someone who knew, by some mystery, how to push me into a new zone of physical feeling. What if he could have named the same gift in me? His skin turned pink in places when I aroused him, like some genetic mark he couldn't control. Blushing, he would call it. We were both more afraid than we could say. Could we have taken what passed between us as less than predestination, but more than an accident? We would lie in his futon on the floor eating Chinese food from foil containers and listening to tapes he'd made of John Cale and Nick Drake, sad songs by boys who dreamed of more than they could realize. He gave me that music, and I still listen to it all the time. I thought I loved him, and he said he loved me. Were we lying? Why did we have to even say those things?

Jed married the next girl he hooked up with after me. I would see him around with her sometimes, at a concert or in a restaurant; for a while we would trade forced hellos, then one night I just ignored him when he passed by, and that was the end of it. I hear he's a father now, living deep in the suburbs of Northern California. I haven't spoken to him since 1985. For years, I thought he was the biggest jerk the patriarchy had produced—the monster I'd yank out of my closet when I was sitting around exchanging tales from the crypt with my pals. But now I think that he was just like me: someone who couldn't say what he really wanted, even to himself.

Later, when I discovered the perverts' open universe, I began to see that the most damaging aspects of our erotic encounters stem not from too much scrutiny being given sex, as conservatives and romantics would say, but from not letting sex come into focus at all. We drown in a sea of implication. Billboard-sized underwear bulges loom over tourists in Times Square, where the strip clubs have been replaced by megastores selling SM-tinted pop tunes by Nine Inch Nails. Teenage girls pierce their bellybuttons and wear vinyl miniskirts to biology class, where they might get a lecture on condoms if the parents' association hasn't barred it, but they won't hear much straight talk about how their own bodies have started to feel. Given no other words for those sensations, they call them love. But their language of love is a lexicon of habits, wedding etiquette, and romance-novel scenes. And for sex, all many get is dirty jokes and a pamphlet about disease.

A terror of clearly seeing sex infuses our culture. No matter how much more enlightened America has become thanks to the ministrations

of Hugh Hefner and Dr. Ruth, most people would not feel able to speak
in plain language about their body's responses and desires with their
best friend or their sister. Sex is trapped within its own euphemisms, the
elaborate codes people have developed to deal with a subject that they
worry will blind them, like some Medusa, if they face it head-on. We all
dread the loss of those innuendoes, whether they involve hearts and
flowers or dark alleys and cheap thrills, because they have served as sur-
rogates for so long that they now seem like the real thing. This is why
sophisticated people with no visible hang-ups often condemn self-named
perverts for taking the mystery out of sex. Beyond mystery, for most
people, sex does not exist.

But if sex is a mystery, then surely it is the spiritual kind, luring us to
its depths with the promise of revelation. A path deserving devotion. It's
not surprising that many sex radicals attach religious significance to
their erotic pursuits, although often such talk simply becomes another
code. The language of the clinician dwells too much on pure physical response to serve the emotional side of sex, just as romance dwells too
much on an imagined heart. What's really needed is a whole new means
of expression, one that integrates sex as a social interaction, a body
rush, a cognitive exploration, an act of unveiling, an occasion for mas-
querade, a source of joy, and an archive of shame.

I invoke Jed because I think he'd be the first to challenge my assertions. Like many people who lead perfectly average and basically happy
erotic lives, he would resist the need to lift the lid on a subject he feels
goes beyond rational comprehension. He would question the polemics
of perverts and try to bring them down to earth. He would refute their
easy assumptions, even as they would refute his. He would probably be
embarrassed to be talking about such things at all—and in that, he's also
like most people, including myself in certain company. So, Jed, wherever
you are, I walk down this darkened avenue of erotic exploration, stopping where I see other people's lights, with you in mind.

A R A B B L E - R O U S E R

As I began my pilgrimage among the Bay Area's practicing voluptuaries,
I could have stumbled into any number of entryways. Heaven knows
several gates had swung open and hit me in the face over the years. Sex

radicals, natural theorists that they are, tend to pursue careers writing, performing, or otherwise creatively framing their erotic activities. Susie Bright and Pat Califia were just two of the celebrity sensualists who'd made their mark on my consciousness: there were also Dorothy Allison, the novelist and keeper of home truths about the daily life of the working-class SM dyke; Ron Athey, whose L.A.-based Club Fuck! gave me firsthand experience in public polymorphous perversity; Lisa Palac, editrix of the now-defunct *Future Sex* magazine and cybersex pioneer; punk-rock drag queen Vaginal Creme Davis . . . and the list goes on, long enough to pack Club Uranus on Vinyl Night. But I decided to start with Carol Queen, the Practicing Pervert, who is, in almost any way you can use the phrase, All of the Above.

I met Carol in the early 1990s, when I hosted a roundtable she appeared on at a U.C. Berkeley feminist conference. I hoped the panel would expose a new audience to these amazing women I'd been discovering through the anticensorship movement, women who were not only artists and writers but sex workers, whether that meant publishing pornography, selling vibrators, starring in dirty videos, or throwing play parties for leatherfolk. Carol had done each and every one of those things. With her sharp features, vintage horn-rimmed glasses, and bleached-blond baby-fine bob, she relishes playing the good girl gone naughty. She is a sex-positive missionary, touring America giving lectures and going on talk radio, facing down the prejudices and fears of the heartland. She has published two books, *Exhibitionism for the Shy* and *Real Live Nude Girl,* written for many publications, staged solo performance pieces, and given advice over the Web. And to develop her expertise, Carol has built up an impressive erotic vitae. She's been a dancer at the Lusty Lady peep show, a high-priced call girl, and a porn star; a performer in educational sex videos, including *How to Female Ejaculate*; a safe-sex-party organizer; activist with the International Coalition of Prostitutes, and an academic, earning a Ph.D. from the Institute for Human Sexuality in San Francisco.

I talked with Carol and her partner, Robert Lawrence, over tea at Mad Magda's, a funky café near their loft in Hayes Valley. They looked like any artist couple, Robert with shaggy hair and craggy, lived-in face, and Carol wearing a theatrical hat and a thoughtful expression. Occasionally, Robert would make some small gesture, like running a fine-toothed ivory comb through Carol's hair, meant to convey to me, the inquiring "vanilla" girl (that's what perverts call people who prefer more conventional sex), the complex power balance of their relationship, in which each switches between dominance and submission. Mostly, though, both talked, in emphatic, digressive paragraphs—a couple of old-style lefties out to smash the state, except their tools were rubber dildoes and manifestos about orgies.

"My ex-girlfriend once said to me, 'I could see it if sex were your business. I could see it if it were your hobby. But everything?' " Carol's laugh was an exclamation point. "I'm the kind of person who gets fascinated. It's a quality that, quite frankly, I don't think we're encouraged to develop—that kind of fascination that leads you to take risks. The mainstream culture doesn't encourage us to go deeply into things. Because it's dangerous. It would fuck up the political system at the very least, and it would fuck up capitalism."

Words like "capitalism" spring to this sex worker's lips because, like her friend Susie Bright, Carol was an activist first. In 1975, she helped found one of the first youth groups for homosexuals in the nation, in her hometown of Eugene, Oregon. "It was an open time," she recalled. "I was getting information and inspiration from popular culture; I was finding other people to play with. But I also was very much aware of the iron hand of the state, because when I was fifteen one of my lovers was an adult. I could have easily gotten sent to juvenile hall—I saw it happen to other girls—and he could have been sent to prison. In this decade, he would have been."

Carol was one of those kids who manage to enjoy being weird in a small town, instead of letting the taunts and the ostracism drive her under. But she craved a larger context. In college at Santa Cruz, she found allies within the lesbian community, but eventually she realized that she couldn't completely stifle her attraction to men. Admitting her bisexuality made her a dissident, like the women of Samois before her. She soon determined that she could flourish in that role.

People like Carol, who have made public lives from what most consider the essence of privacy, constantly get into trouble for being too much trouble themselves. Some of her allies in principled exhibitionism have accused Carol of going too far by actually engaging in prostitution rather than the more vicarious enterprises of pornography and stripping. Some of her colleagues at the Institute for Human Sexuality question the boundaries of her participant-observation. From certain lesbian friends, she gets flak for having taken up with Robert, a gay man ten years her senior who honed his sexual chops in San Francisco's leather underground. Then there are the purists who accuse Carol of selling out, because she's appeared on the Home Box Office–produced program *Sex Bytes*. To some, it seems that sex celebrities like Carol are not fostering revolution, but simply selling themselves.

The line between education and entrepreneurship does blur in the world of radical sex. Critics have argued that sadomasochism in particular has become little more than a cottage industry, its challenge to sexual conventions lost in the push to sell more custom-made whips and how-to books. "The leather conventions have turned into crafts fairs," conceded Robert, who has known more illicit times. "The people that I hung out with in the Catacombs dungeon twenty years ago are now making a living teaching the things they learned, like whip-making.

"There still is an inside," Robert continued. "A group that's out there doing nasty things to each other in the alleyways at night. Then there are the people who buy the clothes and go to the clubs and do their whipping according to the standard."

Robert and Carol seem torn between cherishing the pure illicitness of yesterday's sex underground—where badness ruled, and no one talked about accommodating potential converts—and working toward a distant utopia where the very concept of immoral sex would dissolve. Like everyone fighting in this long and nebulous revolution, they are caught in a strange middle. So much more makes its way to the surface now: films paying tribute to pornographers can be nominated for Academy Awards, a Marquis de Sade–themed restaurant does booming business in Manhattan, a six-foot-tall black drag queen named RuPaul can release a Christmas album on a major record label. Social critics in the 1970s wondered if suburban sex-toy parties would really only change the lives of a few savvy entrepreneurs. Carol, who is quite the saleswoman herself, wonders if today's erotic marketplace may be doing the same, promising novelty to bored customers who soon move on to the next trend.

"What does it means when a culture gets mined for its entertainment potential for the zoogoers?" she mused. "I am not crazy about seeing a scene that is about heartfelt self-expression and the creation of alternatives mined for entertainment potential. On the other hand, there's some little teenager with blue hair in Salt Lake City who's going to tune in to the San Francisco segment of *HBO Sex Bytes* one night and go, 'Oh my God, I could go there.' And he'll end up working at Mad Magda's next week, and it could save his life. Literally. It could stop him from committing suicide."

"This society does not honor sex as an art," added Robert. "It involves a set of skills which can be taught. There is an available body of knowledge. I mean, we're not the first." Robert and Carol proceeded to reel off a list of their forebears, from nineteenth-century nudists, to the denizens of the Weimar Republic, to the polygamous Oneida colony, to England's Hellfire Club and leather Teddy Boys. "We have a lot of ancestors," Carol said with a smile.

"We want to colonize the larger culture!" she went on. "We want to send the pods into space and have the new civilizations flower. Maybe a show like *Sex Bytes* makes the mother of the blue-haired kid think twice. How do we help that mom and that kid make the space they need to live together as a family, and to affect their community? Where do we send out these seedings? In some ways, the least weird ones effect the most profound changes."

Our culture has bred sex as a night-blooming flower, one that often dies when brought into the light. Carol and Robert's sunny frankness can seem almost delusionally optimistic, a refusal to face the fact that many people want that darkness in their erotic lives. Carol acknowledges that it's very hard to get anyone to talk comfortably about sex in public, and for that reason, she and her fellow sex celebrities often come across as blithe advocates of orgiastic bliss. I recall the end of the panel where we'd met years earlier: the students and others in attendance were so nervous and shy that the discussion spiraled into a fantasy-swapping session among the panelists. It felt like they'd given up and agreed to behave like a bunch of afternoon talk-show guests, titillating on command.

"It's not clear to me that the sexually alternative communities have a strategy for talking to people who are different, because I think we're as reactive about them as they are about us," Carol admitted. "When people call it a cultural civil war, I don't think it's too much hyperbole. Because it is about control of the hearts and minds of the folks floating around in the middle. I want the guy in the gray flannel suit to say, 'Why am I living this way? Not only have my wife and I never talked about sex in any meaningful way, but I'm too tired to fuck when I get home from work! How can we change our lives?'

"I sound like I'm trying to liberate heterosexuality," she admitted, a little angry now. "But quite frankly, I think some of the backlash against alternative sexual culture comes from straight people who are suffering, they're working, they're not having enough space or time or love or connection or touch or play in their lives, and in their eyes all these fucking hippies, punks, homosexuals, freaks, whatever, aren't having to put their shoulder to the wheel."

"And the guy in the suit has a memory of a joyous sexual moment somewhere in his life, and he wonders why it went away," added Robert.

Carol doesn't scorn that uptight man. He has been her customer, and she has lovingly loosened him up. He has also been her accuser, and she's argued with him even when he spat on her. She keeps fighting because the man in the suit was also her father. A long way now from home, with her parents both dead, she thinks of them still.

"I can look back on it and know what was up," she said. "My mom had been sexually abused when she was a kid. She never felt like sex was a fun, good thing that she had any control over. Like most women of her generation, she did a certain amount of trading sex for love. It was also clear that my dad was married to this woman who didn't want to have sex with him. They were both good people, but they were totally fucked up about this. It's really heartbreaking. Their inspiration lives at the heart of everything I do."

The ghosts of Carol's parents hover over her as she talks so zealously; she is their psychic avenger. And she is the sister of every weird kid trying to make it out there in wide, gray America, the delicate freak for whom the word "queer" hasn't yet been transformed from a taunt into a badge of pride. For them, she goes on the radio, writes manifestos, causes trouble. Even with all the reaction she gets, she knows there are always more spirits to bother, and to save.

■

AN UNEXPECTED FEMINIST

It's tempting to get swept up in the practicing pervert's vision of a sexually satisfied world, convinced by all the pleasure-talk that with one big pull the veil of repression could unravel. But everybody knows that when push comes to flesh, it's not that simple. When most people think of really hot sex, they conjure images of conventionally luscious people. Since the only bodies displayed in the mass-produced softcore of movies and rock videos belong to models, movie stars, and rock stars—or to their body doubles, that elite club of those whose gifted and gym-formed physiques let imperfect celebrities off the hook—we have few images of less-than-perfect people in passion's throes. Regular folks who express desire are usually the butt of jokes. With Hollywood's models in mind, the curious but average adventurer can't help but feel a little silly in her lingerie or his leather harness, with a bit of a gut hanging out, wrinkles visible under the silk, and a patch of body hair or blotchy skin spoiling the dream of glistening carnal beauty.

I believed in the pantheon of beautiful sexy creatures for a long time; it helped me rationalize my own self-orchestrated string of romantic failures. If only I looked like Madonna, I thought, I'd be a sexual super-star. Then I happened on a scene that completely messed up my assumptions. It was a steamy summer night in the North Mission District, at a sleazy little bar temporarily commandeered by a gang of leather-wearing, pierced-and-tattooed perverts from Los Angeles who called their scene Club Fuck! The night started with a sweaty set by the band Ethyl Meatplow, followed by a piercing ritual enacted by Ron Athey. Then the deejay turned up the mix. Slowly, a mosh pit formed. But instead of the usual hardcore-boy slamming and jostling, these dancers rubbed against each other, bumping and grinding and bending over backward. Women felt each other's breasts; men kissed with tongues. Threesomes formed and broke apart as everyone moved through the fluid mass of bodies. The pit held for a few minutes, then dissolved, as participants made for the bar or the door. I'd been in the middle of it, welcomed into the ecstatic circle.

It was a scene I would find again in queer clubs throughout San Francisco. What made it exciting, beyond the pheromones, was its unspoken egalitarianism. These dance floors weren't dominated by the MET-Rx'd pecs of the pretty boys who cruised the Castro, or the waifish flower-figures of the girls hustling for a fashion gig at straight clubs downtown. Instead, there were bulldykes with major muscles, hairy Radical Faeries in chiffon drag, middle-aged rubber queens, teenage ravers—individuals spanning and blurring the categories of race, size, sex, gender. The occasional gorgeous specimen would hardly be ostracized, but easy beauty was never the point. The spotlight belonged to those with the energy and skill to get fabulous with what they had. The notion of allure as a self-determined quality rather than a God-given gift was as radical as any of the uncommon sex acts in which this exciting menagerie indulged.

Given these experiences, I wasn't surprised when I met one of that era's most outspoken Bay Area pornographers and street-level queer theorists, and he turned out to be a rather short, heavyset, round-faced guy with a mohawk and multiple piercings. Mark Pritchard started his groundbreaking 'zine, *Frighten the Horses,* in 1990, nearly a decade after Pat Califia and Samois opened their assault on boundaries, well into the AIDS epidemic that made redefining eroticism a necessity. The late 1980s and early 1990s signaled the maturity of queer culture, and its exploding presence defined how bohemians thought about virtually everything, most of all gender and sex. Mark was one of those questioners drawn to the queer world after exhausting the edges of straight-dominated alternative America. His bisexuality informed his interest, as did his enjoyment of SM. But most of all, he had a hunger for new circumstances, and the queer nation was where those circumstances lay.

"SM and genderfuck—which means drag, girls putting on a dildo, guys getting fucked in the ass, guys basically being willing to give up some of their gender privilege—are two sides of the same coin," he said over a Mexican meal not far from the East Bay software company where he works his day job. "They're all about making gender identity and sexual identity fluid. When people are able to take control of those things, they can remake themselves, their relationships, and their immediate world into something that really fits them. When I think of myself back in high school, suffering under this system where you had to be a really cute-looking football player or cheerleader and you had to go steady—I just wanted to wreck all the assumptions that those roles were based on, into which so few people could fit!"

Mark spent his youth in suburban Houston, where a surprising guide helped him elaborate his nonconformist impulses into a worldview. "I got copies of *Ms.* magazine whenever I could. I really soaked it up," he said. "I was eighteen in 1974. I missed all the protesting and marching in the streets and stuff, which just seemed so cool. Feminism was the next thing. It was exciting, because when you got right down to it, it was really about sex."

At the university in Austin, Mark lived his erotic life according to *Ms.* code. "I just took the ideology very seriously," he said. "The idea that you would ever treat a woman badly seemed really terrible to me. Included in that was any idea of rough sex. The way I did sex was very soft, very equal. I would literally keep track of the number of times I was on top and that she was on top." He claims he wasn't particularly frustrated by this, but he did get bored with Texas. So he went west in 1979, arriving in San Francisco just after Dan White, the murderer of Mayor George Moscone and gay city councilman Harvey Milk, had been given a wrist-slap five- to seven-and-a-half-year sentence. There was rioting in the streets, and revolution in the air.

Kicking around in the avant-garde performance scene, doing body-contact improvisation and other forms of postmodern dance, Mark met a lot of cool women. His sex life took a radical turn one night when he was in bed with one. "She said to me, 'Mark, pull my hair.' And the rest is history." He chuckled. "I really felt conflicted about what we were doing. But I thought, Well, she's the woman, and she thinks it's okay, so . . ." For a few years Mark explored this new sadomasochistic path in private; along the way he met Cris Gutierrez, whose embrace of bisexuality and nonmonogamy mirrored his own. The two became life partners. In 1989, they became creative partners as well, when they decided to start a magazine to suit their erotic tastes.

"I had already started writing dirty stories, for myself and my friends," Mark said. "It was all sort of very mild, you know, 'the raindrops are falling' kind of thing. I was frankly afraid to get into anything else. It was scary enough for me to write about sex at all. Then doing SM freed me to start writing about other stuff. I looked around, and thought, Jeez, there's no place where I can send this. *On Our Backs* had been out for a while, and I thought it was fantastic. But it was about women, and I didn't really think they were going to take my material.

"The 'zine thing was just starting to happen," he continued. "You'd go into Modern Times Bookstore, and there were all these things starting to pop up." We took a minute to list our favorite sex-friendly 'zines from that era: *Homocore, JD's,* Vaginal Creme Davis's various publishing ventures. "It was so cool!" exclaimed Mark. "And I thought, Jeez, what would a magazine that would publish my stuff look like? I decided to make that kind of magazine."

I asked Mark if he'd ever thought about sending his material to a mass-marketed porn mag. He scoffed. "In my stuff, the guy watches the girls do it—and then they kill him! That's not going to fly at *Penthouse*."

With its fantasies ranging all over the place, daring high-risk subjects such as bestiality, sex between children, heavy bondage, cutting, and more, *Frighten the Horses* made a policy of giving its writers freedom to dream up whatever they wanted. Mark's only rule was that it had to be artistically convincing. "I had no interest in writing or asking for stuff to formula. We got a letter once from some guy who wanted stories specifically about big black guys balling white chicks. It's like, Well, if you want to write that story, okay. But that formulaic stuff we weren't really interested in. And we definitely didn't want to break the law or anything."

The difference between *Frighten the Horses* and, say, *Hustler*—which also publishes pointedly transgressive material—was consciousness. The 'zine's life span coincided with the most bitter conservative backlash against artists in recent memory, the Christian right's attack on the National Endowment for the Arts. *FTH* published regular updates from this battlefield and others. It functioned as a kind of community newsletter, culling information from other sources on subjects including abortion clinic defense and the ban on the RU-486 "abortion pill"; legislation for gay rights; the political struggles of gays in Mexico; and the Supreme Court appointment of accused sexual harasser Clarence Thomas. This aspect of the 'zine politicized its controversial pornographic submissions, and placed the whole project within the context of queer liberation. Scattered between the porn and the news were essays such as Pat Califia's brilliant "Slipping," about the devastating effect of AIDS on queer eroticism, Cris Gutierrez's defense of "lesbian prostitute serial killer" Aileen Wuornos, and Rachel Kaplan's reflections on coming out as bisexual.

Bisexuality was an elemental aspect of the *FTH* sensibility, one that earned it scorn in certain sectors. While more fluid notions of both gender and desire have by now permeated radical sex circles, a decade ago the lines were more rigid. Gay men and women often saw bisexuals as traitors, while straight vanilla types thought they were just going through a phase. By publishing the thoughts and fantasies of open bisexuals, and by commingling a strikingly diverse assortment of fantasies within its pages, *FTH* constructed a paradigm for polymorphousness.

"The funny thing about bisexuality is, it's not about who you're supposed to fuck, it's about who you happen to be fucking now," said
Mark. "Or who you want to fuck. That changes from year to year,
month to month. So it's very, very difficult for bisexuals to organize except against something else. Ultimately, though, I have a very difficult
time distinguishing a bisexual agenda from a feminist agenda. It's just
about fulfilling a personal and sexual destiny."

Mark's insistence about connecting contemporary feminism and radical sex may seem odd to those who've grown accustomed to the antisex
radicalism of Andrea Dworkin and company. But the original women's
liberationists counted sexual self-knowledge and independence among
their main priorities. Prostitutes' rights even made the official agenda of
the National Organization for Women in the early 1970s. Pro-sex feminism continued to thrive in the ensuing decades, although it sometimes
called itself queer and was often at odds with the movement's mainstream. When ill-informed provocateurs like Katie Roiphe declared feminism sexless in the mid-1990s, they overlooked Mark and Cris, Susie
Bright, Pat Califia, and the many others who had kept feminism's talk
about sex alive and hot.

Not every sex radical likes loudmouthed rhetoricians like Mark.
He's given to attacking others if he disagrees with their methods;
when I mentioned him to Carol, she shook her head and told me of
his on-line diatribes against her. His indie sensibilities, manifested in a
preference for the hardest-core porn and the most controversial opinions, combine with an elitist attitude that allows him to dismiss much
of what's floating around out there in the marketplace. "There are
some people who seem to be promoting themselves more than the issues they're talking about," he commented. He didn't seem to consider that he himself might seem a bit of an egotist, since he did start
a magazine to publish his own opinions—and sexual fantasies starring himself.

However pure or personal Mark's motivations were, *Frighten the
Horses* captured better than virtually any other publication I've seen the
embattled, thriving, curious, passionate mood of radical sex as it rose to
the forefront of cultural politics. Eventually, though, his and Cris's energy and financial resources waned, as they almost always do when
your work walks a margin. They live quietly now, in the house they
bought together in Bernal Heights, designing software and putting

money away. They maintain their vow of nonmonogamy, but most nights Mark finds himself at home.

"I've gotten a little more domestic, it's true," he admitted. "You know how in an ice-skating rink they have certain sessions? From one o'clock to three o'clock you're out there on the rink, going around, and then the bell rings and you get off, and the people in the next session come along. I feel like the next session is happening now. And the people who are out there are creating something based on things that my session did, which was in turn was based on the previous generation. There are those who will think they've invented their own world, but it's always a mixture. They do invent some of it, but they look to what came before." Just as Mark did in 1990, remembering what *Ms.* taught him in the back of a Houston bookstore in 1974.

■

TWO ADEPTS

Behind the sexy shared fantasies and passionate ruminations that form the public life of radical sex is a practice, and that's usually where things get complicated. The pervert philosophy might be powerful enough to shake up the social structure, but the action is what transforms people's lives. To understand how, you need to get specific. What exactly is a safeword? What happens in a scene? How do lofty notions like "power exchange" apply to skin on skin? These questions require a franker dialogue, perhaps staged anonymously on a sex-advice line or coaxed out over a bottle of wine with a savvy friend or two. "Have you ever tried . . . ?" you say, and if you can keep your embarrassed snickers down you might learn something.

Nicola Ginzler and Rebecca Hensler have been trading tips for a long time. The two women met at an SM party in the early 1990s and became fast friends. They've never been lovers in the romance-and-property-rights sense of the word, but they do frequently engage in sadomasochistic play together, either alone or with others who strike their fancy. When I visited Nicola's apartment for an evening of enlightening chat, the two had just returned from a day at the mud baths in Mendocino—two sunburned, mellow buddies, the very picture of healthy Bay Area womanhood. Nicola, a dark-haired, pixie-sized woman whose assertive comfort in her strong body belies her diminu-

tiveness, offered me a seltzer while the freckly, voluptuous Rebecca un-
loaded their stuff from a day bag.

At that moment, neither looked much like the usual notion of a dominatrix—although a glance inside Nicola's closet would have revealed a
collection of custom-made leather whips. We sat on the bed in her neat,
elegant studio, snacking on Grape Nuts and Reese's Peanut Butter Cups,
talking long into the night about play-party etiquette, the roles of top
and bottom, the difference between sadomasochism and dominance-
submission, and the fantasy appeal of *Buffy the Vampire Slayer.* Their
insights filled up my tape recorder for hours.

I'd known Nicola back before she found her calling, when she was
going out with boys and playing the femme fatale. Back in the mid-
1980s she wore vampish vintage suits and dated a guy named Mick,
who had a big car. He ended up being the last in a string of male lovers
who'd left her feeling less than satisfied. After leaving him, she placed a
personal ad that took her down a very different road. She was looking
to try sex with women, just because she thought it might be better than
boring. The woman who answered her ad turned out to be ready for a
different kind of thrill, too. Soon Nicola found herself experimenting
with dominance and submission. Ten years later, she is a respected top
in the very community-oriented San Francisco SM leather scene.

And now she was prepared to share her expertise with me. I thought
I'd better start with the basics. Why did she like SM?

"For me, it's a central metaphor for communication, for negotiation
and desire. Not just sexual desire. Anything you want. And pleasure,
also. It's this huge metaphor for negotiating responsibility and pleasure," she ventured.

The writer and performer in Nicola—she has published essays and
fiction in *Frighten the Horses* and other magazines, and held center
stage at various ritual events—was leading her into abstraction. Rebecca
quickly steered our talk back toward the gut. "The first four or five
years of being sexual, I didn't know a lot about what turned me on, and
I certainly didn't know how to express it," she said. "This friend of
mine and I used to have a joke about the fact that we were not getting
what we wanted: it's like, I'm the only one who notices that the CD is
over. Just once in my life I wanted the music to end while I was having
sex and not notice, because I was so wrapped up in the sex. Now that
happens all the time."

I thought Rebecca's granted wish sounded like the kind of thing a straight woman writing to *Cosmopolitan* about her lukewarm marriage might be looking for. Rebecca chuckled. "It's funny that what straight advice columnists tell people to do to bring back romance is something that pervs have already figured out," she agreed. "Setting aside a moment and giving ritual to your pleasure is a powerful thing."

"I think one reason why sex ends up being stilted for straights is lack of community," added Nicola. "There's no one to discuss what you do with, except in a giggling way." For her, finding a formal path toward intimacy was a huge attraction of the SM world. She is a serious woman, prone to dark spells, whose great reserves of emotion needed coaxing out.

"I grew up with virtually no feeling of connection with other people," she explained, her low voice dropping to a murmur. "I had a hideously lonely childhood and adolescence. One of the greatest joys of my life now is that I have learned to connect with people. SM is an extremely important one of many ways that I've been learning that.

"For me it incorporates a huge number of things that work—sexuality, touch, storytelling, voice, goofiness," she continued. "Fantasy, roleplaying, desire, courage. Honesty. Physical exertion. And if you add in that I happen to be wired for a certain amount of sadism, masochism, dominance, and submission, that's a really potent cocktail for me. In the same way that working out is a really potent cocktail for me. Perfectionism. Sweat. Like riding my motorcycle. Acceleration. Fear. Speed. G-force. Cranking the throttle on a bike and getting slammed up against the wall by a lover—it's a really similar feeling. Both are dangerous, and both are safe with certain precautions."

Rebecca finds the same rich offering in radical sex, but she's more earthy about it, maybe because she came to it more easily. Her parents, both academics, let her explore her urges and never withdrew their love when those desires manifested themselves in unconventional ways. They allowed her to have lovers stay the night when she was still in her teens; their main rule was, Be home by midnight. That way they knew she was safe.

"My friends thought my folks were crazy," she recalled. "But they taught me how to think for myself, how to take risks and accept responsibility if I fucked up, and to love myself. A lot of people would think that they were permissive, but the fact is, I never got pregnant. I never had sexual intercourse with a man without birth control. I haven't gotten any sexually transmitted diseases other than your basic yeast infection. My parents prioritized my physical well-being and my mental health and let me make decisions. By my standards, they were very successful."

Because she respected herself, Rebecca sought to form an ethic that accommodated her enjoyment of certain intense sex acts. "Before I learned about negotiation, there was no border between SM and abuse," she admitted. "I had at least two early sexual experiences that involved both. They actually taught me that my SM sexuality existed, but because of how they occurred and my lack of control over them, they were also sexual assaults. At the point when I wanted to stop, I said stop, and the guy I was with didn't. Because there was no safeword, no agreement ahead of time—we didn't even know to do that.

"Then, when I moved to San Francisco, I was having a sexual relationship with someone, and he took me to a play party thrown by someone else he was sleeping with. For the first time, I played with experienced people. I still didn't know much about negotiation, I still kept making big mistakes both as a top and as a bottom. But it began there, because the people he introduced me to were serious about what they were doing, and took me and my desires seriously."

The terminology of formalized kinky sex—"safeword" and "negotiation" and "play"—trips off Rebecca's tongue. The words matter as much as the fetishized spiked heels and tight corsets, because they are the signposts that guide people as they push themselves to physical and emotional extremes. A "scene" is the framework of sexual theater in which SM play occurs. A "safeword" is an agreed-upon term that ends a scene, because a participant has reached a limit. "Play," not sex, describes SM, because sometimes its actors don't engage in genital acts; Nicola, for example, is always fully clothed when topping. "Negotiation" is the series of conversations players have before a scene to define what they want from it. They might choose "sadism"—inflicting pain, via whips, bondage, canes, careful cutting—and "masochism"—enduring that pain—or a less physical power exchange, which is just called "dominance" and "submission." The "top" is the scene's doer, while "bottom" is the one done to, but that doesn't mean (as many outsiders presume) that the bottom is powerless. In fact, the lines easily blur, and in many ways the thrill is in charting the course of a power exchange.

"One girlfriend and I used to do lovely dinners where she would cook for me and serve me, and she would kneel next to me and I would feed her," said Nicola. "Who's topping, who's bottoming? Who knows? That was one of the things that was lovely about it."

Nicola and Rebecca often used adjectives like "lovely" or "awesome" to describe their experiences; they obviously gain much emotional nourishment from them. It distresses both women that so many people can't see past SM's fierce costumes to its ginger explorations. SM can be brutal, like any sex, but the watchful nature of its players usually provides more protection than the average sorority girl or circuit-party boy gets. "Safety is fetishized in San Francisco," said Nicola, who has explored scenes in London, New York, Los Angeles, and Seattle, and walked away grateful to live where she does. An experienced player, she presents a fairly judgmental view of the international scene.

"I do have a responsibility to the community, simply because there's a whole lot of bad play out there," she explained. "By that I mostly mean boring. You see people going *whap-whap-whap* at parties, and it's like, Are you enjoying that? Okay, one person's broken a bit of a sweat and the other is screaming, but are you actually connected with each other, are you liking each other for the moment? And if not, why the fuck are you doing it? Don't do it because you think it's cool. Take a fucking risk, and let your fucking guard down for a minute. That's what I want out of it."

Nicola and Rebecca were telling me that kinky sex is both primal and highly sophisticated. At one moment, Rebecca would interrupt Nicola's stories with a question like "But does it make you wet?" as if that were *the* simple criterion. Then she'd present a knotty anecdote like this one:

"I have an ongoing SM relationship with a woman named Andrea. We get together once a week. One time recently, we were playing with electricity for the first time, with a stun gun. It sounds like this." She picked up the gleaming gadget sitting next to Nicola's bed, pushed a button, and it let off a loud *rat-a-tat-tat*, with a sparky line of blue light. "It doesn't hurt more than being caned; in fact, it hurts a lot less. But Andrea was terrified.

"I tried lots of tricks for calming her down, like shocking myself with it. I talked to her about what it could and couldn't do, and what I was going to do and not do. Eventually she said, 'I'm hitting the point where I'd rather do anything than deal with that.' I untied her, sat the stun gun down between us with the safety on, and said, We're going to talk about this. We talked about why she was afraid, and I offered her the chance to propose doing something else. There were a lot of things she could have offered me at that point that I would have accepted, other extremes that didn't scare her but just hurt.

"Instead, she said she was willing to go on with the stun gun, and we negotiated some things that would scare her less. The sound and the light were terrifying her. So I said, 'Stick your fingers in your ears and close your eyes.' She went from being blindfolded and in rope bondage to sitting on the floor, close to me, with her sight as she wanted it, humming so she didn't have to hear the clicking. I shocked her three or four times. And then I stopped. That was enough. We were able to negotiate through it. It was awesome."

Rebecca has the compassionate manner of a guidance counselor; in fact, she regularly gives instructional workshops to gay and lesbian youth groups, and works the phones at a sex information hotline. As she talked, I pictured her and Andrea sitting cross-legged on the floor, and it looked a lot like couples therapy. Except, of course, for the ropes and the sparkling weapon in Rebecca's hand. I wondered if anyone outside this world would be able to accept the paradoxical connection between inflicting pain and offering empathy. Some veterans of the SM scene have derided younger players for dulling its edge with a blanket of touchy-feely nonsense. Some outsiders think it's just disgusting to try to find a good side to what looks so much like pain.

"I have played with a lot of people who have always felt really, really bad about what they want," Nicola said. "Who have felt sick, fucked up. And I have gotten a real, real charge out of watching someone get what they want for the first time." The dominatrix, as these women have defined her role, is indeed part therapist—but in a very physical way. A memory engraved on the body can push people further out of their habits and anxieties—and closer to their emotional potential—than mere words can. This is a holistic notion, so Californian. But as someone who never knew her own strength until I took a self-defense class and kicked a (well-padded) male instructor in the balls, I can testify that some things can't be learned by the brain alone.

Nicola and Rebecca have their own analogies for SM. Nicola compares it to riding her motorcycle—a love that has proven far more dangerous, since she has survived two debilitating accidents caused by careless motorists. Not just the thrill of mastering such a big machine but the impropriety of it, the way people gawk at this tiny woman on her beast of steel, gives Nicola a kick. She gets the same feeling of grabbing power that others wouldn't suspect when she dresses in her spiky boots and wields her whip at one of Carol Queen's safe-sex parties.

Rebecca, in her more buoyant way, compares kinky sex to gourmet cooking. "Food and sex are both basic human needs and desires and pleasures," she said. "If you like really spicy food, you like really spicy food. Your food involves pain, and that's pretty acceptable. Yet if you like your sex that way, you're a pervert. If you cook for your family or your lover, and also cook for a living, that's acceptable. If you have sex for money, that's not acceptable. If you cook a dinner for twenty-five people, that's fine. If you have sex with that many people, it's a big deal. The comparison goes on and on and on. Fast-food sex! Definitely picking up some porn and buzzing off would be the sexual equivalent of grabbing a burger at McDonald's.

"I am a spiritual and emotional person," she concluded. "But why can't we see sex as an activity"—like savoring a meal—"and then use it for what it's worth?" It seemed a reasonable question. But even for women like these, who have fought to be able to ask it, the answer doesn't come easily. Nicola and Rebecca dotted their testimonial to SM's healing power with references to more ordinary pain: misunderstandings among friends and fellow players, lost lovers, old-fashioned heartbreak. No matter how sophisticated people become, sometimes the human heart weakens. Rebecca talked about the suicide of a friend and lover driven to despair after a failed sex-change operation. Nicola admitted her own frustration at being perceived as nothing more than a rock-hard top, when at times all she craves is a chance to show her own vulnerabilities. "I know my capacity for emotional pain," she said quietly. "It's so up there. What I need is less pain to handle."

Sexual sophistication hasn't stopped these women from making emotional mistakes; SM simply gives them a framework to better understand their hunger. What it offers, and what it requires, is not for everyone; even the most enthusiastic bondage queen would agree to that. But like any art, this one has earned its insights. If it does nothing else, it dramatizes the ways that sex is more, and less, complicated than we think.

■

A   C U R I O U S   G I R L

Like any group of enthusiasts, sex radicals live inside their preoccupation, seeing the world through its window. I've been privy to similar highly trained perspectives in my travels with skateboarders and record collectors, microbrewers and computer geeks. Still, I knew that for most people, all this sex talk would feel a bit excessive. "We are already living in a sexually liberated age," scoffed one vanilla pal when I told him of my inquiries. "Myself, the women I've been with, everyone feels they have a right to have sex and not worry too much about it. We just don't need to think that hard."

It's a kind of sympathetic apathy, this attitude; it works as a double agent in America's ongoing conflict over sexual morality. As Robert Lawrence told me, "Most of the people in this country could give a shit what other people do. 'I'm busy mowing my lawn, dude, leave me alone.' " Americans are accustomed to a certain level of sexual dialogue in their daily lives; they aren't horrified when they turn on HBO and see *Sex Bytes,* and they're mostly amused when basketball jester Dennis Rodman pulls on his nipple rings. If Uncle Harry showed up in leather chaps for Christmas dinner, well, that might be a little weird. But getting used to a gay cousin has become so commonplace that folk singers write songs about it. It's hard to shock most Americans. But it's hard to engage them, too.

Increasing permissiveness unaccompanied by a public examination of what these new freedoms mean—how they challenge such basic concepts as gender, reproduction, even decency—is what really makes the present moment in sexual history a moral free-for-all. In the gap created by the majority's silence, advocates at both ends of the spectrum battle. And because conservatives raise more money and more active support, they usually win. Arenas for sexual expression are shut down, art is censored, sex workers continue to be denied basic civil rights, and some perverts go to jail for what they and their partners consent to in the privacy of their own relationships. It's not far from this battlefield to the next one, where conservatives aim to curtail rights that moderates take for granted, such as the right to reproductive freedom or to engage in free speech on the Internet.

The refusal to measure the weight of our sexual assumptions has another, more insidious effect. The vanilla worldview encompasses more than an undue respect for the missionary position; it includes larger assumptions about how people should fulfill their destinies. Single women, for example, may develop successful careers, supportive friendships, and rich interior lives, but if they have not "landed a man" by a certain age they still feel like failures. Gay men, historically damned as promiscuous monsters, are now threatened with censure in their own ranks if they do not "get married" like straight people do; although there is a civil rights argument to be made for gay marriage, the pair-up-or-perish attitude drives some men to abandon hope and return to high-risk behavior, while discouraging the community as a whole from exploring ways of making the whole range of sex practices safer. Bisexuals, older women involved with younger men, aggressive women who aren't in it for love, gentle men who don't want to take the lead, friends who sometimes have sex with each other, avid masturbators, even celibates—the vanilla myth condemns them all to shame and secrecy. Even many couples who live the dream quietly suffer, fearing they don't live up to its standards but unsure of what to ask for, or how. The idea of "normal sex" continues to keep a whole range of prejudices and fears in place, their impact reaching far beyond the bedroom. And the foundation of them all is the idea that we shouldn't have to think about sex.

One way to shift this paradigm is to boldly pull it in the opposite direction, to become an evangelist of the erotic. The proud perverts I've encountered find much power in this action. Yet in some ways they remain in their own separate category, their fetishes so theatrically unusual that it's not always easy to see the connection to other forms of desire. Yet there are many people, usually less flamboyant, who have made the most of the middle ground between the vanilla-scented and the leather-clad. Laura Miller is one such person: a curious girl, fairly conventional in demeanor and tastes, who found herself immersed in a world of radical sex through a twist of circumstance, and had to figure out her position from there.

Laura currently makes her living as an editor at the on-line magazine *Salon* and a writer for such tony publications as *The New York Times*. But for seven years, she worked a day job at Good Vibrations, the famous sex-toy store in the heart of San Francisco's fashionable Valencia Corridor, and for a while she selected the shop's adult videos. She also served as the company spokesperson, appearing on panels and passing witty sound bites to the press. I've known Laura for many years, but I'd never sat her down and asked her about her time in the sex biz. When we met over a plate of spaghetti in her comfortable studio apartment not far from Good Vibes, I didn't know what I was going to discover about my pal. Would I see her in a whole new light by the time we finished our bottle of Orvieto?

The short answer is no. "I had the same serial-monogamy lifestyle that everybody else was having in my peer group," she said. "I wasn't availing myself of all these supposed opportunities. I just wasn't really interested in them." Watching hundreds of porno movies seems to have affected Laura's mind more than her libido. She is another theorist of sex, as astute as any Foucault follower, with the added bonus of several years' training in the field. Her demeanor is casually elegant, and rather conservative except for a tumble of black curls; conversation animates her, the flow of ideas her perfect drug. It's easy to imagine her in a women's studies department, the hip professor with scores of girl students vying for her mentorship and boy students mooning after her during office hours.

Although she often found herself fighting with antiporn feminists during her time at Good Vibrations, the company's commitment to feminism is one reason Laura sought a job there. Joani Blank had founded the company as an extension of her work in the women's health movement, which convinced her that sexual confidence played a key role in women's ability to care for themselves. It wasn't a big jump from the speculum, the instrument of self-examination routinely distributed in women's studies classes, to the vibrator.

"Good Vibrations is really important because it's pro-masturbation, on a how-to level, and on a supportive ideological level," Laura explained. "Everybody is welcome, but it was specifically designed to make women feel comfortable. It presents sex like a normal part of people's lives, like their hair or something. They need a certain amount of information, they might want some products, they might be interested in finding some alternatives. There's so much basic information that people don't have, that they were able to get in the context of that feeling. It became a haven for so many people."

Working on the sales floor, Laura discovered just how much even sexually experienced people sometimes didn't know. "People were suffering as a result of all these screwy ideas about sex. Not just in terms of big issues, like sexual identity, but simple anatomy. That whole clitoris thing, still people don't always get it. And where would they find it out? Most people get their sex information from *Penthouse* and *Cosmopolitan,* and they're just not that explicit. Or if they are, they're fantasy-oriented. Like, he touches the woman's breasts and she has an orgasm."

I told her I couldn't believe that people still didn't know about clitoral stimulation. She reminded me that many Good Vibes customers, especially those who mail-order, don't live in big cities and don't receive any sex education related to pleasure. And there are other reasons people don't grasp the essentials. Primary among them is romance.

"What's romantic about being really frustrated?" Laura scoffed. "A woman customer would say, 'I have this problem. My boyfriend and I are fucking, I almost never come.' Probably what she needs is more clitoral stimulation, and she'll have to either ask him for it or do it yourself. 'Well,' she would reply, 'that takes all the romance out of it.' So it's so romantic right now that you never get to have an orgasm! It's insane that you have to choose between those things."

Laura had been lucky; her natural inquisitiveness, and a liberal education during her Southern California youth, helped her escape that fate. She took to Good Vibrations like a Rhodes scholar to the British Library's Reading Room. The pornography especially interested her; she'd always liked erotic books, and had made the same tentative forays into blue films countless college students had, surreptitiously slipping into those cheesy revival-house variety shows with titles like "The Hollywood Erotic Film Festival." I'd done the same thing, and been bored; the only image that stuck with me was of a woman rocking back and forth on a basketball while the object of her desire, a lunk without a speaking part, swung a baseball bat outside her window. "The idea of porn was so much more exciting than the actual experience," Laura agreed. "I got past that initial disappointment, which most people don't. And then I started to find some really interesting things."

At Good Vibes, Laura found a good place to take the next step. Her predecessor as mistress of porn was Susie Bright, who had amassed quite a collection for the company. Susie also turned Laura on to *Adult Video News,* the industry's trade publication. "I highly recommend it," Laura enthused. "It's totally fascinating. The gossip column is endless. It's better than any gossip column, except that you don't know who these people are. It's just a great little world."

The world of porn wound up being more engaging to observe than its products. Plodding through tape after tape, Laura witnessed the problems inherent in a shunned medium. "There's no reason for somebody who's talented to be working on a porn movie," she explained. "It's not like Stanley Kubrick would have been a porn director. There's not enough money for him to achieve what he wants to achieve, and there's this formula, and there's no recognition. You never get any critical attention if you make a brilliant porn movie."

Despite its inherent tackiness, Laura says, porn can offer a unique window into sexual experience. "Porn has the potential to show how people's emotions are expressed while they're having sex. Movies that aren't X-rated cannot show that. Porn has permission to, although it almost never does," she explained.

Searching for the rare film that captured the depth of sex, Laura began to realize something about her own erotic life. "To pursue this," she said, struggling a bit to find the words, "I don't want to say that it felt like a male prerogative, because that makes it sound like the important thing about it was that it was male. But there is this thing that men have. Their sexuality is this source of pleasure to them that they fully possess. Women don't often feel that way."

As porn mistress, Laura tapped that rare sense of privilege. "It's like having a car or something," she said. "You can do this thing. It's all yours. I had my own apartment, my VCR, I had this video, it was my experience." She sometimes shared porn with lovers, and regularly discussed it with a few girlfriends, but generally she kept her viewing to herself. The experience engaged her intellectually as well as physically, and Good Vibrations gave her a context in which to explore its various levels of meaning. By the time she gave up the job, weary of the genre's poor production values and generally low level of insight, she had realized something elusive, but fundamental, about sex.

Her epiphany came as a result of her porn viewing, working in the store, and fending off the attacks of moralists. Serving an array of fetishists gave her one piece of the puzzle. "You know what it is? It's a thing about roles," she said. "Perverts realize that you are one way when you're in your regular life, and then you can go into sex and be in a role and that's not necessarily who you are otherwise. I wouldn't want to have a sex life where I'm always a dominatrix or a submissive or whatever, but people who do are really clear about the separation between their real identity in a relationship and the roles they have in sex.

"Romance, on the other hand, is all about imagining yourself in a certain role without admitting it. You want to think, 'I am the kind of person who gets flowers, I am the kind of person who drives men mad with desire.' If that's what you're getting out of your relationships, it doesn't seem like intimacy. It's a fantasy about yourself that you're using this other person to achieve."

Immersed in the sphere of manufactured fantasy, Laura began to see how each person fabricates wet dreams for herself. She saw films serving obsessions so specific, and sold goods to fetishists whose needs seemed so obscure, that her assumptions about what was natural were dislodged. "Did you know that there are videos you can get that are just a woman smoking?" she exclaimed. "No sex, fully clothed, just smoking. One guy wanted scenes with women near fire. Not burning themselves—no one being hurt—just fire really close to their bodies. Maybe two women together having sex in front of a fire, but no men. It's like, Why? It's just mystifying."

She finally came to a conclusion: "Sex doesn't have an inherent meaning. That was what the exposure to different types of people forced me to see. When you live in a society where the diversity of what people are into isn't really acknowledged, certain sex acts seem to have a really fixed meaning. Like, a blow job is always degrading, or something like that. Whereas the reality is that any given act can mean totally different things to different people. The same blow job means one thing to the guy, another thing to the woman, and another thing to whoever might be watching it—as a presence in the room, or somebody seeing a photo or film of it. It could mean one thing while you're doing it and something else the next day. The meaning is really fluid, and you decide what it's going to be."

This meaninglessness, not a dark void but an open field, is what most people can't see about sex. "It wound up being really liberating to me," said Laura. "I started to see that people need those absolute meanings to believe certain things about themselves. Like a guy needing to be with a certain kind of woman because she's a trophy and that makes him feel successful. But being with her won't make him young or successful. And in the meantime he doesn't have a relationship based on who he really is, so he's lonely and unsatisfied."

It seems so obvious. Sex is nothing more than itself, just another activity, as Rebecca said. Yet because we invest so much in it and examine
so little, it becomes a looking glass through which each of us tumbles,
upending fixed meanings, uncovering hungry selves we don't want to
meet. Unable to admit that its patterns read differently for everyone, we
let this mirror world define us.

After all she's learned, Laura has a way of dealing with her judges, internal and external. "Whenever somebody's focusing so much emotional
energy that it turns into hate or anger, they're getting off on it somehow," she said. "So, what are they getting out of it? Realize that this
person is meeting a desire in a certain way. How can you work with
that? Don't be so attached to these huge arguments about right and
wrong."

She flashed a sly look. "Unless that's your fetish," she said.

3

.

GOOD DRUGS

AND BAD DRUGS

" MISADVENTURE " : it's the word that means you did it to yourself. Cops and coroners use it to describe those poor fools who slipped up in the midst of an autoerotic asphyxiation, or danced over a window ledge on a drunken dare, or (like one twenty-three-year-old inmate in Kentucky) tried to eat a Bible to clean out the digestive tract. It also designates drug overdoses, especially if the chemically overloaded corpse belongs to a family ashamed to leave an official record of such an accident. I've always thought "misadventure" an oddly jaunty term, especially for a nation so hell-bent on making drugs and other agents of recklessness seem as grim as possible. It implies adventure, after all—a character-expanding journey of risks worth taking. Not the usual thing associated with pathetic junkies drooling toward unconsciousness in some needle-strewn squat.

There are also misadventures that people survive. Crazy chances seem to be a required element of the bohemian life, a consequence of being open to possibility. Many misadventures I've heard about don't involve chemical overindulgence—there's risky sex; there's sleeping in your car with the locks open—but many do. With the hindsight of years, these stories turn grossly comical, tinged with just the slightest recognition that such wild fun could have gone very wrong. Martin's involves a chunk of cocaine purchased to be shared among five people, which rapidly diminished on his desk as he sat up all night, writing piles of letters he would never send. Another friend, Rose, tells about one night when she dropped Ecstasy, ate mushrooms, and smoked heroin at a party. "My eyes were going around in my head," she told me. "Nobody could look at me, so I had to put on sunglasses." My own misadventure resembled Rose's. I've dubbed it the Night of the Seven Substances: acid, speed, two kinds of mushrooms, alcohol, pot, and hash. Each of these passed my lips during the course of a long evening lost somewhere in 1982, during which I nearly broke up with my boyfriend, wandered through a few strangers' parties, and ended up on the stage of the Kit Kat Club with a few similarly wrecked friends, playing Grendel's mother in an improvised free-jazz opera based on *Beowulf*.

Everyone but the cleanest squeakers has one of these battle stories. People often turn reticent, though, when it comes to discussing their current views on drug use. Saying you get high is like proffering a secret handshake: are you one of us, or one of them? On either side of this loyalty oath is a set of passionate beliefs fed by firmly planted cultural myths and intense personal experience. The most obvious gamble—the fact that by telling you I dropped acid last week, I'm confessing to a crime—is hardly the fundamental one. It's doubtful that you are a narcotics agent. Much more likely, and in many ways, daunting, is the possibility that you are simply clean, and may now suspect me to be endangered, weak, or even sick—just as I may view you as a judge overstepping your jurisdiction.

"Drugs are sometimes sacred, sometimes profane, but always meaningful," writes the sociologist Danny Monroe Wilcox. Every social enclave assumes the meaning its ascribes to a drug to be indisputable. Hippies know that marijuana is mellow and harmless, while "Just Say No" moms know toking leads to disaster. Those same moms swallow Prozac by the handful, while the hippies consider it a government plot, opting instead for the herbally correct St. John's wort. Junkies still on the needle know that heroin doesn't kill you, while junkies who've recovered know it does. Tweaked-out punks know that rushing on speed is like reaching heaven, while straight-edge punks know speed makes your life hell. Incontrovertible evidence can be gathered to support every one of these beliefs. They are all lies, and they are all true.

Around this swirl of contradictory realities has accrued a history of images as distorted as any psychedelic dream. The drug fiend is a common folk devil in America's history of ethnic tension: the Gold Rush–era opium scare was used to justify crimes against Chinese immigrants. At the turn of the century, cocaine was associated with rampaging Southern free blacks. A few decades later, marijuana was supposedly to blame for shiftiness among Mexican migrant workers in the West. Sometimes a group would transform this stigma into a badge of pride. The poet LeRoi Jones (now known as Amiri Baraka) thought that black hipsters in the 1950s sometimes used heroin because the drug's taboo status glamorized the role of the social outcast. "It is one-upmanship of the highest order," he wrote in 1963.

The ultimate one-upmanship of this kind, of course, occurred in the 1960s, when disaffected youth began turning on in vast numbers and making their trips a main source of cultural expression. Hippies made drug use a lifestyle, complete with fashions, music, poster art to hang on bedroom walls, cookbooks and comic books, even a car: the Volkswagen bus, with plenty of space in the back for zoning out. The establishment of this mainstream drug culture created a code of behavior that went beyond tripping itself. In the counterculture's aftermath, suburban kids could go into their local head shops and find information on anarchism, organic gardening, the *Kama Sutra,* shamanism, and kinky spiritual practices. Before hippiedom, drug use in America was the province of degenerates and elites. Now nonconformity had reached the masses, and the drug culture stood for a range of ways ordinary people might reject the status quo and explore their own potential. "Is he on drugs?" my mother wondered, watching Jimi Hendrix burn his guitar when the movie *Monterey Pop* aired on public television. He may have been, but his droopy eyes weren't what clued her in. It was the purple outfit, the experimental music, and the aura of utter individuality that he projected. For both Mom and me, to be "on drugs" meant to show yourself breaking society's rules, with all the perils and possibilities such a crossing entailed.

I was in eighth grade when we saw Jimi on TV, and drugs were about to become more than a fantasy to me. I went to a Beach Boys concert with a friend and her older sister and smoked my first joint. Nothing happened; only later did I find out that you had to try it several times before it took. Waiting for more opportunities, I found some vicarious thrills in the young-adult section of my local library. They were all cast as warnings. *Go Ask Alice,* the ubiquitous diary of an anonymous dead heroin addict, read like an episode of *The Brady Bunch* gone drastically wrong as nice, pretty, perfect Alice slipped closer and closer to her inevitable oblivion. *Teacup Full of Roses* and *Run, Baby, Run* were about inner-city kids, dynamic and tragic and nothing like me. Art Linkletter's daughter was middle-class, though, and I read that she'd jumped from a window after consuming LSD. Stories like hers became hopelessly entangled with the numerous, equally popular books I was reading about mental illness like *Lisa, Bright and Dark* and *Sybil;* desperate accounts of girls who started out only slightly more cracked than I felt. I related to the drug addicts in these books because they were weird and they had ear-shattering fights with their parents. But their stories scared me, too, like the tales of gothic horror I also gobbled up.

All I knew at thirteen was that drugs took you somewhere else, and somewhere else was where I wanted to be. Then, when I was a freshman in high school, a kid in my class named Claude Lorenz walked through a plate-glass sliding door. The rumor was that he had taken PCP. I didn't know Claude, I'd only seen him from a distance across the lunchroom. He was a budding Saturday-night-fever stud, with feathered dark hair and white pants, bad skin, and one of those gold Italian horns hanging from a chain around his neck. After his stupefied dash onto the family patio, Claude became a legend, a looming ghost in the Blanchet High School halls. He wasn't dead, but he never came back; he transferred to a public school. The rumors of his physical deformity and mental collapse were probably greatly exaggerated. But Claude had crossed to another side, and had not returned intact. To my friends and me, he was proof that drugs could be bad, just like our parents said, and since we were not prone to believe our parents about anything, this evidence shocked us.

My baby bohemian friends and I soon settled on an explanation for Claude's fateful inward journey. He had taken PCP—angel dust, an animal tranquilizer favored by crazed criminals. *A bad drug.* Twenty years after that September, I have still avoided angel dust. Never mind that within months of Claude's disappearance from Blanchet I was downing bottles of Robitussin in a juvenile effort at mind expansion, and by junior year I was dropping acid and drinking cupfuls of mushroom tea. Those were all *good drugs,* favored by gentle hippies and genius bands like the Butthole Surfers, promising bliss and visions, not permanently warped frontal lobes. Pot was a good drug, too—organic, even. Heroin was bad because it could addict you, it killed Alice from that book, and besides, shooting up was gross. Cocaine was good because people shared it at parties—it signified generosity. Speed was bad or good, depending on whether you talked to people who got things done at night or people who valued their sleep. Peyote was good if you treated it seriously, taking a whole weekend in the woods to let it work its juju, and bad if you ate it at your cousin's Super Bowl party. Knowing the difference between good and bad drugs was crucial to one's evolution as a druggie. Shadow figures of the Claude Lorenz variety sulked on the edges of our scene, doing the bad drugs and getting into trouble. We stayed clean, as far as we were concerned.

When I moved to San Francisco, my ideas about good drugs changed to suit my new environment. I did more coke and speed, and smoked a fair amount of pot, but I would never buy drugs—that was my boundary. If someone wanted to give me some, I would take them happily, but I would never stoke my hunger by making them instantly available. A few years into this phase, I discovered Ecstasy, which seemed like an utterly good drug; before being outlawed, it had even been used by therapists to get patients in touch with their emotions. I stayed away from crack, because it was the drug of the desperate. Eventually, I also decided speed was bad and acid was bad, because I was getting older and I feared things—a racing pulse, a loss of memory—that had seemed insignificant before. Lately though, I've been feeling nostalgic for all those enlightening acid trips I took as a teen, so I might start thinking of acid as a good drug again.

Taking any drug is a leap into the unknown. As with all dangerous activities, certain precautions can be taken: I can be careful, for example, to limit my intake; I can surround myself with people I trust, and stay in a comfortable environment. I can drink lots of fruit juice to replenish my vitamin supply. The expectations and fears I bring to the experience are harder to control, but I can at least think them through. If I am certain that smoking heroin will lead me toward addiction, for example, I should probably avoid the opportunity to fulfill my own prophecy. But the murky bottom of any drug trip is the melding of two sets of chemicals: those in the substance, and those in the body. This is an unpredictable process. One person's mild high is another's overdose, and although experience can illuminate the limits of one's capacity, those limits can change without prior notice.

Given that our bodies are so mysterious, growing cancers or collapsing from strokes or giving us sudden pain with no warning, it can seem crazy to add to the chaos with a foreign chemical. Staying away from drugs altogether seems like the only sure bet. But the fact is, no one does, not even my mother or your grandmother or the local Baptist minister. "Virtually everyone in this country is a member of a drug culture," writes Wilcox. He points out that his students' parents, who would panic at the sight of little Janey toking a joint to relax, don't hesitate to give their kids someone else's prescription drugs—Mom's Tylenol with codeine, say—to alleviate an earache or bring on sleep. And there's no guarantee on prescription drugs. The *Journal of the American Medical Association* reports that more than 100,000 Americans a year die in the hospital from severe reactions to properly prescribed medication; it's just a risk you take. And death is only the extreme. I know a woman, plunged in deep depression, who continues to make the rounds of psychoactive substances from Prozac to Zoloft to Xanax and beyond. She weighs each drug's set of side effects against the others'; sometimes the headaches or nausea are worse than the depression itself. The only thing she can rely on is an evening joint to bring her down. Her doctor surreptitiously sanctions her marijuana use. He would prefer to limit her to the acceptable substances of his profession, but it seems merciless to leave her defenseless as he fiddles with her serotonin levels.

Trying to maintain an essentially arbitrary divide between good drugs and bad drugs has led America into a weird and often panicked relationship with illicit substances, resulting in the paradox of very high addiction rates despite some of the most punishing drug laws in the world. Even the most taboo drugs, heroin and cocaine, were once widely distributed under the false claim of their curative powers. Rampant drug use was and is encouraged by the medical profession, and often the ills these heavy doses remedied were caused not by physical weakness, but by social problems. The women who became morphine addicts by the thousands in Victorian America often suffered from mythical ailments such as neurasthenia, which historians now acknowledge was probably depression exacerbated by their extreme isolation and the constricting duties of the home. Cocaine was also introduced as medicine—and one of the primary conditions it "cured," ironically, was opium addiction. Foremen on the docks in New Orleans and other sites of hard labor encouraged their workers, often blacks, to use cocaine to help them shoulder brutal workloads.

But patent medicines remained the most popular source of both cocaine and opium, even after their potency and availability were greatly diminished by the Harrison Narcotic Act of 1914. The critic Greil Marcus writes about finding an advertisement for one such elixir in an old junk shop in the Napa Valley of California. The sign illustrated a cure-all potion named "Americanitis." Marveling at the sign's elaborate yet strangely numb portrait of small-town utopia, with a fountain spewing medicine at its center, Marcus wondered, "What is the cure, and what is the disease?" He noted the ubiquity of such medicines at a time when America was changing rapidly, reshaped by waves of industrialization and immigration. "At the beginning of the century, fatigue and depression seemed to be everyone's fate," he writes. What he did not observe is that the cures themselves, presented as safe for unlimited consumption, were one major source of those very maladies.

Perhaps this incredible scam, which victimized scores of hapless consumers when ignorant medical professionals met the unscrupulous venture capitalists manufacturing these tonics, is the buried root of the unrelenting anger characterizing America's official line on drugs. The embarrassing truth is that a century ago anyone could become a raging addict simply by trying to get well. And cure-alls have never stopped being marketed as the sanctioned counterparts to increasingly stigmatized illegal drugs. Often, no difference exists between these legal substances and forbidden ones. Some prescription drugs, especially relaxers like Valium and Quaaludes, developed parallel identities as recreational "downers." Diet pills relied on amphetamine, outlawed in other forms, to help housewives slim. More recently, mood-altering drugs like Prozac have become popular by affecting the levels of serotonin in the brain, which is exactly what the illicit "rave" drug Ecstasy does. The fight to legalize medical marijuana makes obvious how unstable the line between good and bad drugs remains: despite clear benefits to terminally ill patients, marijuana remains banned because of its history as an illicit, countercultural drug.

Those who fear such substances consider their users criminal, and the law enforces their view. Those who embrace them elevate themselves as shamans and anarchists seeking psychic health in a hypocritical society that is medicated to the gills. They argue that cigarettes are more addictive than crack and that alcohol causes tens of thousands more deaths each year than heroin. At the same time, many drug users demonstrate some discomfort with their own behavior, most clearly in the need to constantly label their habits a form of self-medication. Junkies call finding a fix "getting well"; Kurt Cobain, the decade's most famous drug casualty, often told interviewers that heroin was the only reliable cure for his chronic stomach ailments. "It helps me sleep," says an old hippie I know who's a bit chagrined by his perpetual pot smoking. Recasting illegal substances as medicines makes them into good drugs.

But there are no good drugs. There are no bad ones, either. Perhaps we should assess how people take drugs—their ethic of consumption, not their chemical of choice. But it's tricky to make any governing statements at all. Drugs offer an encounter with the random self, a step beyond the rational into aspects of one's physical and psychic being that can be named only when they surge forth. Taking drugs is like taking an airplane ride inside your own head; you can arrive safely or crash, and fastening your seat belt may or may not save you. Many people take this dare without thinking, jumping into an altered state and learning how to direct themselves once they're inside. Few seriously consider the challenges posed: hard tasks, like dealing with buried corners of your psyche, and remaining responsible while relinquishing control. To take drugs is to give up the idea of being able to predict the future, if only for a few hours. Such an experience can offer extremely valuable lessons about the fickle physical world and the need to react according to the moment. But it's very hard to judge the right way to go about it. Chance is not governed by morality.

Nor, some might say, is pleasure. Psychedelic priests and therapists may be right about the cosmic possibilities of acid-washed spiritual discovery, and concerned commentators don't lie when they say today's kids often turn to white powders to numb the cruel impact of their lives. But most people begin—and continue—to get high because it is just plain fun. And unlike sex, drugs are not about sharing that fun with someone else. At its most primal level, getting high is mind masturbation, self-centered and unproductive. It's anticapitalistic, because it wastes time and doesn't earn you anything; it's antisocial, because it doesn't contribute to the well-being of anyone else. Sharing drugs can be as intimate and enriching as sharing sex, but unlike sex, drugs don't present even the basic procreative reason to do so. In fact, the best trip these days, cutting-edge shamans say, is taken not in a communal circle or on a friendly dance floor, but solo, in a darkened, silent room.

This may be the deepest reason we find it so hard to talk about drugs. They represent selfishness, a quality every person possesses but no one wants to reveal. Unlike forms of selfishness that engender admiration—the acquisition of wealth, for example, or the maintenance of beauty—getting high doesn't bolster the myth of self-development, in which narcissism is encouraged as a route to becoming a more productive member of society. Drug takers have cleared out a space in which they can consume, and become consumed by, themselves. It is very difficult—some would say impossible—to connect this private corner to the rest of your life. If there can be an ethic of drugs, it exists in the attempt to do just that.

THE FRACTURED HIGH

When I embarked upon the acid trip whose description starts this book, I had no intention of ever letting my turn-on turn into a drop-out. I was sixteen years old, for God's sake, with everything from sex to college to my first Clash concert ahead of me. The life of a strung-out dope fiend, which I knew about from all those alluringly scary books in the Young Adult section, would not be mine. I believed this not only because I was doing good drugs, but because those drugs made up just one carefully contained corner of my blossoming alternative lifestyle.

Bohemians younger than the baby boom saw the hippie dream of drugs as a "ray of light," as the tripping guru Allen Ginsberg once called them, collapse into darkness. In the 1970s, society itself seemed to overdose, the stoned dreams of a generation dissolving into violence and cynicism. By 1980, when I was sixteen, virtually no one was talking the hippie line about drugs saving the world. Instead, people consumed marijuana and hallucinogens as quietly as possible, afraid of getting busted and uninterested in idealizing their highs. The typical drug-using kid in my high school belonged to the stoner clan: working-class or lower-middle-class arena rockers who lived to party, shoplifted Budweisers from the 7-Eleven to wash down the smoke from their Mexican weed, and tried to pick up underage girls at the roller rink by offering them a toke. Some stoners may have smoked conscientiously, getting into their Rush albums and having profound thoughts in their bedrooms. But most just wanted to get wasted. Their drug use was an extension of their drinking, dulling the brain instead of expanding it.

I never hung out with the stoners at the back door of the wrestling room after school. Their mindless daily toking seemed like a waste of brain cells. If I was going to fry my synapses, I wanted to feel more than numb. I was influenced by the remnants of the psychedelic counterculture as it translated into the free-jazz art-punk of eccentric visionaries like Captain Beefheart, the desert-dwelling abstract artist and musical ranter I learned about from the older kids I'd met following my favorite local bands. Those groups, who dressed in thrift-store rags and went by funny names like Fred and Audio Leter, created dissonant squalls of noise behind free-associating vocals. They took acid, as the hippies had, but in their crayon-colored visions, humor and rawness replaced cosmic musings. They were inventing do-it-yourself psychedelia, created with fingerpaint and stuff pulled from trash bins, emphasizing the acid trip's silly, disjointed vision—its playfulness—instead of its spirituality.

In those first drug days, from high school to early college, getting high was part of touching the imagination's frisky underbelly, turning everyday life into an art project without worrying about how we might one day make careers of our experiments. Most of the crowd I ran with played music, and we would all gather in the parking garage beneath the University of Washington's main campus thoroughfare—Red Square—holding impromptu jam sessions that continued as long as the spirit (and the chemicals) moved us. To denizens of the 1960s New York art scene, these events probably would have looked like "happenings," those spontaneous art fests organized by people like Allan Kaprow and Al Hansen in storefronts and private lofts. When I look back on these minicircuses now, their style reminds me more of what would develop into rave culture: the Ecstasy-fueled moving party scene that would slip into abandoned urban spaces and then vanish, physically realizing postmodern theorist Hakim Bey's idea of the "temporary autonomous zone." Psychedelic art-punk was the bridge between the romantic vision of 1960s performance art as an invasion of everyday life, and the 1990s rave scene's reimagining it as a stealth attack.

One trait of the conscientious drug user is that she chooses her poison to suit the personality she either already possesses or is trying to cultivate. We baby art freaks wanted to be fanciful and fun. We floated down University Avenue on clouds of our own whimsicality. Even when our bodies were chemical-free, we remained oblivious to the other punks on the street: the heroin users, slinking around on a jones for cool, and the speed munchers, hyped up on intensity and the drive for whatever came next.

As I drifted along in my own dimension, a future friend of mine was prowling the night vistas of Northern California, hyped up on speedy acid and indulging her own latent tendencies. Cassandra Cole got turned on by her older brother when she was in high school and he'd just started college; they had a band together, and would spend wired nights making music or talking philosophy. "We would sit around for eight to ten hours, tripping," she remembered years later. "We always had things we were supposed to do, but we'd end up sitting in the car for eight hours, talking about social contract theory and Marxism."

Cassandra liked the way drugs unlocked her mind, just like I did, but the hidden compartments she sought to explore held more intellect than id. She also liked cocaine, which got her brain racing, although the payoff was much too limited. "I didn't criticize cocaine until I had speed, and then I was like, Let's talk about this. Coke lasts for twenty minutes and you spend the whole time thinking about how you're going to get more. Speed lasts for twelve hours, and maybe you want a little bit more, but it's not like you're going to freak out if you don't get another line." Cassandra became a speed devotee because it was more practical than coke, but also because it was cheaper, born of the street, more punk.

When I met Cassandra, it was 1985 in San Francisco, and white powder seemed to be falling from the sky. She and her punk buddies were just one gang zipping around under its influence. Far bigger was the crowd I landed in by having a close friend who got a job in a restaurant. Studies have shown that restaurant and bar employees are the largest single group of drug consumers in the nation. It's no wonder, with all that cash making their pockets itch and those weird hours to organize a life around. Other card-carrying members of the service sector—record-store employees, for example—also partake heavily, especially if their place of employ stays open until midnight and their social lives subsequently extend until dawn. Planet Records had its share of tweakers, as serious speed consumers are called. Still, their noses were barely dusted compared to those of the pros at Martin's restaurant.

The itchy-pocket factor, and the fact that many worked second jobs or went to school during the day, made cocaine the powder of choice among the restaurant crowd. It seemed ridiculous to us that coke was getting a rep as a yuppie drug via books like Jay McInerney's *Bright Lights, Big City* and movies like Woody Allen's *Annie Hall.* In the popular culture of the mid-1980s, coke signified the yuppie's endless, empty desire for more, with no concern for what that "more" might be. This portrait of greed-stoned youth reached its nadir in Bret Easton Ellis's deliberately icky *Less Than Zero,* which depicts a pack of zoned-out rich kids slumping around Los Angeles in their parents' expensive cars, draining the meaning out of every landscape they crossed and encounter they had. In the movie version, Robert Downey, Jr., who would one day land in jail for his real-life addictions, played a private-school boy turned male prostitute. This was supposed to be a portrait of my generation.

Except, I didn't know any rich kids who would sell their bodies for blow. I didn't know any rich kids at all, only working people who liked to party after they got done with a shift. Chemicals hit different people unpredictably, heightening one urge in one person and a different urge in another. Those multiple effects translate into multiple cultural meanings. In the 1980s, cocaine signified the impulsive excesses of the yuppie class; distilled into crack, it became the symbol of desperate inner-city life. Both of these extrapolations reflect reality; in the Reagan era, rich fools did suck millions of dollars up their noses while eating tiny portions of overpriced cuisine and blowing their bonuses on luxury co-ops they later couldn't sell. And crack's pressing high has led to much ghetto violence and family tragedy. But the yuppies' greed and the ghetto's violence weren't rooted only in the drugs; other factors, such as the exacerbating effect of Republican economic policies on the gap between rich and poor, mattered more. Focusing on drugs raises a tangible demon for people to chase. I'm not denying that white powder stimulates compulsive tendencies, or that many people fell heavily under its spell. But doing a line or two after work did not mean throwing all the promise of one's life out the window. Especially if that life was a bit of scramble already.

I believed enough of the negative hype about white powder to be very cautious around it. In the days of Martin's restaurant, I limited my intake to the small amounts offered at social gatherings. I can't say I never did anything foolish under its influence—there was a one-night stand I long regretted, and a couple of others that my friends might think I should regret. In each case, though, the drug simply gave me an extra push toward something I wanted to do anyway. The choice to have sex with that darkly brooding bartender in the front seat of his Toyota was my own; I probably would have done it with nothing more in my system than a few shots of tequila. Not only that, but the drug enhanced the experience, made me feel the rush of this gamble through nerve endings that prickled and buzzed. I loved the erotic groove white powder created, the way everyone suddenly seemed fascinating, how nervousness and languor, which sometimes overwhelm my desire to connect with people, just vanished as I danced around the room catching every sparkling eye. It was a blast, hooking up with all those egos. And it certainly wasn't any more meaningless than sitting around by myself, watching TV. Since I made it a point to keep my outings recreational, and never kept any speed or coke around the house to tempt me, I had plenty of time for other states of mind.

When I did go out on white powder, I entered an after-hours world I'd never have otherwise discovered. This was the biggest benefit I got from these drugs. Acid had illuminated the city's abandoned corners, as we wandered through silent, luminous parks and labyrinthine parking garages. White powder brought me into another hidden environment: I kept company with the minders of the city's common halls long after the doors had been shut to everyone else. A bar or a restaurant after closing becomes a magical zone; all its shifting elements, the music, the flow of alcohol and food, the mood itself, now fall under your command. As the servers, who make all of those mechanics seem natural during open hours, serve themselves, they open up the long history of secrets such rooms are made of. Playing pool at four in the morning in some Valencia Street dive, I could see every stain and rip in the green felt; fetching myself a drink, I discovered where the joint's ice and baseball bat hid.

I also learned the secrets of the gypsies who spent their lives making these establishments feel like everyone's other home. They often had spotty histories, having escaped from unhappy families and neighborhoods literally or spiritually impoverished, promising them little: they were daughters of Central Valley fruit pickers, Los Angeles liquor-store clerks, Oakland civil servants. Others were college kids uneasy at the prospect of life in middle management. Everybody seemed to have a secret, whether it was a crime, an illegitimate child, or simply a dream with which they hadn't quite reconciled. Most were drifters in one way or another, maybe just for a year or two, maybe for a lifetime. The driftier they were, the more the drugs could prove a problem. Marie, my best friend among them, was a satellite bouncing around, with eyes that never settled, a yen for a new boy every night, and a hunger to be brilliant at something, she just didn't know what. She had a lot of trouble with white powder. Its tendency to drive people can make them reach for their desires, pushing the yuppie to scramble for more dough or the sensualist to look for a hot one-night stand. But Marie had nothing specific on the other end of her want. So the drug pushed her right out of herself.

It was Marie's bad habit that finally led me to swear off white powder. I'd met her when we both worked behind the counter one summer in a North Beach café, making messy sandwiches and feeding our friends for free. Martin's restaurant crowd had dissolved, as these families of runaways so often do, and I followed Marie into her ragtag clan, which held court at a very scruffy but cool bar in the Mission District. For nights that turned into weeks and months, she and I tripped through that bar and many others like two electric wires, dangerous to touch, touching everything we could. We were high on being trouble girls, staying up late in bad places. But we were also high on drugs, and after half a year, when I started to feel sick all the time, I decided that following my nose into the bar's back office every afternoon was stretching my body's limits. And, like most drugs, white powder had only a limited amount to teach. I was getting bored with it.

I tried to tell Marie I needed to take a break. She said, Okay, no problem, just still hang around with me. But it wasn't so much fun anymore; we'd go somewhere, she would fly around the place, I'd be bored, grounded. Eventually Marie stopped bothering to land. People were getting mad at her for being there one minute and gone the next. On those rare occasions when she did come down, she plummeted into the nettles of self-hatred. She had abandoned the necessary double consciousness of the conscientious drug user, which keeps you aware that drugs are good and bad at the same time, and that every high is a tightrope over the abyss. "Why can't we stay high all the time?" she asked me once, sitting over lemongrass soup in a Thai restaurant. I didn't know what to say. I felt comfortable in both realities, straight and high, while she had made peace with only one. Like most of the drug abusers I've known, Marie had no problem with being wasted. Her crises began when she got sober. The problems had been there before she'd ever sniffed a line, and she was willing to sacrifice the whole rational world to keep them at bay.

Marie went to the Far East, got even more strung out, and ended up in rehab. She got lucky in there; after many terrified encounters with her own soul, she discovered a self she wanted to hang on to. Now she runs her own boutique in a city far from San Francisco and sticks to red wine. But I lost her for years, and it broke my heart. I know some people will wonder why I don't hate those drugs for what they did to her. Of course I wanted to save Marie when she plunged into the vast emptiness; I felt helpless, furious, betrayed. But it was her emptiness she'd left me for; the drugs just took her there. She would have gone anyway, maybe through sex, or depression, or even suicide. If she'd flung her body from the Golden Gate Bridge, I couldn't have blamed gravity for pulling her down.

So I didn't get mad at drugs. In fact, I came to believe that they deserved a lot more respect than we were giving them. What began to disgust me was the way reckless users (myself included, sometimes) would ingest as if doing so were a normal activity, like drinking a soda. Getting high is never normal. It is profoundly weird—one of the few chances humans have to fully inhabit an alternate sensual reality. Finding the balance between the drug's will and your own is the crucial step in negotiating that reality instead of letting it just crash over you. I learned these lessons by watching people like Marie surrender to a force they'd once controlled. I came to see that drug experiences aren't just about the high. Myriad decisions surround takeoff: how much to ingest, when and how often to do it, what people and places to allow into the trip. I'd grown less meticulous about these things, and too many of my partners in powder didn't pause to consider them at all.

I decided to stop taking drugs in bars or at parties, abandoning the practice of getting high with acquaintances. From now on, I would maximize my psychoactive pleasures by limiting them to communal experiences with close friends. Luckily for me, a drug had emerged that particularly suited these more intimate experiences. It wasn't a hallucinogen, although in certain doses it could make the room spin. Neither was it an amphetamine, though it would keep you up all night. MDMA has been classified as an "empathogen," and before being criminalized in 1985, it was used by therapists to help emotionally blocked patients open up. When I first tried it in 1986, in a glass of juice doctored by one of Isadora's boyfriends, who worked in a U.C. Berkeley chem lab, I immediately understood why kids on the street were calling it the love drug. Six of us sat in Fulton Street's tiny living room that night, and an hour after we'd dropped the drug we were all on one chair.

An orgy of cuddling ensued. Although fucking can be slow fun on MDMA, its real effect is presexual, the baby's plain delight in being enclosed in warmth. That first night, we spent hours trying on all our different clothes, enraptured by the sensation of velvet or cashmere against the skin. Simple emotions match the simple bodily pleasures of the MDMA experience; basically, you just feel really good, in an innocent, indiscriminate rush of loving-kindness. That's not to say the drug will definitely banish negative emotions. It's an intuition opener, and if you've got a bad mood lurking inside it can lure the bummer out. The second time I took it, with the same people and in the same place, I spent a good chunk of the night weeping and wandering the neighborhood in the rain. Things with my mate, David, had not been going well, and the MDMA forced me to admit that I really wanted to break up with him. I could have paid a therapist a lot more than the fifteen bucks I'd paid for that hit and still taken months to overcome my denial. As it was, I started looking for a new apartment the next week. Why in the world, I wondered, had they criminalized this stuff?

The question remains pertinent fifteen years later, as I watch great handfuls of my friends try one psychoactive prescription after another to reach similar, if less intense, states of contentment. Recent research suggests that MDMA may have long-term negative effects, but that could be true of legal mood alterers, too. Drug laws don't represent reasoned judgments about good and bad; they follow notions of normal. If a drug makes you different from the way you would be in the accepted waking state, then it cannot be allowed in a crowded society that only keeps running with everyone's cooperation. MDMA makes people too happy. They don't want to work; they don't need to buy anything. The insight MDMA provides is the same one Buddhists meditate for years to comprehend: that harmony is best achieved by relishing the moment. One of my most memorable MDMA trips involved eight of my favorite intellectual pals. We planned to drop the drug and spend the night discussing its properties. I spent the next five hours sticking my head in the freezer and watching the frigid air move around. I'd never felt satisfaction come so easily.

The culture that rose up around MDMA also celebrated simple pleasures, but being as entrepreneurial as any bohemia, it dressed those pleasures up in shiny colors and sold them in infinite varieties. The subculture coalesced in England, where ravers, as fans of MDMA and electronic music became known, multiplied and spread throughout the land. By the mid-1990s tens of thousands of ravers were gathering at impromptu locations, packing airfields and abandoned warehouses and vanishing with their sound systems by the morning light, half a million of them taking MDMA or some variant each year. The scene was like a new England floating out of the tired gray landscape. The drug fueling it soon gained an appropriately rapturous name: Ecstasy.

Ecstasy altered the consciousness of a generation as profoundly as acid had in hippie America. The rave was a new conceptual art form that outstripped any of the happenings of the 1960s in scale and social impact; its music, a blend of synthesized sounds and samples that did away with the guitar-bass-drum formula, threatened to supersede rock and roll. The inevitable backlash and government crackdown weakened Ecstasy culture's impact in the late 1990s, but the fact that virtually the entire population of England under age twenty-five had sampled the drug presented the possibility of a massive mind shift of the kind the acid priests had only dreamed about. England still awaits the repercussions of this communal blowout.

Ecstasy culture never caught on in the States the way it did in England. Perhaps the thud of the post-1960s psychedelic crash still echoed too loudly to allow for the idealism the scene required. English rave organizers viewed their country's new explosion of grooviness as the second coming of the Summer of Love: one wrote in 1988 that they were "reviving a San Franciscan ideal of 1966, in the 'gathering of the tribes'—young, old, and differing youth factions." In San Francisco itself, however, Ecstasy culture took on a different meaning. My town's hipsters left the huge English-style raves to Midwestern college students, who did manage to organize a few impressive events in the mid-1990s, and instead focused on the links between neo-psychedelic drugs and the nascent cyberculture of virtual reality and the Internet. The fluid identities that people assumed when logging on to Internet chat rooms, momentarily abandoning physical reality as they typed in new names, produced a sense of self not unlike the out-of-body experience of tripping. Even that venerable 1960s drug huckster Timothy Leary got in on this act, spending his last years exploring the links between neo-psychedelics and artificial intelligence, and finally expiring in a triumphant drug haze in 1996 while thousands monitored his final breaths on the World Wide Web.

The advocates of cyberpsychedelics are right, I think, in considering drug use a technology of the spirit—a phrase once used to describe Buddhism, another anarchistic metaphysical practice popular in the 1990s. The avant-garde of 1990s conscientious drug use is deliberately aiming for this kind of soul expansion. Terence McKenna, the scene's most prominent guru, is an ethnobotanist who believes human consciousness evolved because prehistoric people ate psilocybin-fueled mushrooms, stimulating such higher emotions as altruism and empathy. He's a cosmic prankster, specifically chosen by Leary as his heir. McKenna has labored to inform his revelations with scientific data regarding the drug trip and anthropological accounts of non-Western tripping. His acolytes are experimenting with such obscure substances as DMT, a synthetic drug that mirrors chemicals in the brain to produce a fifteen-minute trip more intense than any Westerners have experienced.

"Ecstasy [the mind state, not the drug] is a complex emotion containing elements of you: fear, terror, triumph, surrender, and empathy," McKenna once told an interviewer for *Omni* magazine. "Drugs are not comfortable, and anyone who thinks they are comfortable or even escapist should not toy with drugs unless they're willing to get their noses rubbed in their own stuff."

My own history of tripping has been marked by all of the arduously experienced perceptions McKenna mentions, not to mention a lot of pure enjoyment. Yet I always found that after a while, a drug had given me what it had to offer and I didn't want more. I haven't done any hard drugs since New Year's Eve 1993, when a disappointing Ecstasy trip forced me to admit that my capacity for its exquisite pleasure had receded. Age is certainly a factor; I also can't indulge as heavily in legal drugs like alcohol and nicotine unless I want a whopping headache and a potential cold. I would smoke pot regularly if I could, but my bizarrely low tolerance for it makes a toke more irritating than relaxing. Cocaine just isn't around anymore, although reports from high society say it's made a comeback in fancier apartments than mine. Speed is still off-limits after the scary palpitations it caused. The club kids' current poisons, like the animal tranquilizer ketamine, aim for a level of self-obliteration that doesn't interest me now that I'm actually trying to figure out the whys and wherefores of my life. I feel similarly cautious about DMT; maybe someday, in the right dark room with the right shamanistic friend, I'll give it a try, but the opportunity hasn't presented itself. Heroin—that's another story. But it's not mine, I never even smoked the stuff, so I'll have to look to others to tell it.

To be honest, I find my relative sobriety rather discouraging. The greatest gift drugs gave me was a real knowledge that every passing second is unpredictable, and that's an important insight to hang on to as a weapon against moral ossification and self-centered hopelessness. If establishing a value system is like drawing a map over territory as you cross it, then drugs force you to stop and rub your face into the earth. (Sometimes literally; a fairly sober pal told me he once ate some mushrooms that had him munching the mulch in Golden Gate Park. That was after he threw his glasses away and before his companions asked a homeless person to drive them all home.) Maybe "getting high" is the wrong phrase, after all; in many ways, drugs are about getting low, down to the basics of the instant, the root of the senses, the trickery of time.

It takes focus to do this well. Many people fail, spinning beyond the grasp of themselves, while others luck out and stay intact without even trying. Such unstable narratives make everyone nervous. When I started out pondering what I then thought was the difference between good and bad drugs, I found two stories that seemed to delineate the divide. One concerned Constance Reed and the other friends who first initiated me into the psychoactive sphere; now busy with their adult lives, they still regularly trip on acid and smoke pot without any obvious consequences to their health or happiness. The other followed Cassandra down a dark passage, into the blank womb of heroin, which eventually claimed the life of her lover and nearly destroyed her best friend. Good drugs and bad drugs: the difference couldn't have been clearer. Yet as the stories evolved, I again discovered that nothing was obvious about these categories except the fact that they were awfully easy to shake.

■

TRIPPING WITHIN REASON

The inherent other-consciousness of the drug trip makes trips very hard to discuss in a normal tone of voice. Instead, both sympathetic and damning chroniclers have elevated the user's tale to the realm of the epic, rife with peril and wonder. Odysseus faced no worse trials than the hallucinating wanderer who strives to survive William S. Burroughs's *Naked Lunch*, and later bards of addiction have drawn their tales in similarly otherworldly hues. Their worlds crackle, aflame with the surreal. Or they glow with an aura as cold as the moon, their protagonists corrupted monks who have pledged their souls to a demon realm of steel and blood and ether. "Realistic" drug epics, like Larry Clark's photograph collection *Tulsa,* or Linda Yablonsky's *The Story of Junk,* emanate from a realm of perilous enlightenment and mortal condemnation.

But there are people who manage to balance their chemical explorations with other aspects of their lives. My first tripping buddies fit into this category. They are not outstandingly noble people, nor extralucky ones. They're all in their thirties and have curtailed their chemical excursions now that their bodies are older and their lives more complicated. They don't deny the hazards of filling the brain with foreign substances. Most have endured bad trips, been scared by close calls, and lost some friends to the same substances they had learned to manage. But even if they began their drug adventures believing in the separate reality Burroughs and the others wrote about, they now have regular jobs and homes where they stay in and cook dinner on the weekends. Just as the practicing perverts of San Francisco rewrote the etiquette of sex, conscientious drug users are working to establish a code of conduct about drugs. I turned to them to find out what role drugs might play in an ordinary person's day-to-day life.

"Recreational, recreational, recreational!" That was Ivan Morris talking, waving a marijuana pipe in my face and looking stern. We were sitting at the kitchen in the small ranch house he owns with his wife, my old friend Constance Reed, in the unpretentious lowlands of Seattle. Ivan is one of the dreamiest and most solid men I know. He's a musician—a former member of one of those acid bands we cavorted with back when—and a master builder, one part of him forever flitting after his muse and the other planting his feet and lifting a shovel to dig another foundation. He firmly believes that smoking a nightly pot bowl and dropping a few psychedelics once every few months can be be part of the All-American pursuit of happiness.

I mentioned to him that just that afternoon I'd read an article in a fashion magazine about how marijuana was destroying the nation's young men by making them into zombies unresponsive to women's needs. He glared. "It doesn't fuck you up like alcohol does," he insisted. "I'd much rather cut down a tree after smoking a joint than cut it down after drinking a couple beers. I'd probably have an accident with a chainsaw if I did that."

"He's an active person. He's not a couch potato," added Constance, who was sipping port and finishing the dishes. "When you're smoking pot, you have a tendency to do that thing that you like, more. Ivan will go out and get stoned and dig a huge trench, whereas if he weren't stoned he might dig a small trench. Guys who like to watch TV, they'll sit for hours and watch it, whereas if they weren't stoned, they might watch a little and then go out and do something else. It gives you that focus towards whatever it is you like. Your indulgence."

Ivan and Constance would be excellent poster children for the promotion of good drugs. Responsible citizens, rugged types who hike for miles every weekend and renovate decrepit properties for fun, they have made getting stoned into a healthy hobby as successfully as anyone I know. The ethic they have established is characteristic of mature recreational drug users, despite the fact that its measured tone doesn't fit in to any of our common stories. Constance is even more levelheaded when outlining her views than Ivan. She definitely believes that some drugs are bad—namely opiate and amphetamine derivatives, which she considers too addictive—and she also insists that even the good ones must be approached with the utmost care. Since she started sewing all her own clothes when we were in high school, Constance has always reveled in the practical stuff of life. She even started her tripping career with a full set of instructions.

"I researched the acid thing," she recalled with a grin. "The first time I got high hadn't been a conscious choice—I was making out with someone who had just dosed, and I got some of his buzz. But then I went to the library at my high school and found whatever information I could. There were these instructional videotapes, designed to warn kids away from drugs, and I watched them in the audiovisual room. I could distinguish the hysteria of a movie like *Reefer Madness* from the scientific information some films offered. Once I'd done the research, I made a choice as to whether a drug was dangerous or not."

I love to picture Constance in her Catholic-school uniform, munching on a Snickers bar and scrutinizing old science films about the biological effects of LSD. She never forgot what she'd learned. Constance tried cocaine only once, in a joint laced by a friend; she refused speed and heroin. She also quickly adopted one lesson from Timothy Leary: that set and setting are crucial aspects of a good trip. Parties, clubs, and crowded city streets were not appropriate. Anything with a patch of green and a wide open space was. She carefully chose her companions: a few close friends, at least a few of them more experienced than her. "Doug was older, he was in his twenties, and he would always guide us to these places where we weren't going to get caught," she said of our favorite chaperon during those days, an impish trumpeter with a special gift for climbing trees.

It's debatable, how safe our rambles really were. Doug once toppled out of a tree he was bonding with and broke a rib, and another particularly wild buddy disappeared for several days on a psychedelic bike ride. Both boys had ingested more alcohol than anything else. Constance would say they were out for trouble, not measuring their consumption, setting forth in a reckless mood. "It's really just down to your willpower against your surroundings and your cravings," she explained. "You use your judgment when you administer the drugs to yourself."

For all her pragmatic talk, Constance admits she's occasionally taken a dare. "I once did acid during class in high school," she admitted. "It was a kind of academic exercise. My friend and I took half a hit each. We were sitting there and my friend was watching her arm melt. If I'd seen my arm melt—which never happened, I wasn't prone to hallucinations—I would have said to myself, 'I'm on drugs, I'd better not fixate on it.' But she just went for it, muttering to herself about it and fondling her arm. I was trying to restrain her, going, 'Knock it off!' "

Luckily, the nuns at Constance's school already thought she and her friend were pretty weird, and apparently chalked up this theatrical behavior to hormonal angst. Constance had successfully tested her own mettle. She kept her equilibrium from then on, except for a brief span in college, far away from home, when a couple of careless highs led her to give up tripping. This phase lasted about as long as the average frat boy's party phase, before he renounces his extremes and becomes a lawyer. "I was like a swing set, going from one extreme to another, before coming back to the people I started out with," she explained. Eventually she came back to Seattle and her old crowd, hooked up with her unresolved teenage crush, Ivan, and reacquainted herself with drugs.

Ivan had gone through a straight phase, too, dating a sorority girl and concentrating on his guitar playing. He and Constance returned to the secret glowing universe at a party known in Washington State hippie-punk circles as Mungfest. "It's the annual acidfest." Ivan laughed. "Twenty miles up a dirt road, there are twenty campsites set up, and everybody at each campsite is tipping back the home-brewed beer they brought."

"And people are wandering around naked in the creek at midnight," Constance chimed in.

"Someone dyed their white dog green one year," Ivan declared.

Mungfest is a typical 1990s-style freak festival, a bit like the gatherings of the 1960s, minus the delusion that the group's combined energy will somehow change the social order. Like England's raves, Mungfest operates as one of Hakim Bey's temporary autonomous zones—for about forty-eight hours, it arises, a domain with its own rules and resources, and then everybody packs up their tents and instruments and evaporates. For Constance and Ivan, it's a holiday, the annual ritual that keeps them in touch with their ebullient insides. They take care to keep their spirits, and their intake, light, because they've seen the consequences of unanticipated intensity.

Constance has watched friends break down when high, suddenly devastated by memories they didn't even realize they possessed. Once she sat for eight hours in her college laundry room with a housemate, trying to talk her back from such a scary encounter. "Something she was repressing stopped being repressed," Constance said. "She didn't expect it to happen, or even know it was there." This is what a bad trip is, according to Constance: an unscheduled meeting with the darker parts of yourself. Her methods of measured consumption don't eliminate the chances of such unpleasant encounters, but they reduce them.

As Constance and Ivan see it, the problem with drugs is exactly the same as the problem with every other American act of consumption: excess. "It's gluttony," Constance insisted. "If you're a glutton about anything, you turn desire into a need. Whatever you use drugs for, to relax, to free your mind, to play, when it gets to be a need, that's the problem. Like my need for burritos. I would weigh four hundred pounds if I ate as many burritos as I craved. You set limits; you have to. It's all a matter of discipline."

A few nights later, I sat at another dining room table with Hank Quinn and Iris Dickey, another young married couple who are old friends of Constance and Ivan, and heard about an instance of drug gluttony. The setting was Mungfest, the previous year. It was the year when Iris went wild.

"My bad trip," she began with a rueful shake of the head. "I decided I could take as many mushrooms as this notorious Mungfest wildman who calls himself Forrest. *After* taking a hit of acid. I was just way too high. Sick to my stomach, couldn't figure out that I was sick to my stomach. Had to pee, couldn't figure out I had to pee. The lights were on in Forrest's camper, so I went over there, saying 'Forrest, I'm too high,' whimpering. And he was in the same predicament—he couldn't get out of the camper!! Finally he did. He said, 'Let's sit down.' I just kept saying, 'I'm too high.' Then he told me, 'You feel like you have to throw up.' I was like, 'Aah, yeah!' So I went over to a corner and made him hold my glasses, and I hurled. Then we went and sat in front of the camper some more, and tried to figure out what we were going to do. Finally we decided, Forget it, we're not going to be able to make it out of this campsite. So we just sat there watching, talking to people coming by.

"The relationships you make when you're on acid, it's never quite the same afterward. I felt this total camaraderie with Forrest. We were sitting there for hours. We thought years had passed. Every once in a while we'd laugh or something. We weren't talking. And I remember Forrest said, 'I'm making sense to you, aren't I?' "

This little saga is a classic in the annals of the too far gone, an apt illustration of the consequences of irresponsible tripping. It is not, you will note, the story of someone who jumped out of a window. I'm not saying such accidents have never occurred, but far more typical is the semifrozen state Iris and Forrest experienced. The worst part about their trip is that they were grounded, unable to enjoy the vistas psychedelics can uncover. They ate lots of drugs, and then just sat there. What a waste.

I had a similar experience once, tripping on Ecstasy. The drug came on too strong and I had to get into bed while the door frame menacingly multiplied. In a flash, my housemates and fellow trippers found me; they talked me through the worst, until I could move around again. That's the other important lesson offered by Iris's story—that even at their highest, conscientious trippers watch out for each other. Psychedelics may put your head in another dominion, but they also increase your attention to every little action. If somebody's having a bad time, all she usually needs to do is show signs of it for a nearby ally to notice and make it a project to help her down.

The most dangerous moment in a psychedelic trip is usually the end, when the pesky ego reenters the building and starts throwing around bad advice. Iris's husband Hank, a saxophone player who often gigs with Ivan, had a little encounter with the law at that very instant a few years back.

"When I got arrested for driving while intoxicated, that was the second day of Mungfest," he said. "I wasn't flying, but I was on the tail end of it. It was morning, and I was trying to talk Forrest into not going to work. He was going to call in sick, so we had a couple beers. Then Forrest decided he had to go to work and talked me into driving him. I shouldn't have been driving, with the beer and the leftover acid mixing inside. We came around this corner, and there was this cop. I had empty beer bottles in my pockets—because I didn't want to litter! When I got out of the car, the beer bottles just fell out. That was a bad trip."

Hank knows he should have just stayed at Mungfest and let the experience he'd ingested play out. He maintains that it was alcohol, not drugs, that ultimately screwed up his judgment. Hank is something of a world traveler, and in the lands of holy tripping, where drugs have sometimes been used to attain spiritual insight, the bottle was the most evil influence he saw. "I've seen incredible alcoholism in India," he said. "The way that the Indians drink is just to get wasted. There was one time I was going out with these guys and we went to the liquor store. They were all buying bottles of gin and vodka. I thought, There's plenty of alcohol, I'll just buy a couple beers. And then the guys just threw the bottles' caps away and drank them."

Hank and Iris think that bringing drug and alcohol use out in the open would lead to saner habits. "If kids could learn to drink like they do in France, instead of by stealing a six-pack from their parents' fridge, or shoplifting, it would be better," Hank said. "When I was a Boy

Scout, we had the one guy who'd rip off jugs of gallon wine. That's why one of the first times I got drunk it was on Bali Hai." He scrunched up his face at the memory of the nauseating drink, his point made: surreptitious consumption leads to intentional inebriation, not connoisseurship.

Iris has other reasons for advocating legalization, conclusions she couldn't avoid after working for a few years as a medical technician in a hospital. "I had a lot of patients who smoked pot," she explained. "For a lot of the chronic pain and nausea people, especially diabetics, it's the only thing that works. And the medical establishment is like, 'Oh no, don't do that. Let's give you some morphine instead!' I think pot is a lot safer."

Hank and Iris stopped believing in the official line between good and bad drugs long ago. Now, they're trying to make those distinctions for themselves, and sometimes they reach pretty startling conclusions. Hank sometimes talks about marijuana as a wonder drug. When he had his appendix out, his doctor prescribed him codeine. But codeine makes him feel ill, so he traded it for pot. He has musician friends who smoke instead of taking Inderal to alleviate performance anxiety. He even thinks that weed could do the trick that Prozac is working on the millions these days, mellowing them out and cheering them up. He's more suspicious of over-the-counter painkillers than he is of weed. "Ibuprofen makes me deaf," he insisted. "And I understand it makes people blind, too."

The evidence of Hank's life doesn't always support his declarations; he has to admit that marijuana is probably no more of a cure-all than those patent medicines of old, and possibly as much of a problem. "I'm actually trying to cut down now," he confessed. "My problem with pot is I get depressed. I fall into the trap of believing society's judgments. It's really easy for me to say, Oh, yeah, there's nothing I can do. But I'm the one who smokes all the time. If I was in school again, I wouldn't smoke. I don't smoke before I go to my music lessons."

I've known Hank for a lot of years, and I've seen these moods come over him, especially when he's hungry for work and sick of the lack of respect and compensation he gets for pursuing experimental music in a culture that prefers easy listening. When his blues get too heavy to bear, he tapers off the pipe and spends his afternoons bike riding. He could go totally clean and sober, and that might make him more aggressive about his musical career, but the art he loves will always be marginal.

Perhaps he would be more motivated to go mainstream and pursue the usual American narcotics, like money and useless leisure toys. Maybe he'd own a sport utility vehicle and get drunk on the weekends and drive it around, the way his fisherman brother did before he joined Alcoholics Anonymous.

Or maybe he would work to change the things in society that bug him. That's the biggest irony about regular drug use—not that it's a threat to American prosperity, but that it actually helps keep the system in place. The soothing effect of marijuana helps Hank contain his rage, and he imagines it does the same for many people beneath the poverty line. "How are people going to fry hamburgers if they can't smoke pot?" he asked. "How in the hell are you going to get people to work at McDonald's?"

The dream of equal opportunity has always been a white lie; just ask the kid who sells you your next McChicken sandwich. Getting stoned is a small rebellion that keeps the worker thinking the system isn't killing him after all. Pot wipes out concerns about time, the linchpin of efficient capitalism. Smoking dope is a form of time theft.

Since the advent of homegrown weed—which U.S. Drug Enforcement Administration records show is the main target of the criminal justice system's official War on Drugs, despite the fact that marijuana is the least harmful of illicit substances—the marijuana trade also operates as an All-American shadow economy, a network of entrepreneurs excluded by necessity from the accepted routes of advertising, distribution, taxation, and regulation. "What is the war on drugs if not a war on competition?" argued Hank, spinning out a typical pot smoker's conspiracy theory. "The government makes money from its drug connections in other countries, so they can run their private armies, and in this area you have homegrown. The marijuana here does not come from Mexico, it comes from people's basements." It may or may not be the case that the CIA is protecting its own interests in the War on Drugs. What can be said is that by targeting marijuana growers, seizing their property, sentencing them to long prison terms, and even, sometimes, killing them, the DEA sends out a strong signal against what libertarians call living off the grid.

People like Hank and Iris have sneaked off the edge anyway, becoming experts in a subject no one likes to talk about. Their counterparts in the sex world, the practicing perverts, have been able to push a different awkward cultural conversation forward a little, because the law does not restrict them quite as much. Few such authorities exist in the drug world; it's simply too dangerous. There are the folks at *High Times* magazine, and the activists working to legalize pot through organizations like the National Organization to Reform Marijuana Laws (NORML). Both Ivan and Hank have been known to quote from Leary and other drug gurus who made their mark in the 1960s, when the cultural conversation about drugs briefly went from a whisper to a scream. They've put together their own theories from their own experience and from this underground material, trying to separate crackpot musings from useful information.

Hank and Iris have witnessed the War on Drugs in their own backyard. They live in what the City of Seattle unironically calls a "Weed and Seed Neighborhood." Police resources are channeled into these low-income blocks to catch small-time drug operators. So nobody in their house ever smokes near the windows, and when Hank and Ivan are driving to a gig, they don't fire up the pipe until they're in the theater parking lot. One time, though, Hank got a little closer to the DEA than he'd ever wanted to be. He wasn't getting busted. He was listening to testimony at a methamphetamine trial.

Methamphetamine—speed—messes with its users much more seriously than pot does. Intemperate use leads to breakdowns like the one my San Francisco friend Marie went through before she landed in rehab. Yet despite the fact that meth is also a homegrown industry, and a toxic one that leads to exploding makeshift labs spewing waste over the landscape, marijuana busts outnumber meth busts a thousand to one. And it happened that a meth bust coincided with Hank's round of jury duty.

How, I asked in wonder, did he of all people get assigned to a drug trial? "The questioner asked if I was a member of NORML or any organization that wants to legalize drugs. I'm not," he said. "And then when they asked if I sympathized with their views, I didn't speak up." Way to infiltrate the system, dude. But the fact is, Hank is a guy who actually respects the law once it's set in motion. He readily admitted to driving while intoxicated when the cop pulled him over after Mungfest, and now he swore to make his judgments according to the state's rules.

"They had somebody who was caught selling meth, and they used him as an undercover agent," he recalled, a look of disgust creeping over his face. "This was some poor bastard who was looking at being away from his wife and kids for twenty years unless he let them wire him up and send him in." The dealer-turned-agent fingered two men, one of whom was definitely trading in speed. The other may have been in on the operation, or he may have just let a friend in trouble stay the night. "We ended up finding him guilty because of how the law is written," Hank said. "He had knowledge. The state was all happy because he was the big catch."

"Was he a kingpin?" I asked, thinking of *Scarface* and *NYPD Blue*.

" 'Kingpin' is not the right word for somebody in a four-hundred-fifty-dollar rental house in Everett," Hank scoffed. "The guy had five kids. He had not handled the drugs, and was not directly involved in the sale. I argued for three hours trying to get him off. And I was the only one. I could have hung the jury, but I swore to uphold our damn law. It made me ill, once I did it."

"That guy was like you, with everyone you're talking to for this book," Hank said, throwing me a fish eye. "If any of us were actually selling drugs, you would be part of the conspiracy."

His statement made the veggie chili Iris had served for dinner rumble in my stomach. It's easy to get caught up in inventing your own morality, and I for one think it's also a noble quest. But reworking the rules about drugs makes you a genuine member of the criminal class. Even a person who would never deal, who dislikes the thought of offering a potentially dangerous choice to someone else, can get significant jail time merely for possessing drugs for personal use. If the DEA thinks you're growing your own little garden in the basement, the law says agents can rip up your house, even burn it down, without having any actual evidence. It's happened. The most responsible drug users can end up in the worst circumstances.

And of course, the drugs—or the you inside, whom the drugs beckon out—can lead to trouble, too. My Northwestern friends have avoided falling down that hole by moderating their intake and keeping their priorities straight. "I smoked crack once," Hank revealed. "It did make me feel that elation, and I really wanted more. But I said to myself, I'm a poor musician. I do not need this in my life." Not everyone he has known has been able to make such decisions. One childhood friend, a former glue sniffer, overdosed on a mix of speed and cocaine and died. A former band member got strung out on heroin and disappeared from the scene. Another is clean and sober now, after some desolate years as a junkie and petty thief in New York.

One thing that helps my Northwestern friends stay on track, I think, is their unwavering belief in the good-drug theory. They treat their trips like wilderness treks; like Everest climbers, they know the mountain isn't evil, but the way you go up can kill you. They stay away from peaks they consider too high. I have always done the same. That's why I thought it would be easy for me to paint an unambiguous portrait of a bad drug, one guaranteed to send users howling into the void. Heroin: the unredeemable taboo, the trip too dangerous for anyone. I even had a personal tragedy to pull out as an example, the story of a friend who climbed too far and fell all the way down. Here, I thought, was a story of risks I'd never take, one that everyone would understand. So I went to dig up some painful memories. I ended up finding more complexities.

■

T H E   T U E S D A Y - T H U R S D A Y   C L U B

When I opened the letter from Cassandra on a soot-colored weekday seven years ago, I was standing at the big white desk in my first New York apartment, the one I would eventually abandon to the fleas the former tenant's dog had carried in. The note was an uncharacteristically formal gesture from a friend given to impromptu afternoon phone calls. I knew it would contain something Cassandra didn't want me to hear in the high, giddy music of her voice, something she wanted me to have time to digest. I looked up into a corridor of Brooklyn backyards. Their worn-out trees and valiant little green patches were so different from the light-kissed expanses of San Francisco, the home I'd left my heart in, just like that dumb song said I would. Cassandra's words made me feel locked up inside those little squares; they threw up another wall between me and what was quickly becoming my past. "I am writing to tell you something very sad. Tim Bateson died on December 9 in his apartment in the Outer Mission."

She had recorded the news as if it were a line in a newspaper obituary, using the plainest language to make it solid and real. Tim had been Cassandra's boyfriend when I first met her skipping class on the lawn in front of the Humanities Building at San Francisco State University. They were a golden couple, punk-rock style—she an aspiring poet with cranberry-colored hair and the best collection of Doc Martens boots in town, he a political rabble-rouser with an angel face behind his wire-rimmed spectacles. I had always been a little in awe of their careless beauty. And of their confident drug consumption, which I only took part in once or twice. This was years before my serious white-powder phase; at twenty-one, I hadn't moved beyond what I thought was the safe stuff. But Cassandra had a reputation as a speed freak, and the word on Tim was that he did just about everything.

"He did tons of drugs," Cassandra verified one summer morning last year, sorting the laundry in the North Beach apartment she shares with her husband, Dennis Chang. "He was always doing drugs. One of the first times I met him, I think it was the first time I slept with him, he brought in Ecstasy in two juice bottles to our philosophy of science class. And he gave one to me. I remember thinking, This is fucking crazy.

"I knew it had the Ecstasy in it. The class was already going on when he came in. We were sitting all the way on the other side of the room from the door, so we couldn't leave. And I felt it coming on at the end, and I'm sitting here in class, going, 'Ahhh, I've got to get the fuck out of here. It's time to go.' And he's freaking out sitting next to me, having a good time."

Tim didn't seem to feel the need to control his tripping the way Cassandra did. Ever since she'd started taking speed on a regular basis, in her freshman year of college, Cassandra had set down certain ground rules and never broken them. Her pals Rose Linden and Damien Armstrong would want to stay up all night doing line after line. Damien particularly advocated this nocturnal life, since he was going through a gothic-rock phase, listening to Siouxsie and the Banshees and dressing like a vampire. Cassandra just said no.

"I was the only one who realized you had to sleep," she explained. "You cannot manage otherwise. You go completely nuts. I had this thing, that you had to close your eyes and be asleep before the sun rose. I'd drink a few beers, tack up the blankets on my windows, and demand to be left alone for five hours."

Cassandra enjoyed drawing boundaries around her drug use; like Constance challenging herself by dropping acid at school, she was exhilarated by the tangle between her volition and the drug's seductions. To her, taking drugs was an extreme sport, like surfing, another one of her passions. Or it was a variation on traveling in remote corners of the world, which she did whenever she could raise the money to buy a cut-rate plane ticket. It seems ridiculous to her that this one dangerous activity would be designated morally corrupt, when all the others weren't. "My view was, I do it all the time, I don't see anything wrong with it," she said. "I still feel that way."

For all his bravado, Tim did not share her sense of rectitude. He never approved of his own chemical indulgences. "He thought he was doing something really bad, something he had to hide from people. That the drugs had something on him," Cassandra said. The way Tim introduced Cassandra to heroin illustrated his shame. "We had this logic test and everybody in the class failed," she recalled. "I was just so bummed out. I never failed anything! And Tim said, 'Let's do heroin.' " Cassandra agreed, although the one time she'd done the drug before—on the night of Ronald Reagan's reelection—she'd puked herself raw. She repeated that performance with Tim. But he kept at her to try again. She did, and then she liked it.

"It was really fun!" she insisted. "But he always had a habit of getting it when he was depressed. Like if we'd had a fight, he'd go do heroin. He'd come over to my house really high, offering some. Of course, I had a really hard time saying no."

For Cassandra, heroin simply added to her menu of bliss. This attitude is hardly in sync with the way most people view the drug. Heroin's legend calls it the baddest of highs, the opposite of hippie mind expansion. "I have made a very big decision," sang Lou Reed in the Velvet Underground's junkie anthem named for the drug, "I am going to nullify my life." To artistic outsiders like Reed, heroin was the visceral route to existential alienation. Opiates smother the senses in a swoon of euphoria; withdrawal causes an opposite all-encompassing effect, a sickness beyond compare. In between these two totally absorbing states, serious heroin users see nothing. By the early 1970s, heroin had basically been the death of several counterculture stars—Joplin, Hendrix, Morrison—and its rise officially signaled the dawn of a new cultural Dark Ages. By the 1990s, when heroin became chic among fashion models and grunge rockers—claiming a new batch of famous lives, the most emblematic being that of Nirvana leader Kurt Cobain—it had become a pure indicator of cultural decay.

But some heroin users, Cassandra included, contend that the aura surrounding heroin, not the drug itself, create its lethal pull. Ann Marlowe, a New York writer whose 1995 *Village Voice* cover story "Listening to Heroin" presented one of the few contemporary descriptions of heroin use that didn't veer directly into those stereotypes, agrees. "Society systematically overestimates heroin, like every other luxury good, inflating its pleasures and dangers, creating a myth of irresistibility to rival any snack food's advertising claims," she wrote. When I read that piece, I dismissed Marlowe's claims as a junkie's rationalization. But when I started exploring the scientific literature about heroin addiction, and sized it up next to Cassandra's accounts, I reconsidered. It's not like in the movies or the rock songs, I discovered, where one shot sends innocents reeling toward destruction. Becoming a junkie takes a certain amount of determination. What appears to be a lack of will is in fact a serious commitment to the downward spiral.

Half the people in Cassandra and Tim's drug clique eventually made that pledge. The others dabbled and stayed free. "I'll never forget the first time we did heroin," said Rose, sitting on the couch one Friday night in her Ivy Street studio with Damien. "Damien got it for his roommate, Sam, even though Damien wasn't all that interested, because he had the drug connection. And I'll never forget Sam saying—"

"—'I will become a junkie,' " Damien put in.

"He said, 'I could be a junkie if I wanted, huh?' I heard Sam say that and I knew he was going to do it, because he wanted something he could do and be proud of."

"It was an identity thing," Damien continued. "That was his entrance into countercultural existence or something. But heroin just wasn't fun for me. I just thought it was a really boring drug. Plus, I had nobody to fall back on; I didn't have the economic possibility of becoming a junkie. Sam had a huge inheritance, so he didn't have to worry about money."

Sam became a junkie because he thought it would be cool. Cassandra's best friend, Rachel, became a junkie because she could never admit she might—she constantly rejected Cassandra's warnings that her binges were becoming a problem, and her need to maintain the illusion of normality stopped her from tempering herself at all. Rachel's lover, George, a motorcycle boy Cassandra describes as a "slimeball," became a junkie because it fit in with his idea of the rough life. Tim became a junkie because he couldn't settle into anything else.

"I think part of Tim's struggle was this horrible fear," Cassandra said. "He desperately needed me, because I was publishing my poetry, and I represented somebody who could be creative and be successful at it. He really wanted to be a writer, that's the fucking really horribly sad thing. He just couldn't do it. He could never *make* anything. Because he had that huge fear of facing himself. He decided to do drugs instead."

It still pains Cassandra to talk about this aspect of Tim, more than his drug dilemmas or the many ways he played with her heart and her head. When I set out to tell his story, I wanted to talk to her and Rose and Damien together. Cassandra refused at the last minute. I thought it was because she was still angry that both of her friends had had brief affairs with Tim when she was still seeing him. It turned out that she didn't want to listen to them condemn him for dying, for being stupid enough not to keep his problems under control. Even now, she feels nothing but sympathy.

Damien and Rose remembered Tim much more fondly than Cassandra had warned me they would. "He was the first heterosexual man I had as a friend in my entire life," exclaimed Rose. "He extended something to me that I couldn't find anywhere else. He wasn't a loser. Sexually, he wasn't trustworthy. But at the time, he was sick on drugs."

"I take a different view of that," said Damien. "Because he was also seducing me. It wasn't the drugs. He was open to anything, and he felt that he communicated most clearly sexually. He wanted closeness. He wanted to connect. Cassandra would be in his bedroom, and he would be showing me out of the house. Tim would refuse to unlock the door, and [he'd] just attack me and make out with me, right there in the hall. It was pleasurable, but at the same time it was like, 'Cassandra is a really good friend of mine. We are overstepping something here!'

"That was something unique about Tim," Damien concluded. "He didn't have a strong sense of boundaries. He was always trying to break things down."

"Which is something an artist would do," added Rose.

"He had an artistic temperament," Damien agreed. "He just didn't have any discipline."

Whether it was a lack of discipline or an overwhelming sense of worthlessness that drove Tim to self-obliteration, two years into his relationship with Cassandra, he had become a mess. "He became addicted and kicked several times," said Cassandra. He wasn't the only one inching toward crisis. By this time, the circle's drug use had taken on a ritual aspect. They called their gathering the Tuesday-Thursday Club.

"I was Cassandra's roommate then," said Damien. "We'd all gotten into heroin. Cassandra and Tim and George and Rachel and I started doing it every Tuesday and Thursday. After a while I realized we weren't doing anything else anymore."

"There were very few people who would just do Tuesday and Thursday," Cassandra admitted. "It was sort of a general rule, but people would drift into days and days. It wasn't like we planned anything out. I would lounge around endlessly with Rachel, reading books and doing drugs. I think the only thing I ate during that time was mixed nuts, no peanuts."

The Tuesday-Thursday Club rose up like a sheltering edifice, drawing everyone in. "I remember lying in bed with Damien, holding hands with him, and listening to music, with both of our eyes closed," she continued. "It was really great, just a really sensual experience. Sharing something with somebody. And Damien's room was like a womb. It was five-by-five, with a big potted tree, a bed, and a huge stereo. We'd just lie there, and be like, 'Ooh, this is nice.' "

"It was a huge group hug when we did heroin," Damien agreed. "Seven people in a bed, and my soundtrack to it." The drug tuned them in to the same low frequency. Eventually, though, some people started tinkering with the dial. "I always did a really small amount," Damien said. "I was never into getting higher and higher and higher. Cassandra and I were the two people who did a little piece, to sorta get high. Then after a while I would get nervous on it and start bitching at everyone else. Saying, 'You're really boring, this is really boring. I don't meet new people, I don't do new things.' "

At this point, the story of the Tuesday-Thursday Club turns a corner to become more like the old familiar variety of heroin horror tales, at least for most of the characters involved. Rachel and George started living the junkie clichés—stealing from their friends, getting dope sick, embracing denial. Tim was the first to clean up, partly because Cassandra had finally put an end to their relationship, and also because he'd just reached that point on the circular map of his drug use. "He was always in and out," Cassandra remarked. "I remember having a conversation with him at this point, about how George and Rachel were really bad, and how they needed to clean up. He was talking about how he couldn't be around them, because they would come over, high, and want to talk about getting off drugs. God, they would be so irritating."

Cassandra finally got fed up with the lie that the Tuesday-Thursday Club had become. Damien had done the same a few months earlier. Each moved into a new house, a different life. Both of them still insist that their refusal to fool themselves was why they escaped the bog into which their friends sank. The other saving grace was their passion to create, the focus that Tim could never find. Cassandra had immersed herself in her poetry, and Damien was seriously working on the first of his short films. Drugs just didn't give them as much satisfaction as they found in these pursuits.

"The main imperative in my life is to create my art," said Damien. "Doing heroin is counterproductive to that, regardless of what any number of rock stars might have said. You can't continue to produce and to function. I'll go all the way out to that edge, but there's an automatic mechanism in me that snaps and pulls me back."

Both Cassandra and Damien also stressed the importance of healthy fear, the kind that neither dissolves into obliviousness nor curdles into shame. George and Rachel both pretended they weren't junkies until their drained bodies and wallets forced the truth out. George fled first, getting sober on his own. Rachel struggled. "It was just so hard," said Cassandra, looking pained. "Every time we'd go out she would insist that she wasn't high. She was working, she had a job. But she was just a mess, she looked awful. Everybody knew she was a junkie. She just went through some really hideous times, alone with herself and drugs. Like trying to shoot herself up and not having the veins, or trying to kick someplace and realizing she had this tiny bit of heroin and shooting up again. Finally she went into a rehab center for a month, because she was really bad off by then."

A common bit of wisdom from Alcoholics Anonymous states that addicts will never betray the poisons they love unless they hit bottom, their orifices filling with the filthy muck of their lives until they either suffocate or move on. That's what happened to the junkies in the Tuesday-Thursday Club. They plunged down, further than they ever thought they could go, and then they had the luck and the resources to bounce back. All except one, who never got low enough to ricochet all the way out. Tim.

"He would clean up for long periods of time, and he would go back to it," said Damien. "He always thought he could control it, no matter what proof there was in his world. So many of his friends were junkies. It changed their lives considerably. But Tim, I don't think it ever changed his life. He thought he could go away from it and come back."

It's not clear whether Tim really made himself oblivious to the wreckage all around him, or if he convinced himself he could keep afloat above it. His shame made him keep his deepest feelings to himself. He carried his addiction around like original sin, hidden behind good intentions and moments of clarity. I last saw Tim at Cassandra's wedding, looking fresh and a bit chubby (the clean man's bloat) in a vintage suit. He talked about the work he'd found as a hospice counselor, helping AIDS patients at the local hospital deal with their pain. He said he still liked the housepainting he did on the side, for money. Maybe in the future, he speculated, he'd finally get that career in politics off the ground, somewhere in the realm of environmental activism. His hopefulness seemed like small talk.

I was just glad he was clean again. For a couple of years, he stayed that way. Cassandra and Dennis started making their home together; Damien kept at his films. Rachel moved to the wilderness and took up mountain biking. George stayed off on his own. Rose went to graduate school. Sam kicked around, working at staying sober. I moved to Berkeley and then to New York. Then that letter came.

"I was in Indonesia when Tim died," remembered Cassandra. "I hadn't talked to him in six months. It wasn't like anything that anybody decided. We were doing different things." The turn of events shut Cassandra down. "I remember people wanting to talk to me about it when I came back. They would say, 'Aren't you mad? Don't you feel angry, don't you think he should have taken better care of himself, that he shouldn't have done it?' But to me, it was just incredibly sad. He never, ever got to figure anything out. He never had the chance to say to himself, 'I get it.' Which everybody else gets the chance to do.

"It irritated me that so many people were mad at him." She was crying again, crying still. "Saying, 'Fuck him for dying!' Saying that he'd brought it on himself because he was weak, or that he was fucked up for leaving us. That just rang completely hollow for me. I didn't give a shit about how he died! I still don't care. The fact is that he's gone. I will never, ever walk down the street and by chance run into him. All that other shit just doesn't matter."

The logic of blame that Cassandra so resents is not only cruel; it doesn't exactly apply to Tim's death. "He had just started to do heroin again," she explained. "He hadn't been doing a lot, and it was just one of those quirky accidents. It wasn't like there was enough heroin or anything else in his system to kill him. The autopsy showed that. He choked on his own vomit and he died. It was a fucking accident."

Tim had swum too far into the treacherous surf, he hadn't protected himself, and he'd been drawn under by a freak wave. It's a metaphor Cassandra understands. These days, a new mom with a mortgage to pay and a graduate degree to complete, she limits her high-risk activity to the waters of Ocean Beach. But despite the loss of her old love to the vicissitudes of his own psyche and the accidental revolt of his digestive system, and even after watching her best friend fight for her life and almost lose, Cassandra does not harbor regret. Not for herself, and not for Tim.

"He wasn't leading a miserable life," she insisted. "He would think about things. I remember having conversations with him in those last years, about his childhood, and his dad, who did not respect him. Tim was finally being able to think about what exactly made him angry about their relationship. If he had done that just for another year and then died, that's a whole other year. It's not like he'd waived his personality because he did heroin. He still counted."

As for herself, she refuses to disavow the speed, which she finally quit because it was making her heart hurt, or the heroin, which if not for the baby she might do again. Cassandra's drug years taught her as much as any other part of her life, and, she dares to say, gave her as much joy. And she doesn't want Tim's memory to be swallowed by the mythology of drugs. She wants him to be remembered for his kindheartedness and his sense of humor; for his audacious opinions and his light, almost golden eyes. She is also willing to remember the bad side—his lack of commitment, the terrible affliction of his doubt. But please, she wants me to say, don't read this and think he was just another junkie. Drugs may have killed him, they definitely haunted him, but they were not the sum total of his life.

One afternoon in the dark of a screening room, Damien found himself confronted with an aspect of Tim's life that had been veiled by the mystique of his death. "I was watching this independent film about housepainters," he said. "And when the credits rolled at the end, the dedication was to Tim. It was such a shock. This filmmaker knew him as a craftsman, not just a junkie. I found the director's number and called, just to say, 'I knew him, too, we were once really close friends.' "

Drugs are not the sum total of anyone's life, whether the user in question is a miserable addict, a gleeful experimenter, or one of the millions of people who make indulgence part of their special occasions. The challenge drugs pose to anyone is the chance to not think in absolutes. I am not willing to say that conscientious drug use must be part of everyone's healthy self-development. If you prefer getting your endorphins through marathon running or tattoos, that's great. But I do think that the judgments society passes can be as ingrained and careless as the habits of smokers, sniffers, and shooters. These condemnations can ruin the lives of people doing nothing more than growing a garden, and they can stop problem users from ever trusting themselves enough to try to get free. "Drugs do exist, and they've always existed," Cassandra said at the end of our conversation. "I can't imagine a civilization without it. We can't have a pure society." The fantasy that we can—and the assumption that we would want to—may be as dangerous a head trip as any of the ones we find it so hard to talk about.

THE CULTURED

PROLETARIAT

I KNOW it's old school, but I like the word "slacker." It curls side-ways out of the mouth, causing whoever says it to mix a sneer with a smile. A sensuous barb, it contains its own alibi: although its meaning is self-deprecating, the pleasure of the word itself, its first syllable all loose and its second snapping into action, reveals its inner cockiness.

When I dragged myself and a double latte to a morning press screen-ing of *Slacker*, the 1991 Richard Linklater film whose title made ubiqui-tous that slumpy, beautiful word, I was shocked awake by a mirror image: the dubiously employed oddballs the film depicted were the Texas cousins of my friends and neighbors. As "slacker" slipped into common usage, though, most members of my generation recoiled. They didn't want their prospects as junior executives or Gap clerks messed up by the suggestion that they disdained an honest day's drudgery. In one mid-1990s survey, nearly 90 percent of workers under age thirty-five de-clared their unswerving company loyalty and job satisfaction. That's cool; they're scared. No theorist of slack ever said this lifestyle was for the timid middle. It's always been a bohemian thing.

Bohemian attitudes toward work invent a different rhythm than the routine flow of the career-bound. To slackers, employment is optimal when it comes as punctuation—just enough to pay for rent and groceries and to refresh the social skills a bit, and then it's back to whatever real business occupies you. Skinning salmon in an Alaskan fish factory might seem like a no-way-out proposition, but for my friend Maria, a writer who lives frugally in Montana the rest of the year, it's a manageable summer gig. Other people I know have used copyediting, computer data entry, and sex work as stopgaps. They've managed to not let these potentially dehumanizing jobs defeat them.

More regular work, to be satisfying, must contain the capacity for play, which means some degree of independence and surprise. A bike messenger risks life and limb delivering bullshit memos from one faceless office building to another, but she gets the physical thrill of riding and she can dress any way she wants. A waiter can transform his job into a nightly performance, entrepreneurially earning tips in accordance with the success of his carefully perfected persona. A video-store clerk stands or stocks all night, but if she's a film freak she can get first crack at the latest releases and use her expertise to guide and impress her favorite customers. These gigs all seem pretty low-level to the outside world, but under the right circumstances each satisfies the primary bohemian concern of being a whole person, all the time.

Since most conventional jobs don't encourage such highly individual expressiveness, the average bohemian worker is an antiworker by necessity. These days, he can be found among the legion working what the novelist and Generation X herald Douglas Coupland dubbed "McJobs": sous-chefs, flower deliverers, concert ticket-takers, strippers, swing-shift data entry clerks, bookstore cashiers. Not everyone who works this kind of job is a bohemian; in fact, as America completes its transformation from an industrial to a service economy, such positions are becoming standard. Political economists call this an age of "just in time" production, in which most jobs will be temporary and extremely fluid in nature, and ideas of worker empowerment formed on the factory floor no longer fit very well.

In the 1980s and 1990s, the myth of corporate benevolence and picket-fence consumerism has drifted further and further into disrepair. Manically merging companies lay off workers en masse, from the lowest-level support staffers all the way up to the once-untouchable executive managers, while their CEOs continue to rake in obscene salaries.

Chain stores replace local merchants in even the smallest towns, erasing all trace of small entrepreneurship. The burgeoning ranks of freelancers, wandering from assignment to assignment, have few ways of finding strength in community. Workaholism is up, but job satisfaction is down; people cram their hours with tasks that don't interest them because they're terrified that if they stop, they'll be let go, and have nothing to do at all. It seems dumb, even in boom times, to believe in the prospect of ongoing gainful employment. No wonder everybody hates their jobs.

Some bohemians try to better their lot through established political routes, starting unions or staging formal protests against harassment and exploitation. Others, the slackers, have engaged in less traceable forms of rebellion. Their actions have consequences, some of them dangerous. But they are the means by which many survive, materially and spiritually, in the treacherously evolving world of work.

SERVICE WITH A SMILE

The heaving chests of strongmen assembling auto parts in Diego Rivera's murals; the hunched backs of illegal immigrants picking strawberries in dusty California; the worn fingers of sweatshop seamstresses in Indonesian factories: these are the images that conjure the word "worker," in all its weary nobility. Few would augment them with a picture of a skinny, wan, bespectacled clerk in a faded Public Enemy T-shirt and jeans, arms full of to-be-shelved paperback copies of *Chicken Soup for the Soul*. Yet that figure represents the American worker just as accurately. Culture is our country's main export now; people watch our prime-time soaps in Israel, read our potboilers in France, and play our computer games in Senegal. The production and distribution of these products of fantasy rely on a veritable army of underlings who realize the concepts of the biz's highly rewarded "creatives" and then get them out to the world.

This cultured proletariat consists of workers, usually on the service side of the production cycle, whose interest or even expertise about whatever dream they're distributing matches them, in some small way, to their tasks. The connection may be slight: thousands of copy shops give clerks the means to produce their fanzines, their poetry chapbooks, and flyers for their bands. Or it may be intimate, as for freelance magazine copyeditors who hope someday to place articles in the publications paying them a benefits-free hourly wage. A boutique filled with knock-offs of hip designer clothes isn't selling a "cultural" product in the old-fashioned sense of "culture," but its salespeople read fashion the way bookworms read books, and they approach their jobs like art dealers. The staff at a health food co-op sees the social complexities involved in the way we eat. Under this wide definition, the cultured proletariat includes anyone who works with goods or services that reflect her cultural interests, but whose primary tasks remain menial and unrelated to that specialty.

Sometimes the cultured proletariat will hijack a non-culture-related institution; there are, for example, very hip strip joints staffed by feminists like Isadora, and temporary-worker agencies designed to employ struggling actors. Still, ground zero for the cultured proletariat remains the commercial end of the arts. Peter Schwendener, a writer working as a cashier at a Chicago Barnes & Noble superstore, ruminated on this milieu in a 1995 essay. "If one presses further, into the dark heart of the average bookstore employee, one discovers that the only thing worthy of being called a job is something in, or vaguely related to, the arts," he explained. That he spent most of his time selling travel guides to execs on a lunch break didn't rattle Schwendener, as long as he could count on seeing those untouched volumes of Trollope on the store's literature shelves.

Bookstore clerking is one of the classic bohemian avenues of employment, along with café jobs and various forms of servility to established artists, as assistants, models, or helpmates-slash-muses. In the 1990s, however, literature no longer sits at the apex of the cultural sphere. That prime spot belongs to the movies and rock and roll. Taking tickets in a movie theater was the baby auteur's favorite gig until video stores came around; now most towns boast a Video Edge where self-styled psychotronic cinema experts discourse on the merits of Rudy Ray Moore while avoiding their real task, which is to file copies of *Titanic*. The legendary director François Truffaut learned his medium as a critic writing for *Cahiers du Cinéma*; Quentin Tarantino, the splatter-punk Truffaut, acquired his expertise by working in—what else?—a video store.

Video clerks didn't invent the particular blend of snobbery and kid enthusiasm that Tarantino made famous. It originated with the notoriously snot-nosed rebels who populate the world of record retail. It may be simply that I got my own work education in a record store, but I'm convinced that nowhere else is the stage so perfectly set for exploring the antiwork ethic of the cultured proletariat. Besides being the art form most beloved by modern bohemians, popular music is an entrepreneurial realm that challenges the hierarchies of rich and poor. On the one hand, it's about making your own style through creative consumerism (Elvis owning blue suede shoes); on the other, it's about generating your own fun in ways that defy money's power to exclude (Elvis crashing a rich girl's party and charming her with his guitar). To negotiate this paradox, which is increasingly present in all aspects of popular culture, the record-store clerk needs a spark of defiance that feeds every transaction, an attitudinal punch that says this money stuff is just a means to an end. The music industry can charge whatever it wants for the CD jewel box, as long as everyone gets the impression that the music inside is still free.

The spirit of the clerks is what maintains this impression, no matter how much managers attribute it to gimmicks like listening booths or interactive promotional displays. The clerks embody the contradiction between pop's internal spark and the package that makes that spark sellable. Few hire on for the wage, which is notoriously low, or because the job itself is interesting, since filing and running a cash register are obviously not. They come because music gives shape and substance to their lives. And rock and roll does something else that other avocations don't, at least not directly: as it grants the sense of personal freedom that all such enthusiasms import, it tells its fans that this freedom is their right and fighting for it is their obligation. No other escape fantasy comes with such explicit instructions as those offered by the Sex Pistols in "Anarchy in the U.K." or Sly and the Family Stone in "Thank You (Falettinme Be Mice Elf Agin)" or Public Enemy in "Don't Believe the Hype." Especially since the rock era, pop has promoted an antiestablishment philosophy, suggesting small and large ways that folks can escape the roles dictated by race, gender, and social position. It inspires fans to dye their hair green and wear thigh-high leather boots; or to defy their parents, skip school, tell off the boss; or even, sometimes, to take a new turn and change their lives completely.

The music lover believes in obeying the beat of her heart, but she still has to make a living. A few months after I moved to California, I surrendered to the drudgery of stocking and ringing up purchases in a Bay

Area superstore because it allowed me to be around the thing that made all drudgery bearable. The gang I worked with at Planet Records included skateboard punks and grassroots democrats, jazz snobs and gay liberationists, Satan worshipers, Buddhists, sexual libertines, published poets, performance artists, a working funk musician, a future minor rock star, and one certified antisocial freak who worked swing shift at a spaghetti factory. Few of us could have landed jobs at a downtown department store, much less climbed the ladder toward anything resembling a corporate career. Looking back now, most agree that it was the best and worst of gigs, a pit we were all glad to escape, but also a haven that allowed us to be ourselves.

"I look in the want ads every now and then, and I go, 'What are these things?' " said Murray Shuman, who worked at Planet for twelve years, off and on. His vocation, unpaid, is jazz guitar. "Insurance adjustor. Systems analyst. I know people are getting paid for them," he continued. "But I cannot imagine myself doing any of them." He laughed when I asked him what he thought it took to be a record-store type. "I'm the pinnacle of the profile," he says, "because I don't want to go to work."

It's hard to imagine how any workplace can function when this viewpoint is shared by 95 percent of its staff. I'm convinced that the management at most major record stores understands how a little bit of cheek directed by clerks toward customers can translate into glamour; such behavior proves that rock's seeds of rebellion haven't all shriveled up under the fluorescent-lit chill of big business. Allan Moyle's dead-on cartoonish 1995 B-movie, *Empire Records,* captured this relationship brilliantly. Moyle presents his store as a nonstop carnival, where the adorably quirky staff dances wildly in the aisles, flirts and feuds with customers, eats hash brownies, and causes good-natured mayhem—all of which just makes the shop that much more popular. The movie's climactic scene has a juvenile delinquent metal fan named Warren, recently busted for shoplifting, bursting back into the store and waving a pistol around while he delivers a hysterical monologue about how much he's always longed to be one of those aura-spewing cashiers. "All I ever wanted was to work at Empire Records!" he cries, revealing the dream of aisle lurkers everywhere. Of course, having demonstrated such a flair for rash theatrics, Warren gets the job.

I was like Warren (minus the gun) when I was fifteen, buying my

Elvis Costello albums at Tower Records in Seattle and gawking at the coolness of the guys who took my cash. My fantasy was about as off the mark as Warren's, too; I had no concept of the degrading nature of the minimum wage, or the psychic toll that chronic underemployment takes on smart but somewhat socially inept people. Those things I would learn about later, when I got up my courage to walk into one of the biggest stores in the Bay Area and discovered Elliott Frey, an old mate from my high-school acid punk days, behind the front counter. In time, Planet Records also taught me the spirit of resistance, and a way to rewrite the work ethic to honor passion before obligation, intuition before tradition, and a sense of human decency before procedure.

At Planet, I joined the cultured proletariat. My coworkers taught me the slacker mentality, with all its risks and possibilities. The first step is the simple refusal to take one's prescribed duties as an employee more seriously than other aspects of your life. After that, the doors open up wide. All you have to do is a little work.

■

MUSIC WHORES

Planet was the living theater of employee attitude. My time there was the mid-eighties, the exact moment when the music industry made its biggest karmic compromise by forcing the switch to compact discs, a ripoff if there ever was one. During these years, Planet grew, and big bucks became the bottom line. Through this change, Planet's workers waged a nonstop war of disorganized protest against the transformation of what was once a sanctuary for music-mad oddballs into a Wal-Mart of sound. My Planet crew's story may very well sound like yours, if you're part of the cultured proletariat, or in any segment of the service sector, or just trying to keep afloat in a job market that means to sink you. It's a farce with tragic turns, an epic on the head of a pin. Like many tales of everyday adventure, it presents more insights than clear morals and ends in a mess of questions. Getting to those questions is the point.

Is there such as thing as a good job? Pundits and politicos have debated this matter since Marx, but we self-styled music whores knew the answer: not in this world. Our solution to this problem was the usual bohemian one: to bend whatever tiny corner we could occupy into some new shape, to try things a different way. Under the noses of the buying public, in places like Planet nationwide, the struggle to maintain some free space within an increasingly confining work paradigm roars on.

When I tracked down a handful of my old record-store mates to get their views on surviving and resisting wage slavery, I discovered them mostly still redefining respectable employment, but doing much more than surviving. Many have their own businesses; others have built successful double lives, finding ways to make money and still save room for the passions that aren't so easily sold. Still others, like Murray, get by in the shadow world of night shifts and temping, consciously refusing to enter work's mainstream. None have sold their souls to the company store.

What does it take to be a good worker? One month into my new San Francisco life, all I knew was that I didn't possess that quality. I'd tried employment agencies, but the interviewers took one look at my thrift-store suits and two-tone hair and said they didn't have anything in the arts; one sent me to an interview with a manufacturer of movie-theater popcorn machines. My career as a waitress ended after one week spent in a North Beach restaurant where all the cooks spoke Spanish, the owner spoke Italian, the other waitresses spoke French and I had to descend a spiral staircase to get my plates of spaghetti. I got fired. I had no manual skills except the ability to play "Dream On" on the electric guitar. My savings account dwindled until it was like a candle wick about to be engulfed in wax. That's when I walked into Planet, saw Elliott, and found my new purpose in life

Signing on at 25 cents more than minimum wage, I made my way into the back room and began my sentimental education. One of the great things wage work offers middle-class kids is a chance to know people from worlds way beyond your parents' manicured lawn. In Seattle, I'd sold German sausages at the Food Circus and bused dishes at a Mexican joint, so I'd met a few fellow travelers from other points on the map. But nothing prepared me for Planet's United Nations of freakdom.

Suddenly I was working in the tape room with Justin Turner, a/k/a Justina, a Kewpie-voiced Diana Ross admirer of indeterminate sexual preference who lived in a hallway in the Sunset District and worked on a spaghetti-factory assembly line for extra cash. The night manager, Arnold Francia, was a libertarian drummer who surfed at Ocean Beach on his days off. In the classical room lurked Larry Henzel, a frustrated

Franz Liszt who'd lay his scores out all over the boxing table and point out the exact passages that were too weird for the general public to appreciate, in between rants about *The Exorcist* and tips on the finer points of bondage. Murray, our jazz expert, had once played with a Southern California country-rock band but now studied Zen, swam laps on his lunch break, and moonlighted driving hack; he was my educator in the nocturnal city, taking me to the best all-night Chinese restaurants and Japanese bowling alleys after our shared shift ended at two A.M. From Lester Han I learned about reggae and Caribbean poetry; he was a Korean kid from Concord with a mighty island fixation. From Elliott, who affected a beatnik style and would eventually become a renowned avant-garde guitarist, I learned about the blues. These men were my friends, my mates; even though I was a young woman ready for anything, Planet's comradely atmosphere discouraged us from playing games, sexual or otherwise. Not until much later, after nearly a decade climbing the ladder in the journalism world, would I feel this easily equal to the men with whom I shared my job.

My Planet sisters matched the boys for toughness, most cultivating some variation on bohemia's freeform style of sexy-strong womanhood. Mona worked at Planet, as did my Fulton Street housemates: glamorous Edie, cosmic Isadora, style-defining Lucy. So did a host of other young women defiantly preoccupied with discovering themselves. Maggie Meade kept huskies, knew karate, and spent her free time stumping for Greenpeace. Terri Curtis, a Beatlemaniac dyke fresh out of the closet and loving it, flaunted her hot punk-rock girlfriend, who called herself Spike and used to feel her up behind the counter as she rang up customer sales. Terri was one of the wildest ones; one of the mildest, Bettina Watts, was a blue-mohawked performance artist. She just had an unassuming personality beneath that nouveau facade.

I'd known some arty kids in my New Wave days in Seattle, but here was a whole colony of rabid individualists, of every race, class, sexual persuasion, and artistic passion I could imagine. The funny thing was, at Planet, we all seemed so normal. "Granted, Planet was known for harboring certain eccentrics, but most of us were pretty nice kids," said Ted Rockwell, who came to work there after getting fired from Macy's for having pink streaks in his hair. "We had a shared ethic. Don't do unto others what you wouldn't want done to yourself." Planet's workers were militant about letting each other be. In our ranks we endured the usual assholes, sexual harassers, Goody Two-shoes, and rats, but those people rarely lasted. Planet produced its own kind of peer pressure. If you didn't fit in at not fitting in, you left.

These motley people formed a secret society, as self-schooled masters of a wild array of esoteric knowledge. "It could have been a university, almost," recalled Elliott. "A lot of the people who worked there were probably qualified to teach at that level about their areas of expertise. And there they were, working for five or six or seven bucks an hour." People like Lester, who could recite the entire catalog of King Tubby's 1960s Kingston sessions without stopping for breath, or Terri, who'd begun collecting Paul McCartney paraphernalia at age nine, devoted considerable energy and smarts to pursuits that increased their status not a whit in the outside world. What good did it do Lester to be a reggaehead? It wasn't going to get him a job in the financial district. For the most part, it wouldn't have any effect on his status as a Planet worker, either, since the skills required for his day-to-day livelihood involved no more than making change and fitting rectangular containers for sound into bins.

"There were those rare customers that you really liked, because they actually wanted you to use your skills to recommend records," said my Fulton Street housemate Paul, who signed up at Planet to subsidize an internship at a recording studio. "When David Byrne from the Talking Heads came into the store asking for a record by War, and we didn't have it but I knew I had it at home, that was cool. But for the most part, you didn't get to use your skills." The split between what most of us brought to the job and what we were actually called on to use made Planet seem more like a resource for the employees than vice versa. We used the store like a classroom and a library, opening up dozens of deep-catalog albums every day, playing our weird favorites until the manager came screaming, terrified we'd drive all the Michael Jackson fans from the store. We were like Talmudic scholars, dedicated to our studies and outraged at the thought that any menial activity might interrupt them. Some Planet workers applied this scholarship to their own musical pursuits; others were simply record-store geeks. Connoisseurship didn't increase anyone's social status, since—unlike an education in literature or politics—an intimate knowledge of dub or the Beatles or weird Greek pop isn't widely considered part of being a refined person. It was a private matter, almost circular, pursued only for the love of it.

We flocked to each other because we all shared this holy devotion to music, though we tended to diverge on matters of genre and style. We succumbed to the phenomenon of record-store taste: the pathological pursuit of the strange that occupies anyone who spends long, boring hours amid rows of albums, and which at Planet led to a cultish fascination with the blind German folksinger Heino. But when it came down to serious allegiances, everyone went her own way. Mona preferred 1960s soul, Ted dug New Wave, Paul liked funk, and Tracy mooned endlessly over scruffy indie rockers like Alex Chilton. I did my own mooning over Billy Bragg and Brian Eno, but stayed interested in other people's passions. I gained much esoteric knowledge from an MBA who fancied himself an authority on Brahms, and shared long conversations and lots of backroom smokes with a drummer who specialized in industrial rock but liked Tibetan chant. Loving music had pushed all of us off the track—away from the normal pursuit of career, mate, and family, on an endless quest for that vibrating high, the plunge beyond time that comes only when you submerge yourself beneath the waterline of amplified sound. We were addicts, in a way, but also adepts, enlightened by a noise most people considered no more than a pleasant distraction. What was left for us but to practice our art of listening?

At Planet, workers had very little formal power, but most were intent on maintaining a sense of personal authority. It wasn't enough to keep our passions to ourselves; there had to be some manifestation of this different kind of power. So we made our work lives into a walking theater piece. Sometimes this redefinition of the term "job performance" got literal. "Ted and I used to do *Cabaret* standing on the front counter!" exclaimed Terri. "I'd always be Liza." The store's P.A. system, meant for warning shoppers to move their cars from the loading zone, offered many opportunities for impromptu diva turns. In my Elvis phase, I'd read titillating excerpts from Priscilla Presley's memoir into the microphone, paying special attention to the ones about the King's predilection for white cotton panties. The stereo system also ignited hyperbolic arguments over playlist selection, as whoever was running the front-counter cash register did battle with his fellow shift workers for turntable dominance. These comical taste wars could provoke the most mild-mannered of us to action. "Once Justina played that damn Madonna single 'Live to Tell' twelve times in a row," recalled Ash Greene, a folkie songwriter who definitely qualifies as the quiet type. "I just had to go down there and break it over his head." With such displays, Planet workers would take what most people thought was ridiculous about their lives—their unhealthy fixation on pop—and show it off. If people thought we were freaks, we would run the carnival.

During my first year at Planet, our P. T. Barnum was Arnold, the night-shift manager. Arnold still gets his paycheck from Planet, although he broke the usual lifer pattern by taking a decade off to sell skate-boards, then trade commodities, then raise bees. He has a remarkably instrumental approach to the workplace: whatever position he's in, he quietly assumes the role of partner, and without blatantly breaking any rules adjusts company policy until it makes sense to him. Because he's an eminently sensible guy, the results usually please his employers. "I'm sure the company would not have agreed with everything that he did, but he knew what was important," said Murray of Arnold. "And that makes a great in-charge person. Somebody who didn't rule with an iron fist and at the same time, got the job done."

Arnold was part of a troika of managers who stood between the floor crew and administration. They were housemates in a flat downstairs from my pals at Steiner Street: Carlo Firelli, a veteran of the city's steami-est dance floors in the middle of a lifelong Planet career that has never interfered with his after-hours pursuits; Stan Sorenson, who might have been a regular guy if not for his aerobic-level obsessiveness; and Arnold. Their flat was a frequent after-work destination for Planet clerks, and its revelry raged on most nights until dawn. "The nine o'clock shift would come in, then the midnight shift," recalled Stan. "The whole household was Planet, the people living upstairs worked at Planet. It wasn't just a great party, it was something more." Other managers (about ten occu-pied the zone between the floor workers and the two top dogs) wielded authority with various degrees of awkwardness, but these three some-how managed to hold their ground as both friends and foremen. Arnold did this better than anybody. He'd taken the night job because he didn't want anybody else there to boss him around, and he respected that same impulse in all of us.

"I was just a baby-sitter with keys," Arnold says, chuckling. But he's wrong. Nights with Arnold were the only time many of us felt an ounce of respect emanating from the Planet machine. He knew our tiny pay-checks kept us broke, so he'd buy sacks of potatoes for us to mi-crowave, and sticks of butter to slather on them. He made sure we got fed in deeper ways, too. When my register shift was over, he'd let me type out my assignments for my creative writing classes on the clanky old manual in the back room, watching me ruminate for hours and then simply demanding a copy of my finished work. "Sign it, so when you're famous, I can sell it," he'd say. Once a month on a Wednesday, when the floors got waxed and the store required all-night supervision, he'd haul in his drum kit and organize a jam session that had old hands like Murray teaching new tricks to the punk kids. "I learned a lot from those sessions," said Anthony Marchand, who came to Planet when his goth-rock band relocated from New Orleans. "I was exposed to so many different styles." Arnold grinned when I reported Anthony's fond memory. "I remember him turning to me and saying, 'Wow, this was the first time I ever played *music*,' " he said. "That put a big smile on Murray's face."

Any day might bring a new sly stroke of generosity from Arnold, but his shining moment came every Christmas, when he'd organize a massive feast on the long tables we'd use to seal boxes of returned merchandise. The fact of working on the holiday came as a blessing for most of us, who were either far from our families or wishing we were. We liked getting paid time and a half, but we loved the chance to be with our adopted clan. The corporate offices and the store manager authorized some kind of celebration. Arnold figured, Why not make it count? He rigged a barbecue to the chute where the heater emptied its fumes, and smoked a couple of salmon, island style. Others brought their own offerings: vats of potato salad, a HoneyBaked ham from Mona, Lester's vegetarian ital stew. Isadora baked a pan of hash brownies; Arnold limited consumption to one per register shift. He let us sneak our spiked eggnog behind the register and looked the other way when someone gave teenagers escaping family gatherings a healthy Yule discount. "Hey, get away from your family, come to Planet!" he'd exclaim when some local newsperson would shove a microphone in front of his face and ask how awful it was to work on holidays. "Doesn't this look like more fun?"

Christmas gave Arnold—and all of us—the ultimate chance to exploit Planet management's desire that the store maintain a rock-and-roll image. By turning the token gesture of an office party into an all-day bacchanal, we made what was supposed to be a safety valve into temporary anarchy. This was Arnold's genius; as Murray said, he knew what was important. He didn't hesitate to reprimand a clerk who broke the rules in a blatant or clumsy fashion, but he'd also stand up to a manager who used those same rules sadistically against the rank and file. "I just liked going up against them," he said of the store's bland general manager and his martinet assistant, whom we all called Bubbles. But he did so for a reason: to preserve the store's precious sense of play, the ark of our humanity.

Finally Arnold's trickster impulses did him in. One day, he found a flyer on the floor of the back room, advertising a phone-sex service. Perhaps he was nostalgic for the seventies, when erotic encounters between employees were rampant and even a few customers got caught doing it against the tape-room wall. Or maybe he just thought he'd push Bubbles hard that day. He photocopied the flyer and put one in everybody's box. Bubbles's secretary and secret girlfriend, a Southern Baptist, complained. Fearing a sexual harassment suit, Bubbles made sure Arnold got canned.

By this time, Planet had begun to change. The first compact discs had sneaked into our aisles, weird little ghosts of vinyl that looked like giant dimes but cost three times as much as an LP. Bubbles ascended, eventually becoming the boss, and his fondness for the details of middle management seriously constricted the liberties that made the job bearable. The potatoes and the hash brownies disappeared. But most clerks still had their ways to resist, and we carried on the battle for autonomy. We just took it further behind the scenes.

◾

SCAMMING

I remember the moment I felt the money train run over me. It was the fall of 1986, two years plus since I'd signed my first Planet time sheet. I walked into the back room, an hour late as usual for my one morning shift, and saw the boxes from Columbia, piled up in the corner in a brown cardboard mass. "You know what that is?" said Guy Gillete, the store's distribution manager, giving me his cynical Texas grin. "That's Broooce! And it's on sale for $34.95. Start pricing, baby." I pried open a carton, and sure enough, there was the five-album monster *Bruce Springsteen & the E Street Band/Live, 1975–85*, with the Boss's denim-clad booty on the cover and a list price higher than any rock box I'd seen. What hurt me wasn't the fact of the collection, which I knew fans would cherish, but the quantity the store had ordered. You see, I'd once loved Bruce Springsteen, pored for hours over his lyrics, daydreamed about being the girl riding shotgun in his wreck of a car. And although I understood that millions felt as close to him as I once had, never had he seemed like such a commodity, his art rolled out onto the floor and sold like a radial tire.

As I knelt there affixing orange stickers to intimate spots on Bruce's reproduced body, Bubbles burst through the backroom door. "Get those boxes out there!" he barked. "We're gonna make a lot of green today!" I could no longer pretend that my beloved store existed for any reason but to line the drawers of management desks with cash. Bubbles could have been selling ties for all he cared. I knew the little tricks upper management worked, lying to *Billboard* about the store sales charts to get more promotional goods from the label reps, giving copious discounts to their friends and lame local celebrities like Robin Williams even as they watched the scapegoated clerks like hawks. And I knew that if I were ever busted for the hundreds of albums I'd stolen right under their noses, I would not hang my head in shame as I walked out the door. I would stand straight up, give them the finger, and move on.

"It was horrible to sit there for four hours during your reg shift, ringing up and ringing up and ringing up," remembered my old flatmate Lucy. "It was like working fast food." For us, the tiniest cogs in the overwhelming mechanism of the music industry, it was easy to feel crushed. The best solution was to create our own economy, a shadow world where desire and ingenuity, not the ownership of a Gold Card, earned you what you needed to enrich your life. With the albums flying out of the store like so many cartons of french fries, taking one home for yourself felt like an act of liberation, not just for you, but for the music. Our system of scams, barter, and charity helped us stave off the alienation we felt while we helped turn music to salable goods. It also allowed many of us to survive the minimum wage.

The world of workplace subversion is bigger than you think. In offices and stores everywhere, employees stage mini wildcat strikes, abscond with huge quantities of company property, and generally chip away at the institutional structures that support but also oppress them. Management knows this; most big corporations, including Planet, have insurance guarding against "shrinkage," one popular euphemism for employee theft. But scamming still destabilizes power relations in the

workplace, allowing those beleaguered members of the cultured proletariat to maintain a little control over the flow of the product they love.
If it's done carelessly, it can backfire and cause serious damage to employees themselves. Since Planet was a workplace where almost everybody tested this balance, it offered a serious education in the ethics of
fair exchange, as people devised their own rules to protest the idea that
everything and everyone could be reduced to a discounted commodity.
Over the three years I worked at Planet, I saw many people walk this
high wire, and nearly fell off myself.

Some scams were visible, basically forms of protest. The most common of this kind was time theft. The desire to secure a little leisure while
on the clock is probably universal, but at Planet certain people turned it
into a spectacle. Paul was particularly adept at this, sitting sullenly in
the info booth for four-hour stretches, not moving. If he wasn't in his
spot, or behind the register, he wasn't in the store. "I figured, during my
reg shift I'd sold a million dollars' worth of goods, and made ten dollars
for myself," he explained. "So I could go sit somewhere for four hours. I
would just sit there and watch them buy—there goes fifty dollars, there
goes the fifteenth copy of *Thriller* in an hour. That's all Planet deserved
from me at that point."

Murray recalls drawing a similar line in the mid-1970s, but his had
to do with taste. The then-manager tried to institute a policy by which
employees would push certain hit records. "I wouldn't do it. I will not
sell garbage," he said. "I'll do everything to propagate the real musical
things." Murray won that clash. "At that time we'd play things that
drove people out of the store. Minimalist stuff like Steve Reich. And I
would tell the customers to buy things like that."

One ploy common among the store buyers, who ordered the records
that filled particular sections, would be to distribute their favorites to
friends at a whopping discount, then report high sales for these obscure
titles. If a regular customer showed what one of us thought was excellent taste, that person would unexpectedly find the cost of her purchases
going down. This not only created goodwill between the store and genuine music aficionados, it upped the "sales" of worthy artists, for whom
we felt it was our duty to fight.

The main struggle in our lives, though, was survival on minimum
wage. To do this certain employees developed scams that truly qualified
as white-collar crime. Legend has it that in the glory days, back when

the industry still felt its own portliness and Bubbles had not yet descended on the store, workers were removing product and cash by the truckload. "Our stupid wages were always our excuse, but I do think morally it went way beyond that," said Mona, who started clerk life at a suburban Arizona store in the late 1970s. "It got really bad. It was so easy, it was impossible to stop. It was like gambling, because you were gambling with your job." Mona and her then-boyfriend, a shift manager, had credit card scams, return scams, goods scams, and her personal favorite, the gift certificate scam.

"This was before they installed machines on the cash register that validated the sale of certificates," she explained. "You were just supposed to tear the right-hand corner off. So my boyfriend just said, 'Don't tear the corners off the gift certificates when you get them in your drawer.' Then he'd sell them to a friend, and that guy could come into the store and use them—legitimately. It seemed so simple, because it was just paper! It wasn't even money. It really seemed fake."

After several years of healthy supplements to her unlivable wage, Mona left the suburbs to finish her undergraduate degree at San Francisco State. Wanting to shake that gambler's bug, she tried to find employment somewhere other than a record store. "I thought, This is sick, I've got to get out of it. I worked in a couple of bookstores. But one closed down, and at the other I got fired for refusing to chase a shoplifter." She found herself at Planet. By this time, she'd developed a set of principles she would not violate. "I saw people get greedy, which I never did," she explained. "They took stupid chances. They wanted it, now. It was the high of stealing. But I never wanted to get high. It wasn't worth losing everything."

Mona curbed her greedy tendencies by sharing the wealth. "I was always so generous with the money," she said. "I gave my sister-in-law money when she was broke, I'd send her hundreds of dollars. I would purposely work the drawer to get extra and send it to her."

Mona viewed her dips into Planet's till as part entrepreneurship, part charity, the activity that won her soul back. Others, like Ted Rockwell, enjoyed scamming as a brain-teasing game; he recalls working one cash drawer scam that required total mathematical precision, with even one slipped digit revealing the whole con. Others, especially the merchandise lifters, saw it as an aspect of good citizenship in the shadow community. Terri, for example, worked a deal with a couple of used-record-store clerks; they'd give her a list of their new-release needs, and she'd deliver them for trade. Paul bartered with his pals who worked for a local movie theater chain: albums for film passes. We all sought out worthies like ourselves. Anyone willing to live on Doritos rather than give up constant immersion in an art world or an alternative lifestyle earned a spot in our underground. If they could give back, great. If not, we still earned karmic points for keeping nonconformists happy.

Although we rarely discussed our methods, most people tacitly acknowledged these principles: steal for the right reason; don't get too selfish; don't endanger anyone but yourself. Anyone who took so much that it drew attention to the store's overall shrinkage was committing a crime against his fellows, and earned scorn. Equally bad were the Goody Two-shoes who tried to curry favor with Bubbles by exposing others. The worst were those who transformed from one of "us" into one of "them." Nothing could have been more corrupt, in our eyes, than joining the Planet establishment.

This strict, if unspoken, promotion of antiwork principles caused a conundrum for certain employees who chose to abide by the company rules. Bettina, who worked at Planet for most of the eighties, was one of these tame cats. The girl had blue hair and composed avant-garde electronic music; it was hard to believe she didn't scam. "I always walk the line between being good and being wild," she explained. "My aesthetic and my interests, my ideologies and beliefs are rebellious. But in terms of my behavior, I always follow the rules. I am what I am, and it doesn't happen to fit inside a boundary. I'm a boundary-stander."

Because she could chat with Bubbles at a cocktail party and still get along with her partner at filing cassettes, Bettina was a logical choice to become a shift manager. Now, seven years after leaving Planet, she still wonders if taking the promotion made sense. "If you were a supervisor, there was no way you could completely be seen [as] on the worker's side," she argued. "You were the one who could bust them for not dusting or coming back too late from break. You wanted to look the other way, but if you did, people would take advantage of it. It would get so far out of hand you'd be in trouble." Unable to fully internalize management's profits-first value system, but unwilling to turn it upside-down in a subversive move, Bettina found herself caught in the middle. She doesn't regret her refusal to scam, because she still views that kind of sabotage as a placebo that doesn't solve workers' real problems. She does mention one coworker's example, however, as a form of protest she wishes she'd tried.

"In general, if you wanted to get paid more, you'd have to go over to management's side," she said. "Justina never fell prey to this. He just refused to be promoted. Finally Bubbles gave up and just started paying him as if he were a manager because he was just there for so long. That was smart of Justina, to hold out."

Justin, a.k.a. Justina, was one of Planet's truly strange fish. Little was known about his private life, except that he worked at the spaghetti factory and lived in a group house in the Sunset District. His moods were equally hard to determine; he wore a facade of cheerfulness so rigid that it seemed like a weapon, a pipe bomb about to explode. His sarcasm knew no bounds, but he also genuinely enjoyed what others considered camp culture, especially schlocky pop, with which he tortured us whenever he could commandeer the stereo. His appearance, like the music he adored, couldn't have been more ordinary: he was a medium-sized chocolate-brown man with an unstyled, close-cropped Afro, and he always wore a brown plaid shirt and black gabardine pants. He was less outwardly bohemian than any of us, yet in his reticent way he swam further outside the norm. "Justin stood out in his Justin-ness," said Ash, smiling. Ash worked alongside him in the tape room for three years. "He was this very highly excitable, very smart, but also completely, deeply strange person who did have another side that he never wanted to show to anybody. He was really a trip."

The other thing that made Justin so unusual was the ferocious way he worked. He would never sneak out the back for a smoke or laze in the information booth with the rest of the crew. From the first minute of his shift to the end, he'd file and straighten the tapes, mouthing off all the while in a totally controlled, cutting way. And he would ignore every compliment Bubbles casually dropped. "The way he worked was a statement," said Ash. "It was his own personalized fuck-you—the other side of everybody else's scams."

Justin left Planet in the spring of 1996, and he declined to speak to me about his tenure there—"I prefer to think of it as a long, bad dream," he told me over the phone. Yet other conversations kept circling back to his example. It reminds me of the by-the-book factory protests old union hands would stage. Assembly-line workers would perform their tasks exactly as dictated, not cutting one corner, with a production slowdown the inevitable result. These actions proved that workers' ingenious innovations were what made the factories run smoothly in the first place. Justin's by-the-book clerking exposed a similar reality: if we were to perform our jobs as they were designed, the store would be filled with furious robots and lose the sense of play that made it a desirable place to shop. Justin's example forced Bubbles and the rest of management to see exactly how dangerous it is to steal someone's humanity.

By enacting this nightmare of the model worker, Justin also avoided the moral quandary that most of us wrestled with. For all the small disruptions and individual triumphs scamming offered, it also was, in some ways, exactly what the corporation expected. "You're passing on what you're getting from above," Ash noted. "Our managers were such sociopathic assholes. The employees saw them be that way, so they thought, We don't have to be human." Ash reminded me that whenever management felt the staff needed disciplining they'd simply fire some sap who thought she had her ass covered, as an example. I was almost one of those saps, so I knew what he meant. I left Planet when Bubbles warned me that the "heat" might be on me soon; my displays of attitude were exceeding the limit, and management's awareness of my tendency to pilfer albums I liked didn't give me much room to protest. I could have reformed, become a Goody Two-shoes, but that wasn't in my nature. So I found a job in a café and said the hell with it. Half a dozen veteran workers left under similar circumstances around the same time; management had succeeded in cleaning house, and could start a new cycle fresh.

In his article "A Little Larceny Can Do a Lot for Employee Morale," the management consultant L. R. Zeitler explained how workplace subversion can be used as a tool to keep employees in their place. He interviewed several scamming workers and discovered that their schemes preoccupied them so thoroughly that they became far less disgruntled with their jobs. "Theft serves as a safety valve for employee frustration," he wrote. "It permits management to avoid the responsibility and cost of job enrichment or salary increases at a relatively low amount of money per man per year." Considering Zeitler's argument, I wondered whether I'd been the one ripped off—whether, for all our prideful anarchistic behavior my mates and I had all been a bunch of suckers playing right into management's hands. The few attempts to organize the shop along traditional labor union lines had failed miserably. "Management would take everybody out for a huge Italian dinner, and the union would give them doughnuts," Murray remembered of one disastrous attempt to organize during the 1970s. "People were scared they'd have to punch time cards and wear a suit to work." Voting the union down, Planet workers preserved their freedom, and with it the minimum wage.

■

THE ANTIWORK ETHIC

When I asked Mona whether she'd have pulled her scams if Planet had paid her eight dollars an hour instead of four, she regarded me blankly. "I can't even answer that question," she said. Twice as much cash would have made her material circumstances easier, but low pay was not the root of Mona's problem, despite its painful effects. Underpayment was but one link in a chain of exploitation that started with the artists who signed away self-control for a right to play the shell game of aspiring stardom, and extended all the way down to the customer paying ten times the material value of the musical product some persuasive video promo told her to buy. People still manage to gather meaning from the art that leaks through all the layers of commerce, and believe the paradox of music staying free; the Planet crew was devoted to doing that, otherwise we would have been building real careers or waiting tables for the tips. Yet the fact that we loved the essence of this merchandise made us pained witnesses to its strange insignificance within the industry built around it, and to our own irrelevance as well. We didn't need to read Marx to grasp how something's actual worth gets lost when it is turned into a product, or how a worker's potential is squeezed by the mold of a job description. We looked at Bruce Springsteen in a box and felt it instinctively.

If we had managed to organize a union, we might have secured better pay for ourselves and passed down improved benefits to the next generation of wage slaves. The value of our work would have increased in terms of dollars and cents, and that would have been a good thing. Perhaps we were foolish not to pursue such efforts more aggressively, reconciling with the worker identity in order to better conditions within that role. For better or worse, we were engaged in a different challenge—to change the dominant culture of work, which depends on managers and laborers alike to participate willingly in a system that inevitably forces them to serve not themselves, not their chosen communities, but the impersonal flow of goods out and money in. Aware that we could never totally stop that flow—not at Planet, and not in the larger world—we sought just to interrupt it, and to assert our own opinions about what mattered within the small unobstructed spaces we made.

In the gaps that open up when the system falls even slightly into disarray, workers can act like people, using their imaginations, creating communities, cultivating a sense of play. There's a larger philosophical point to be made here, too. By being a broken spoke in the wheel of commodity culture, the rebellious member of the cultured proletariat honors the many aspects of human life that exist independent of the holy shrine of packaged goods. Scamming makes price irrelevant; loafing steals back time. Rock and roll had taught us there was no way to live outside consumerism. So we stood right in the middle of it and tried to fuck it up.

Planet's antiworkers never organized their methods or their thoughts. Elsewhere in San Francisco, similar neo-proles did. The 'zine *Processed World* surfaced in 1981, as an organ for temporary office workers to share stories of sabotage and resistance. It soon gained a national reputation within the bohemian scene as a forum for new views on the worker's plight. *PW* didn't present some utopian vision of the "alternative" workplace; its contributors generally agreed that any participation in commodity culture, whether you worked at Macy's or in a health food co-op, led to your inevitable exploitation. The 'zine focused instead on what employees might do to disrupt the machines they found themselves caught up in. Its utopia was a world where the machines would all fall apart.

I sought out one of *PW*'s founders, Chris Carlsson, for some political perspective on my Planet crew's antics. We met in his office on Market Street in San Francisco; he's a friendly, somewhat pedantic guy with a beard and an ever-present bicycle, more like an old New Lefty than a punk rocker. Like many of my old cronies, Carlsson found entrepreneurship the best way to survive the strictures of the work world, although he dreams of a time when work as it's now known would become entirely obsolete. "There's just something fundamentally perverse about arranging society around the buying and selling of human time," he opined. "We become slaves to a way of life that becomes 'natural' and inevitable. As though everybody's always sold themselves to some stupid-ass job." *PW* waged a decade-long war against that assumption, publishing on paper pirated from its editors' various temp jobs. With regular features like "Downtime," which chronicled ways temps kept their sanity by breaking office equipment or pinching stationery, and features that ranged from a young gay man's chronicle of a double life spent hustling and housecleaning to a general forum on the question of the possibility of "The Good Job" (conclusion, same as the Planet crew's: there isn't one), *PW* brought to the surface a chaotic web of covert activity and gave it a political context. For most of its life, the 'zine concentrated on the realm of office work, where it documented the same sort of trouble the Planet crew was stirring in retail.

Like most groups running on few resources beyond its members' love, *PW* eventually fell apart. Carlsson and a few of his old *PW* comrades now run an independent typesetting business and devote their spare time to organizing an interactive history project documenting the daily lives of San Franciscans. When I shared my ideas about the shadow values we explored at Planet through our scams and pranks, he got a bit grim. "People you can trust, who you can share things with, and alternative distribution networks of actually needed things are healthy developments," he acknowledged. "But actually building more assertive political initiatives, based on those connections and those communities—that hasn't happened yet. Nobody sticks around long enough. The networks required to talk about any real subversive or revolutionary political movement never get fully established, because people quit their jobs and go looking for another job. The burden is on you to get on with your life. Nobody ever thinks, I'm going to stay in this shitty situation and get together with the other people who are in it and change it."

When I consider the final outcome of our wild years at Planet, I have to admit Carlsson's right. A few of my compatriots still work there, mostly the shift managers; they've made their deals and their peace, and they try to keep the place humane for the workers they supervise. The rest have scattered far and wide, some opening up their own record shops or starting other business, many others surviving as squeaky wheels in somebody else's machine. Mona is a librarian in the Midwest; she lets her assistants take really long lunch breaks and thanks her lucky stars she's not selling anything anymore. Murray drives his cab and writes pop songs only he ever hears. Ash is a used-book buyer in one of San Francisco's major bookstores, and a published poet, which is all he really cares about. Elliott runs a recording studio; Ted is a freelance editor of film books. Bettina mines the shrinking vein of government grants to finance her musical experiments. Then there's me, doing my little dance with the mainstream, wondering if I've sold out.

Not long ago, I shared a plate of Malaysian noodles with Arnold. He's back at Planet after his adventures beekeeping in Montana and selling stocks in Marin. He works the marketing side now, and stays out of the politics of running the stores. He tells me they're hiring a lot of part-timers, kids who still live at home and have neither the need nor the ingenuity to scam. The onslaught of compact discs, and the rise of other superstores, have pushed Planet's atmosphere even further toward conformity; hardly anybody tries to get away with anything. "Those times we were there, you've got to enjoy those times. Those were the really good times," he said.

Walking through the old store a few days later, I could see what Arnold meant. I could see no sign of that famous Planet attitude, no surly looks in the eyes of the kids behind the cash register. Then I realized that I was simply on the other side of it now. To the sly members of the cultured proletariat I looked like an average customer, not a fellow traveler who knew and approved of their tricks. The refinement of the antiwork ethic is a stealth activity, and its effects aren't immediately obvious. The kids running Planet today have their own methods of challenging the drudgery and putting their priorities in motion. I thought about what Mona had said about a clerk she'd encountered in a chain record store near her house in the Midwest. "He was in his late twenties, and obviously had been working there a while," she said. "He was a kind of scruffy guy, wearing a cardigan, with a few earrings. I asked him if he liked his job. And he looked at me and he said, 'They pay shit. But I love music.' " I'll bet that guy runs scams and goofs off whenever he can. And I'll bet he entertains a little dream of worker revolt now and then.

5

.

SOUL TRASH

O N C E I considered writing a manifesto. The subject was not workers' rights, or women's liberation, anarchism or the California condor. The subject was junk. Used furniture, to be exact, although when I began to consider the scope of my revolutionary plan I knew I'd have to include vintage clothing, dog-eared books, and bargain-bin records as well. The two objects that prompted my fervor were an orange crate rescued from a trash pile not far from Planet, and a green love seat that Edie dragged off the street around the corner from our house.

The crate sat in the corner of my bedroom atop two of its plastic cousins, which had carried milk to my corner store before I'd spirited them upstairs to Fulton Street. It's illegal to steal milk crates, since they're the property of the dairy industry—I'd actually once been busted while taking several across the Canadian border in the trunk of my parents' car—but everyone I knew furnished large portions of their flats with them in grimy red and gray and blue, filling them with vinyl or socks, making platform beds or desks with the crates as legs. They were the epitome of bohemian functional. My wooden crate, though, was something different. Sturdy, not plastic but the true flesh of one lost tree, stained by time and rotted fruit and imprinted with the word "Sun-land" in New Century Schoolbook lettering, it seemed like an emissary from a different age. Probably, it had been assembled in a Tijuana factory in 1982. Yet when I draped dozens of Mardi Gras beads from its corners, glued a Mexican Tarot card to its uppermost edge, and hung my U-Framed-It album cover of *The Women Blues of Champion Jack Dupree* above it, this makeshift accessories holder metamorphosed into my own Rosetta stone, unlocking a code of everyday magic. The box was rubbish, no doubt. But I had turned it to treasure.

With the crate I had perfected the aesthetic of salvage, my search for the soul in trash. This quest had begun in childhood at our church rummage sale, a compost heap of broken lamps and auto parts and corduroy coats where I'd dig for hours, searching for who knows what. In the piles I discovered the subterranean fecundity of the material world, where all those shiny goods bought new every season lived on, accumulating dirt and history until they shed the familiar skin of the mass-produced and acquired the strange aura of the obsolescent, the unwanted, the unique. As I grew older, I searched elsewhere for this miracle, spending hours diving into piles of musty men's shirts at the South Seattle Goodwill, finding the perfect wool gabardine suit at the Ladies Cancer League Thrift Shop. When I moved to San Francisco, I joined a tribe devoted to this curious pursuit. We were poor; that was part of it. But we didn't prowl dumpsters for cast-off furniture simply out of desperation; we did it because we were spelunkers, mesmerized by the dark of this cave.

The three hundred vintage dresses that lined Isadora's room, the tiny plastic boxes Lucy filled with curiosities she'd bought on the sidewalk in Chinatown, the wing tips Ted must have pilfered from the closet of Cary Grant—these things were at once utterly disposable and golden, somebody else's discards that spoke their worth only to us. As I saw it, my orange crate represented the apex of this empathic sensibility. Edie's love seat, however, raised the question of its limits. A lovely 1970s knockoff of a French chaise, with sage-green satin cushions and a delicate curve to the back, the piece fit perfectly into our pastiche of a living room. There was one problem, though. It reeked of cat piss. Edie and I diligently cleansed the cushions for hours, progressing from Soft Scrub to Lysol to pure ammonia. The love seat acquired interesting new stains from our efforts, but the smell lingered. In fact, it grew rancid. We were torn; we thought we could redeem anything, and we believed that a little odor, which after all did form a chapter in the chair's biography, should enhance rather than destroy its value. But our noses did not hold such noble ideals. After a month of anguish, we dumped the thing back on the street.

It was then, contemplating why we'd fallen so hard for such garbage, that I devised my manifesto. I had come to believe that anyone with a little ingenuity could survive in the average American city with virtually no money, through a combination of bartering, gift exchange, recycling, and scavenging. Thrift was not my motive; my friends and I were profligate, constantly accumulating more funky stuff, then discarding it without a second thought. We constantly reaped the gifts of the street, hoarding its trash as if the city itself were an honored guest at our potlatch, eager to reciprocate for the great boon we'd given it: ourselves. If everyone treated the material world like a harvest or a mine instead of a factory showroom, I thought, we could become free in ways we'd never imagined.

I never finished my manifesto, and these days I'm more inclined to questions than to pronouncements. But I know why junk and not some more weighty topic inspired me. In a way, the big decisions, like where and how to live and work, come easier; you make them and stick by them for a while, and they take you somewhere. But choices about what and how to buy arise daily. I knew as well as any socialist that the getting-and-spending trap kept most Americans fat and unhappy. In the 1980s, yuppies were ravaging the world, their sweatshop-produced Sharper Image toys driving the American marketplace further and further into chaotic imbalance. To step into their consumer culture felt morally and personally dangerous.

Nor could the solution be found in scrimping and saving. This was the ethic I grew up with. My parents were born into the Depression and raised me on creative-scrimping stories. But they'd bought their own house during the 1950s, and they believed in the transformative power of a redone kitchen and an automatic garage-door opener. My dad worked hard so we could shop at Sears and eat London broil on Sundays. He and my mother took a stern attitude toward luxury, vigilantly guarding their nest egg. Their planning kept us in shoes and Catholic school, and decades later it allows them a comfortable retirement. But growing up, I hated the way products ruled over us, as they did over

everyone I knew, making our dads work overtime and our moms squint
for hours at coupon books. There seemed no way out of this hamster
cage. The rich moms I knew (rich to me, anyway, which was really
upper-middle-class) hunted for the same bargains my mom did, only
they did it at Nordstrom's, not Sears. And their husbands seemed to
spend as many late nights doing corporate homework at the kitchen
table as my dad did.

Faced with a choice between suburban self-denial and yuppie dis-
soluteness, we foragers just said no to both. At Fulton Street we were all
trying to survive on nothing, not only because we had no money but
also because we were emotionally and politically driven to do so. Tom
Wolfe called a similar impulse among 1960s hipsters "poverty chic,"
and condemned it as a convenient way to avoid the issue of class. His
argument resonates today, as self-styled insiders of all kinds draw lines
around themselves by identifying certain others as consumers of, not actors in, bohemia. For an activist like Chris Carlsson of *Processed World,*
such an enemy is the "typical lifestyle anarchist of the 1990s, who wears
black leather and earrings and just says, 'Fuck everything.' " For punks,
it was the New Waver, the popster more devoted to getting the right
shade of fuchsia in his hair than to inducing anarchy. In the 1960s, the
politicos hated the hippies who spent their days dyeing batik instead of
supporting the Panthers. A few years earlier, North Beach chronicler
Ralph J. Gleason had decried fakers, too, calling them amateur Beats.
The consumer-bohemian has always been the counterculture's pariah,
standing at its gateway as a living illustration of who (perhaps you?)
should not be allowed in.

It is not unwise to be skeptical of style, especially now, when brand
loyalty often demands more attention than any deeper commitment,
whether religious faith or political conviction. Taking a risk on a used
leather jacket puts far less on the line than quitting your job to become a
poet, and while buying organic cotton sheets does benefit the earth to
some small degree, it's really doesn't earn you the right to feel utterly
self-satisfied. Tom Wolfe was bemused by middle-class liberals donning
Army surplus socks, as if that made a difference in the People's Struggle;
in fact, Wolfe argued, this condescending act insulted the People, who'd
much rather have Brooks Brothers silks around their ankles. Yet Wolfe
and the chorus of others who've protested this kind of "slumming" miss
a couple of vital points.

First, not all radicals have wads of cash in the pockets of their fatigues; even those from middle-class backgrounds often sacrifice those resources to pursue their less traveled paths. Perhaps some can run home to Daddy when the going gets rough, but many others are cut off from their families, or choose not to use those connections. Besides, the middle class, which admittedly produces the biggest chunk of the bohemian demographic, ranges widely from high to low. Just because my dad worked as an accountant and not a pipefitter at Boeing doesn't mean he made enough to keep us in loafers and ponies. We were a motel-vacation, Hamburger Helper kind of family, and when I left home I received a generous lump sum of $5,000 to tide me through five more years of public university and launch me into my lucrative career (my weekly pay at my first journalism job: $150). My folks gave me what they could, which was a lot. But it wasn't enough for me to live on the Gold Card.

It's really beside the point whether the woman in the fake-fur jacket shopping at Value Village really could afford Versace at Bloomingdale's. Her choice to participate in a different economic sphere helps that sphere thrive. And it *is* thriving, overlapping at points with the mainstream. The elements that figure in the bohemian economy are the same ones often raised by economists as solutions to the waste, overextension, and enforced obsolescence created by the corporate marketplace.

Take barter, for example. In 1996, around 20 percent of the economic transactions in the world involved some kind of trade; the most famous modern example was Pepsi's 1990 swap of cola syrup for Stolichnaya vodka, allowing Russians to rot their teeth and Americans to ravage their livers at bargain rates for both companies. In international trade, barter provides a way to deal with the wildly shifting currencies of developing countries; vodka is always worth something, no matter what the ruble's worth. On a more down-to-earth level, as the average American's buying power slips, barter becomes a practical element of everyday life. Informal neighborly exchanges are commonplace, but in some communities small agencies have formed to organize such deals, connecting housepainters to chiropractors and auto mechanics to Spanish teachers for trades. In an age of escalating prices and diminished job security, the development of barter skills promises more flexibility to just about everyone. Yet this practice is considered part of the shadow world of dangerous deals and low-rent neighborhoods; most middle-class Americans (even those who do it without thinking, like the woman who baby-sits her sister's kids in exchange for a homemade birthday cake) consider barter below them.

Bohemians barter as much as they can, partly because their talents usually exceed the contents of their pocketbooks. For centuries, artists have swapped paintings for rent or poems for meals. Why should any one thing belong to any one person forever? At Fulton Street the women established a clothes lending library, which Paul observed with great amusement. "You guys really should have bickered more," he says now. " 'Oh look, Ann's going out with my sweater.' But there was this environment of put it on, fine, whatever." Sometimes we'd get into conflicts—I remember one bitter dispute over a pair of boots that Edie tried to repossess after I'd had them resoled—but these were rare. Treating things casually allowed us to consider our shared assets abundant, even though in the normal world they hardly amounted to much.

Our exchange of services operated in the same spirit. We all had perfected our little tricks in the workplace, and hoarding the subverted wealth seemed small and mean. Building a barter system allowed us to behave like modern-day Merry Men, stealing from the rich and giving to the poor. The more generous we were with each other, the greater the benefits each would receive. And we had the satisfaction of seeing a small stream of stuff diverted from the profit-making corporate machine and toward a community that really appreciated it. Our circle was a route to self-sufficiency, a kind of survivalism practiced deep within the urban forest. During my register shift at Planet, I could give a deal to Martin, who'd serve me a free meal at his restaurant later that evening and tell me about the great value another pal had given him trading books in at the bookstore; then I'd meet Edie for a movie, courtesy of our buddy Gene, who'd be sitting in the ticket booth in a shirt he'd purchased at deep discount during Isadora's work hours at a Haight Street vintage clothing store. As the exchange moved forward and back, it formed a protective ring around us, making it possible to avoid desperation while we pursued our unremunerative dreams.

I'm sure these barter circles still form in every pink-haired ghetto in America, but only a few businesspeople have caught on to the system's potential as a part of the official economy. One pioneer is Buffalo Exchange, the used-clothing chain first established by the veteran Swedish flea marketer Kerstin Block and her husband, Spencer, in Tucson in 1974. Buffalo figured greatly in our life at Fulton Street. Isadora and

Lucy both got jobs at the chain's San Francisco store when it opened in 1986, and all of us shopped there regularly, which in our chic crowd could mean three or four times a week. Buffalo was hardly the first vintage store in town—there'd been a grand tradition of rags and bags since the Summer of Love—but it adopted a revolutionary new policy. You could bring your own clothes; the clerks would sift through them, and whatever they liked they'd put in a pile that they would purchase from you for cash or trade. The cash made an immediate ground-level difference in our lives—adding to our rent money when those minimum-wage paychecks ran short—but it was the trade that really changed the game. Suddenly you could increase your sartorial capital without putting up a red cent; you could play the fashion game without getting into the rat race. For women, this made a huge difference, because even in bohemian circles our status still depended largely on our appearance; it was easier to get jobs, make connections, and score dates if you looked sharp. Anyway, we were clotheshorses, using iconoclastic style to distinguish ourselves in opposition to a beauty standard that didn't suggest we were naturally worth much. Clothes gave us a sense of power, and Buffalo gave us a way to keep recharging.

Buffalo Exchange taps into the bohemian economy, grafting one of its veins onto a more "legitimate" capitalist venture. Nobody loses in this deal. The stores bestow fair trade for items and charge decent prices to nontrading customers. Kerstin Block considers her business part of the recycling industry, but actually Buffalo promotes reuse, the preservation of goods for their natural lifetimes rather than the span dictated by the marketplace. Buffalo's small suggestion is that we can't escape consumerism, but we can find new ways to explore its potential.

Most people dip into the culture of reuse the same way they barter, without thinking about it. Staging a garage sale, passing on hand-me-downs, trading in old college textbooks for cash or a few new novels at the used-book store—any of these activities makes you a reuser. Nearly everyone buys houses used. Some large retailers, like Urban Outfitters, have even integrated used stock into their inventory, while others, like Filene's Basement, simulate the rummage-sale atmosphere with stuffed, chaotic bins of discount wares. But aside from marveling at the good deal, shoppers rarely consider the difference between picking up a pair of ski boots at the local church bazaar and charging new Nikes at the Athlete's Foot.

Reuse allows things to retain their value as they circulate. An object's worth does not diminish with each hand it passes through; in some cases, as with collectibles, it may increase, and usually it stays the same. Workers are rewarded for their skills at trade—their ability to assess the quality of a jumper or a book, and their help in keeping these items moving in and out of the store. It doesn't matter if something returns in two weeks' time, that simply gives someone else the opportunity to enjoy it for a while. Instead of the traditional model of scrimping or the yuppie game of showing off, both of which rate people by how much they can obtain, reuse lends status to those who share. You're not somebody in the social milieu of a Buffalo Exchange store until you offer up clothes as cool as the ones you're walking out with. At the heart of this circular economy is a notion that Americans fantasize about but rarely believe: that where we live, there's enough to go around.

Clothing stores in bohemian enclaves nationwide have copied the Buffalo Exchange method. In my utopia, there'd be many more, trading not just clothes and books and records, but tools, sporting goods, car parts, furniture, stereo equipment. Maybe we're on our way to that reality. Buffalo Exchange has sixteen outlets scattered around the West. Many fashion-forward teens today consider shopping at thrift stores an integral part of assembling a cool look, dependent as that look is on cues from earlier eras, like Adidas sweat jackets and anything polyester. The fashion industry has responded to the used-clothing trend by skimming its surface; so many designers now specialize in fake-vintage designs that one women's glossy declared the 1990s to be "about revival, full stop." But anyone who's spent a weekend rummaging in a Buffalo Exchange, coming away with four pairs of pants, three sweaters, a pair of boots, and two dresses for under her hundred bucks in trade, knows that an Anna Sui outfit that looks vintage but costs new lacks an essential element. That essence doesn't come from the look of your leather jacket—it's all about how you got it.

■

T H E   O R B I T   O F   T H E   G I F T

Anthropologists have long examined other cultures' economic systems to shed light on our own; one such system is the way of the gift. Many scholars have marveled at the cartoonish bounties of the Native American potlatch and the Polynesian marriage ceremony, trying to figure out why anyone would want to give so much away. In 1983, the poet Lewis Hyde published a book on this subject, *The Gift: Imagination and the Erotic Life of Property*. Examining various cultural traditions, myths, and works of literature, Hyde concludes that gifts are not like other objects we acquire. They are anarchist property, resistant to permanent ownership; they gain worth only if the spirit of giving, if not the actual objects, keeps moving. In the potlatch, one tribal chief may receive twenty cords of pine from another, but his wealth is only confirmed when he gives back one hundred pounds of salmon. Traces of this ethic survive in modern society. If I give you a present for your birthday in June, and our mutual best friend's birthday falls in September and you surprise him with nothing, somehow my generosity seems a little foolish. Hyde applies the gift's logic to art: if your back window presents a beautiful scene, it gains value when inspiration leads you to paint that scene, hang it in a gallery, and give the gift of your vision to me. He argues for an economy of generosity, and explores how it survives in the cutthroat world of the savings and loan.

At twenty I was a struggling baby poet and a devotee of Hyde's book. Its visions of faraway islanders and fairytale witches working gift magic fed a young working girl's romantic urge to escape the drudgery of the cash-register-bound, rent-paying day-to-day life. Rereading Hyde's words nearly a decade later, I realized how closely his ideas relate to the unspoken transactions we engaged in at and around Fulton Street. Our scamming barter circle operated on the potlatch principle: just like a Kwakiutl chief, I would offer bounty at Planet Records without asking for anything in exchange, and my buddies would return the favor when I wanted food or a new shirt. We never had quotas, because to do so would have set the value of our encounters and stopped their natural motion.

Trading clothes at Buffalo was a somewhat different matter, since money changed hands. Going to Goodwill appeared, on the surface, to be nothing more than regular shopping. But as I thought more about it, I began to see in the secondhand world the same traces of the gift that Hyde finds in art. Hyde feared the effects of mass culture on the gift; he wrote of the dangers of the art market and of conspicuous consumption in general, which jettisons precious boons like play and inspiration in favor of outwardly defined status and the acquisitive bottom line. I sur-

vey the landscape of upscale malls and junk bonds and can't argue with
his warnings. But the spirit he so values—of reciprocation, of imagination—survives in the bohemian economy, offering ways to temper the
hunger and cynicism late capitalism stimulates, and to find the meaning
in things without becoming enslaved to their market value.

"We long to have the world flow through us like air or food," wrote
Hyde. "We are thirsty and hungry for something that can only be carried inside bodies. But consumer goods merely bait this lust, they do not
satisfy it. The consumer of commodities is invited to a meal without
passion, a consumption that leads to neither satiation nor fire."

Since there's no getting around commodity capitalism (even monks
shop for soap at Wal-Mart), the question is how to gain that well-fed
feeling from our visits to the marketplace. The answer is hidden in
Hyde's observation that it's about flow. To be content with what you
have in a society that pushes you to want ever more requires either an
impossible level of self-denial, or a new definition of possession. If ownership were defined by use instead of acquisition—if instead of stopping
the movement of things through the world, everyone carried what they
liked for as long as it served them and then passed it on—then you
wouldn't have to deny yourself anything, because you'd get just as much
as you gave. The hunger for things would still arise, like the craving for
oxygen, but it could be satisfied in the same way that need is, with a
motion in and a motion out.

This is a fantasy, I know; people who work in the secondhand trade
would say so themselves. But it's enacted, clearly, in certain aspects of
the bohemian economy—in straightforward barter, in scavenging, and
in bohemian commerce. It's visible within circles scattered all over the
world. Consider one such circle, part of the used clothing trade in San
Francisco—a small group of people who, although they compete in the
larger marketplace, have helped each other establish and maintain their
businesses and their lifestyles as postmodern recyclers. Each came to this
vocation because they received a gift of inspiration from material goods;
their souls were touched and they felt compelled to share what they had
learned. All of them care about the bottom line, and a few can get
downright competitive. But there's a difference between their way of doing business and the way that's come to dominate the marketplace. They
move in the orbit of the gift, and it's taught them how survive in a vora-
cious world.

■

THE RAG QUEEN

The guide who took my hand and led me into this particular territory was Lucy D'Amico, my old Fulton Street flatmate. Lucy had landed a job at Buffalo Exchange not long after it opened on Haight Street. She moved on eventually, and for a few years I wasn't sure what she was up to besides living in a big house she'd inherited from her grandmother, down in Glen Park. Then I began to hear rumors that she was in business for herself, that she was making money, that some considered her the best in her field. "She's selling stuff wholesale to all the stores on Haight Street," Lester told me when I reached him at his bookstore. "And to the Japanese."

It didn't surprise me that Lucy had found a way to turn her fascination with weird scraps and trinkets into a career; she'd always been a digger, filling her room with artifacts she'd excavated, greeting her housemates with a squeal of "Check this out!" and a quick fashion show. But vintage wholesaling was something I'd never heard of. For good reason, I discovered when I met with Lucy at her South San Francisco warehouse. Although many Bay Area clotheshorses eked out small incomes by buying and selling to Buffalo and its main competition, a shop across the street called Wasteland, or setting up tables at local flea markets, Lucy was the only individual she knew doing it on a grand scale.

"Grand" may not be the most accurate word to describe the mood in Lucy's warehouse, but for anyone interested in vintage clothing, it's spectacular. A thousand square feet of nearly raw space in the back of a nondescript office park, to the trained eye it's a regular Magic Mountain: piles of cashmere coats, button-fly Levi's, evening gowns, work shirts, fedoras, windbreakers, and other essentials for the millennial wardrobe extend from floor to ceiling, separated by a narrow path that leads to Lucy's phone and the bathroom. Should you need to relieve yourself in said bathroom, you'd have to stave off an avalanche of ladies' sweaters, lest it bury you on the commode. As we talked, Lucy punctuated the conversation with quick runs to one garbage bag or another. "Here's an example of what I mean by rare!" she'd announce, displaying a worn blue athletic sneaker. After all these years, she still got the same thrill from showing off her discoveries: "Check it out!"

Lucy and I have parallel histories of rummaging. Like me, she grew up in a conservative Catholic family in the middle-class suburbs and lived a moderately miserable teenage existence until she stumbled onto punk rock. The Ivory-washed jocks and fast-lane stoners in her neighborhood had treated Lucy vaguely like a weirdo ever since she could remember; punk told her, You *are* a weirdo, and that can be your pride and your source of kinship. Lucy and her friend Ginger would take the BART to San Francisco to catch shows at legendary clubs like the Mabuhay and the Vats. But only a few guys would talk to the suburban chicks and they felt pretty lonely. "We always felt like outsiders," she admitted. They could manage more credibility on their own ground, but no cool bands made it to Vallejo. "There weren't any clubs in the suburbs," Lucy said. "There were thrift stores."

At five feet tall and around a hundred pounds, with her olive-black hair and old-country Italian features, Lucy never saw herself in the pages of *Seventeen*. For irregular-sized girls like Lucy and me, the Salvation Army and its allies granted power denied by the traditional salons of femininity. "One reason I got interested in clothing in high school was that I didn't like the way I looked," she said. "I didn't think I looked pretty, and when you're in high school your confidence level is so low. So I tried to make the extra effort." In thrift stores, fashion's paradigms crumble. Style forms around taking a chance, trolling for odd items that complement your own off-kilter vibe. Certain practical pressures vanish; there's no standard size in a thrift store, so Lucy didn't have to look on in envy at the racks of size 8 adorables while picking through the arid field of the petites rack. And while she soon discovered that thrift mavens, too, cultivate looks and trends that demand attention and ingenuity, Lucy felt that kind of peer pressure as a challenge she could meet.

At her local St. Vincent's, Lucy first learned the art of networking. "They had a Jewelry World, with racks of rhinestones." She laughed. "Ginger wore tons of that stuff, and she got to know the lady who worked the counter. She'd save us stuff. We'd come in there every couple of days and she'd be like, 'Oh, girls! Have I got something for you!'" The middle-aged charity shop employee, someone who might have turned up her nose at these two punk girls if she'd run into them on the bus, became their ally because she saw the same pearls they did in dustpiles. Later, Lucy would find this camaraderie in a peer group, when she and her fellow Buffalo girls embarked upon their Haight Street reign.

"When I first started, Buffalo had the same kind of feeling Planet had for us," she remembered. "Everyone was pretty close. Each girl had her own thing—maybe one was more into the arts, one was more into nightlife. And we all had our own fashion interests. But there were certain things we all liked. There was a look."

That look still strolls down San Francisco's bohemian avenues, even though most of the original Buffalo girls are gone. Its main quality is whimsy, a sense of clothing as costume—matching hat, purse, and pumps, or skirt and blouse so wittily mismatched that they reconfigure glamour. Often the look revels in color, in the sweep of a cotton ruffle and the sheen of leather or nylon on skin. It has its roots in hippie San Francisco, when freethinking women wore the patchwork of many nations in a flamboyant, offhand swirl, but it's sharper, more aware of itself. The style developed via punk and New Wave, as bands from the Clash to the B-52's to the Human League turned social critique into raucous dance hits, and wore outfits that further played out their ideas. Lately it has manifested in a fascination with the once-passé trends of the 1970s, from disco dresses to rainbow jeans. By taking older styles out of context, this approach to vintage clothing exposes the artifice of all social scenes, including the present day's. We become who we are by design, the look said, and it's best to be your own designer.

Postmodernists called this style pastiche; the cultural critic Angela McRobbie, whose writing on British jumble sales was the first to acknowledge thrift-store dressing's social significance, compared it to dress-up. Lucy uses the same term, stressing the playful, hopeful mood her shiny, happy outfits evoke. There's a serious aspect to this child's game: it challenges the dominant mood of women's fashion, which, despite the insistence by skinny editors of glossy magazines that it's all about fun, is actually about constraint. Year after year, followers of couture are expected to adjust their bodies and their budgets to fit a new trend, decided upon by mostly male designers to suit ninety-eight-pound-weakling models. The experience of shopping for such outfits is one notch less stressful than all the dieting, hair-bleaching, waxing, and plucking that go into making the bodies that women squeeze into costumes cut for somebody else, as the watchful clerk balances her disdain for her customer with her need to make a sale. Following mainstream

fashion feels serious for two reasons: one, high style is presented as natural law by the clothing industry, with women staking their very worth
on being able to fit the bill; and two, it's so damn expensive. For all but
the proverbially too rich and too thin, looking properly glamorous is a
bloody battle.

Now, that excellent Qiana gown at the Goodwill might not fit, either.
A vintage shopper endures her share of frustration and embarrassment.
But with everything so cheap, and the look you're aiming for so fanciful, it's hard to get too worked up. Lucy says her time at Buffalo was
like living inside a grab bag. "Someone would come in and sell a shirt
and I'd be like, 'That shirt would go *perfect* with a skirt I have at
home!'" she said. "Every day we were bringing back clothes we'd had
for a couple weeks and selling them back." The Buffalo girls envied
each other's finds sometimes, but the general mood was noncompetitive.
"From those girls, I got excited," she said. "I wouldn't think, They look
better than me; it would spur me on. And it was just so fun, such a silly
thing."

With their lucky finds and their goofy gorgeousness, the Buffalo girls
possessed the spirit of the gift. This is how women are supposed to feel
about fashion, according to women's magazines. But only by seizing the
fashion system for themselves could Lucy and her friends find pleasure
in it. Mainstream fashion relies on a sense of distance to stimulate need;
looking good is a goal that most women strive for all their lives, alienat-
ing themselves from their real bodies and desires in the process. Conversely, Haight Street fashion valued immediacy; what you could find in
the shop that day became your starting point for that evening. "There
were so many chances to get the perfect match," said Lucy. "It was
heaven."

Sorting through the bounty at Buffalo, Lucy became proficient at pre-
dicting how certain styles became trendy, moving from the corner of a
charity shop to the front racks of her boutique. She eventually decided
to put this knack to use for herself. She quit her job, supporting herself
by selling her excess vintage finds to her old coworkers. At first her rest-
less rounds from estate sale to swap meet and back to the Buffalo trade-
in counter still felt like a hobby; then she realized she was making
decent money, and the more she expanded, the more she raked in. One
day, while perusing polyester in a San Jose Goodwill, she met a Japanese
woman who'd seen her around the bins; they worked out a deal, and

now Lucy wholesales to her friend, who in turn sells to chic marts in her native country. Lucy has a special gift for satisfying the Asian market, partly because her size 3-to-5 is their average, and she can judge what might appeal to them by what looks right on her. She's met some fanatical Japanese collectors, who'll pay hundreds of dollars for the right athletic sweatshirt from the 1950s. "It has to have the double triangle embroidered at the neckline, front and back," she said. In the great stream of recycled culture, collectors are the ones who construct dams. But Lucy likes the collectors because they make her money, and her old scavenger-hunt instinct is stimulated by the quest for valuable stuff.

Lucy thinks the funniest thing is that the world of fashion, where as a kid she'd felt so shaky, made a place for her after all. Actually, she created that place for herself, inventing a role in a corner of the industry far from the hierarchies of the couture houses and the big retail chains. Her little spot is no paradise; sometimes fellow sellers try to steal her sources or her customers. But the community is small enough that unethical acts usually come back to haunt wrongdoers, and Lucy is known as a solid sender, the fairest entrepreneur in her line. These days she's feeling confident enough to consider taking on the big time, maybe selling to a chain like Urban Outfitters. The mainstream seems to have caught on to her ways. A few days before we met, Lucy had popped into Macy's to check out those fake-vintage designer fashions and stumbled across a weird reflection. "I applied at Macy's once, and they wouldn't hire me because of the way I looked," she said. "I had dreadlocks then. I swept my hair up and wore a little fifties suit, but they said I'd have to change. Now I go in there, and everybody looks weird! It makes me mad," she said. But she was smiling. It's funny, sometimes, how the world comes to you.

■

THE MINISTERING ANGEL

A few doors down from the crowded racks of overcoats and cocktail dresses of Buffalo Exchange, one of Lucy's companions in vintage-queendom plays gracious hostess in her own garden of modern antiquities. Lauren Welch was a Buffalo girl for three years, a specialist in the rockabilly look. With her platinum-blond ponytail and her baby-doll features, she could transform herself into the dream squeeze in a fantasy scenario of greaser boys on motorbikes, drive-in dates, and rumbles. Her version of Buffalo girl finesse emphasized precision, not adventure. She cared about the past, and felt driven to keep some small part of it breathing through her careful attention to its remains. In her rockabilly duds, she felt like an authority.

The revivalist approach to vintage clothing that Lauren pursued in her youth is practiced by collectors and fashion plates, who can be just as bad as the mainstream fashion industry in making rules about what's cool. The chilly flawlessness of the swing-revival or rockabilly looks, or the fervent embrace of 1970s style that made unflattering bellbottoms hot again in the mid-1990s, can turn into cultural necrophilia. The circular energy of the gift may be lost in pursuit of flawlessness. Eventually Lauren began to wonder if her nostalgia was controlling her more than she was directing it.

"That scene was so strict," said Lauren, leaning back in a Louis XIV–style patio chair in the front window of her shop. "Your eyeliner has to be perfect. Your seams up the back have to be perfect. I started to wear vintage clothes to find my own individual style, and then suddenly it turned into what everybody else was doing. It almost felt like I was trapped."

Lauren didn't see any way out but to flee the rockabilly crowd altogether. She quit her job at Buffalo, sold her poodle skirts, and rented a warehouse space across the bay in Oakland, near the railroad tracks. There she began the transition that would lead her back, five years later, to a different spot on Haight Street. She stopped concentrating on clothes, turning her attention toward decorative home furnishings and objets d'art. She loosened up her tastes, seeing what would happen if she combined elements from different eras in an outfit or a room display. And she changed her way of making money, abandoning the exhibitionism of the shop clerk for the more fluid, interactive life of the flea marketer.

"I bought my old truck, a 1951 Dodge, and started bringing stuff to the Marin Flea Market on the weekends," Lauren recalled. "It was really scary and weird at first. You gotta get there at two A.M. and you sleep in your car. You'd get out in the mud and the dirt, and you'd have your big boots on. I didn't know anybody when I started, but then I met Clarissa Stephens, my partner in this shop. We were—we are—the only two young women in this business. We've been working together ever since."

Both Clarissa and Lauren were trying to move past their youthful grounding in the punk scene and develop an aesthetic of their own. They shored each other up in the face of come-ons and brush-offs from the overwhelmingly male, middle-aged, roughneck crew dominating the flea market. Lauren also took heart from the community of artists with whom she shared her warehouse home. "Everybody was designing and building furniture out of recycled products, or making clothing, or throwing pots, or painting. It all really inspired me to do something."

Lauren began to focus on objects that seemed like heirlooms—not antiques, with their high price tags and collectible aura—but decorative items a mother might pass down to a daughter: pieces of Belgian lace, Mexican tapestries, a rustic rocking chair. Lauren's interest in this otherwise-known-as-junk stemmed from the way she used it to make her own home feel unique and secure; she hoped her customers would create such environments for themselves. After a few years on the flea market scene, Clarissa and Lauren decided to settle down on Haight Street and open a shop that would show people the possibilities of recycled domesticity.

Such an interest in homemaking as a popular art form is common among the aficionados of junk culture; Western-themed bed and breakfasts and houses that are shrines to Victoriana exist around the country. But few autodidact interior designers can claim as visceral a motivation for their obsessions as Lauren. One disastrous night when she was fifteen, storms literally ripped apart her childhood home, with Lauren and her mother inside. Lauren survived. But her mother fell, along with her living room, down that Santa Cruz cliff and into the rocky sea.

"My life was saved by a chair," said Lauren. "The people who found me said that an antique chair, made so well from solid oak, stopped me from being crushed. It covered me." Lauren can talk about the incident now, even theorize about it, although the loss of her mother still stings like a salted wound. "Clarissa's mom died when she was young, too," she revealed. "We both got into this business after our mothers were gone." By creating a space devoted to preserving materials once beloved and then discarded, Lauren believes, she honors the spirit of her mother, who collected and furnished their home with antiques. "Her house was a work of art, like mine," she said.

If the modern condition is a slippery loneliness, with people roaming from connection to connection wondering why all this contact doesn't

satisfy, treasured objects form the record of our desire to rest. Not the
things we acquire to to keep moving—the new car, the status-proving
gizmos, the keep-up-with-the-Joneses home furnishings—but those that
weigh us down a little make us more ourselves. A pile of rocks gathered
from every beach I've ever walked, a shelf full of books on medieval
saints, my father's high-school pin, every record Brian Eno has ever
made, the plastic animals from atop the ice cream cake at my sixteenth
birthday party: these are my rabbit's feet, guarding me against the great
danger in this crowded world: that I'll lose myself. They are also messages, the first words in all my stories, my biography in junk. Gifts we
share in the showing, rather than through physical exchange, they allow
us to know each other in ways that our running, quotidian selves can't
share. Come visit me and stay awhile, and I'll take you through my collection. And you, among your things, could do the same for me.

It is the job of the dealer to assess an object's worth on the current
market; whether she trades in stocks or sock monkeys, she will make
the most profit if she separates her goods from these unquantifiable,
personal values. Lauren encounters the purely capitalist side of her trade
all the time—the antiques hoarders who beat each other out at estate
sales, the flea-market customers who show up at four in the morning
with flashlights in hand to get to the good stuff first. She concentrates
on decorative items, considered less valuable than collectibles, to avoid
this competitive aspect of the trade. But she has to watch the bottom
line, so her shop sells soap and candles, the items most popular among
the tourists who frequent Haight Street, alongside its 1920s glass bead
necklaces. "It's very frightening," said Lauren. "Our belief system has
shifted. At first we were like, 'No way, no new stuff.' But it's about
money."

Lauren has worked out a rationalization for the store's foray into
manufactured ephemera: she hopes the aura of the store itself will infuse
these more disposable things with a bit of talismanic magic. Some of her
items are very expensive, and she doesn't want the kids who come in to
be scared away. "This parlor set is six thousand dollars," she said, ges-
turing to the wrought-iron chairs we're perched on, which are one hundred years old. "I guess it's like if somebody loves the French parlor set,
at least they can buy a little piece of soap to remind them of it."

Maybe Lauren has finally learned the capitalist's trick of displacing
gratification—"Come to the Disneyland gift shop and take a bit of the

Matterhorn home with you"—but she seems to be sincere in her hope that her shoppers will leave her store with more than the sum of their purchases. Lauren knows what it's like to lose everything, and to rebuild your life from a literal pile of wreckage. Her ordeal has given her the ability to see the worth of people's belongings in the way they use them. "If you don't have a family, or are trying to break away from them, creating your own environment is really important," she concluded. "It allows for stability in an unstable world."

The dream of the House Beautiful is fundamental to membership in conventional society, as I'd discovered growing up at Steiner Street. The old bohemian trick of valuing what others overlook expands the definition of that dream and makes it accessible to those whose budgets and sensibilities don't fit the norm. In a society where consumerism is citizenship, that's a blow for democracy. I left Lauren's shop with a bar of soap and a few new ideas about how to furnish a home.

■

THE SALVAGER

"I see the world through thrift-store eyes," said Veronica Dowd when I met her for a cocktail at the Golden Palm, a dive turned hipster bar in the Mission District. Veronica is a friend of Lucy and Lauren; they both singled her out as their prime example of dedication to the recycled life. In a low-cut leopardskin blouse and black capri pants, her Bakelite bracelet catching the dim glow of the table lamp, Veronica had no problem convincing me she's a total vintage girl; even her demeanor, a mix of Audrey Hepburn and Doris Day, seems slightly alien to the contemporary moment. Unlike the other people in this gift circle, Veronica has not used her interest in the secondhand trade to elevate and solidify her social position. As some would see it, her passion has led her to take a step down. But she doesn't care what other people think. A few months before I met her, Veronica quit her job at a fancy vintage boutique and became assistant manager of her local Salvation Army store.

"It's funny when I tell people what I do for a living," she said. "Unless you tell the right people, it's like, God, what an unglamorous job! But tell an antique dealer, and it's a different story." Veronica enlisted in the Salvation Army for one reason only—immersion in a constantly shifting whirlpool of stuff. Her round face lights up when she talks about the truckload of goodies greeting her at the store's warehouse every morning. Then there are the bags full of donations that cross the front counter, especially on New Year's Eve, as people scramble for their tax write-offs. "You're constantly sorting and separating through qualities of stuff," Veronica explained. "It's a treasure hunt, a mishmash." She has to engage in a little workplace subversion to enjoy the full fruits of her position, since store policy dictates that all goods go on the floor before employees claim them. Veronica doesn't get busted, not only because she's careful but also because her interest is extremely rare within a company the vast majority of whose workers are "transitional," meaning partially disabled, recovering from drugs, or recently released from prison. "They all want the new stuff," she said, speaking of the discount items some manufacturers donate. "Three boxes of new goods come in and they're like, Toilet paper! Wow! Toothpaste! I have no competition. All the stuff I want is old."

Of all the people I've met who pursue the used, Veronica is the most devoted. Although she's made a living selling her finds to Buffalo Exchange and other shops for several years, she's not primarily concerned with making her passion a business. Thrifting is the thing that has made Veronica into herself—the quest, the grubbing, the rehabilitation of what others have discarded, gives her not just pleasure but a sense of purpose. Like Lauren, she turned on to secondhand stuff after a crisis disrupted her family home when she was a teenager. One Christmas she was visiting friends in San Francisco, and her mother, with whom she'd been living in Arizona, phoned her up and told her not to come back home. No explanation, just good-bye. Her friends, a mom and daughter, took her in and taught her the ways of the vintage world. A few years later the family opened a shop on Haight Street specializing in Western gear, and they gave Veronica her first job in the trade.

From having no status, not even a family to claim, to a secure role within a community—that's where thrifting took Veronica. It's striking how this transformation comes up again and again in the stories I hear. Secondhand culture has its snobs and its dirty players, but the presumption that anything can be restored extends to identity, and so its habitués support each other's experiments in self-invention. The logic of the conventional world of goods, which presumes that one's position can be read in the cut of one's suit, goes out the window at the flea market. With it goes the logic of social status itself. A frontier mood prevails within these enclaves, a sense that we have all gone past the comfortable terrain of the mall to strip ourselves clean and start anew. For Veronica, who unexpectedly did have to start anew, this atmosphere allowed her to feel like a pioneer instead of a lost girl.

Veronica is always making herself over. "I'm a theme person," she said. "My first theme was Western—cutout boots, cowgirl clothes, gabardine. Then in college I studied Egyptology, and I started thinking, The Egyptians, they know it all. I started collecting Egyptian objects, got a hieroglyphic tattoo, had that hairstyle with the bob and the bangs. My friends called me Bevis the Egyptian girl. Then I started taking flamenco dancing, and I would dress in Mexican fiesta skirts. Now I like leopard, I like fruit. In my house, the bedroom's cowboy, the living room is 1960s modern, and the bathroom has a sea motif." She blessed me with a goofy grin. "It's gotta have a theme."

Critics of collecting deride the practice for its narcissism; Jean Baudrillard called collectibles the perfect pets, since they represent the personalities of their owners with no involvement required beyond occasional dusting. He considered it regressive to direct so much energy inward. Yet such a cruel judgment doesn't take into account the need to protect oneself against the hazardous turns of one's own life and the tendency of the powerful to degrade the powerless. Veronica has faced some serious hairpin turns in her thirty years; not only was she abandoned by her mother, at twenty-three she married a punk who turned out to be a junkie, and it took her nearly a decade to stop trying to save the relationship and just get out. Thrifting gave her a practical means to earn money when caring for her dope-sick husband made holding down a steady job difficult. Securing the Salvation Army position gave her the courage to leave him altogether. "Maybe all my themes give a sense of order to my life," she suggested, to herself as much as to me. "It's something concrete to go on."

Lucy found a way in to her own sexiness through secondhand stuff; Lauren uncovered a link to her past. Veronica, still struggling harder than either of these women, uses her vintage obsession as a basic means of self-defense. "I use it as therapy," she attests. This remark connects with the traditional suggestion that women shop to feel better, and at times Veronica's palpable insecurity makes her seem as trapped as Lauren once was, her identity overshadowed by the aura of her persona.

But the fact is that very few ladies who shop can turn that consumer impulse into a genuinely productive element of their lives, while in the secondhand world the roles of consumer and trader are so blurred that every serious participant actively affects the scene. By bartering and selling as well as buying, Veronica sees her good taste pay off. And she binds herself to the gift circle, which repays her in fellowship as well as cash. Unlike the anonymous exchange of the shop clerk and purchaser, the interactions that make up Veronica's thrifting life demand a certain intimacy, which leads to fair exchange and even generosity instead of exploitation. "I really hold them in the highest regard," she said of Lucy and Lauren, both of whom she's traded with. "They're my mentors."

Like many kids who grow up on the fringe, without the usual family or class-based support systems, Veronica has taken a while to find a solid place from which to grow. She never expected the Salvation Army to provide that place, but it makes sense to her now. "Right now I feel like I could work in a thrift store forever," she said. "But I have the basic skills now to get a better job. I'm in a transitional phase. I just turned thirty, I'm getting divorced. I'm ready for a new theme. It'll come."

THE RECLASSIFIER

Tony Meredith sits in a pristine conference room so sleek and futuristic it could have been built for the set of *2001: A Space Odyssey*. Tony himself resembles a twenty-first century astronaut: his round Scandinavian face offering an open gaze from above a cream-colored turtleneck, his long legs and wide torso an accidental image of genetically engineered harmony, he's a man in touch with his own potential. Lately, he can't help but be—he's the It Boy of the San Francisco design world, and all because of an ingenious bit of junk rejuvenation.

A while ago, Tony was leafing through one of the catalogs carried by the fancy furniture store where he works, and he came across some hand-blown pastel glass lamps made by an Italian firm. "I thought, What if I were to make something like this using a standard product that I could find anywhere?" he said. "All these things racked up in my head, and then I just popped up with Tupperware! It's heat-resistant, it transmits light gorgeously. It's malleable. I came up with these," he said, turning the pages of his portfolio to a photograph of three soothing orbs, former containers of leftovers in lime green, apricot orange, and pale blue. "They hit some insane nerve. It went through the roof."

I'd first seen Tony's vintage Tupperware lamps earlier in the year, when they held an honored spot in the famous window displays of the New York haute department store Barney's. At the time, I didn't connect the designer's surname with that of an exceedingly fashionable vintage princess I'd known during my San Francisco years. It turns out Tony is her little brother, and part of the same circle occupied by the other recyclers I'd met. A bit younger than Lucy, Lauren, or Veronica—he's twenty-six— and more preoccupied with making it on a grand scale, Tony doesn't spend his days amid musty piles of charity-store castoffs; he's as jazzed by the latest in coffee tables as he is by a great Danish Modern couch. With the Tupperware lamps, though, he joined the growing legion of artists taking the enough-stuff aesthetic to a wider audience. Tony prefers the term "reclassification": he's not technically recycling, which would involve melting down the plastic and structuring it into an entirely new form. I suspect he also likes the scientific tone, since his take on secondhand culture is back-to-the-future, a kind of triumph over the past.

"I have this weird utopian fantasy of everyone living in the same Plexiglas white box with a centralized heating duct and everything really plain," he confessed. "Material culture is very weird to me. I want less. But I'm a designer, so I grapple with this all the time. I guess my way of justifying it is by working with things like Tupperware. I'm creating a new product, but I'm not creating new mass or matter."

Most recyclers I meet, while professing a similar fear about the world's capacity to harbor endless new things, have grown entangled in the clutter of belongings and the values those things represent. Veronica sees herself in a 1950s pillbox hat, but then she has to grapple with the part of her that doesn't feel like the old-fashioned girl she looks like when she puts it on. Lauren fills her house with a century's worth of mementos even as she fights nostalgia for her own lost childhood. These are the complexities of claiming a legacy. The ghosts in Tony's Tupperware are more vaporish than these other specters; perhaps it's because the product itself has always seemed oddly separate from its own context. These highly artificial containers were designed to neutralize the most vital element in the modern household: homemade food. Tupperware turns Mother's meatloaf into a semblance of the preservative-filled convenience food you could buy at the supermarket. It makes accumulation clean. Tupperware's translucent presence embodies the contradictory spirit of American materialism, which urges us to keep buying as if to fill a bottomless bowl, to equalize every experience by reducing it to a purchase, to become like plastic containers ourselves, resisting attachment so as to always be available for the next sale.

By filling Tupperware with light, Tony's lamps suggest that it might be wise to ponder this emptiness and to see what it leaves us with. "Tupperware was a way for people to socialize," he said. "In the 1950s, when these fingerprint subdivisions were built with no markets around, people bought it to store more food, and it was marketed through parties. In the city, you meet people in your doorway. In the suburbs you see someone two acres away in their yard, watering. Or maybe they drive by at eighty miles an hour. You can't talk to them." Tony sees his lamps as the embodiment of the Tupperware party, beacons of warmth penetrating plastic, meant not so much to illuminate as to draw people in. He considers Tupperware a democratizing force, like Coke, because "whether you're rich or poor you can't get a more delicious Coke. It's utopian in that way." It's also Orwellian, obscuring hierarchies with the lie that we are all the same when it comes to what we buy.

All these meanings emanate from Tony's Tupperware lamps precisely because he has changed the object's original function. Storing yesterday's Jell-O isn't really a concern for the city dwellers who make up Tony's audience and his peer group, for whom Chinese take-out and Power Bars are more the norm. But his lamps challenge them to see the nine lives in everything, in a practical sense as well as a cultural one. This is the cutting edge of secondhand culture, where the flow of things changing hands and histories eradicates the difference between old and new. Lucy has a plan for sweaters that recalls Tony's innovation: she'll cut the arms out of one, substitute those of another, and forge a mutant design that's both familiar and utterly original. I remember my orange crate back on Fulton Street, its ordinariness still visible beneath the bright beads that covered it, still a box but not just a box: a reservoir of messages shared and still forming.

The acolytes of secondhand dig out the hidden vocabularies of durable goods, to discover how they spoke to those who first used them and what they might say to us now. Tony can interpret four decades of Tupperware, tell you what each era's chosen colors represent, trace the dialogue between one company and its customers through the curves of a polyethylene water glass. The conversation he uncovers is dominated by the manufacturer's mandate to determine its product's specific use, and to convince buyers that there's always another need to satisfy. But another level exists, where the user decides the terms, and the dead essence of the mass-produced is animated by one person's imaginative possession. People know that it is possible to find pleasure and profundity in the material, because they do it every day, despite the dull redundancy of mass consumerism. The marketplace is global; we can't live on some space station outside it. The question is how to stay human within it.

Tony Meredith's follow-up to the Tupperware lamps was Seating Unit, a foam-rubber pad that conforms to the body's shape—a totally portable, interchangeable office chair. He dreams of a postmodern city where everyone would have the same things, all made of recycled materials; in this pristine environment, hierarchy would dissolve, because everyone would equally have not. This seems a far cry from the cultivated fetishism of the secondhand world, but in fact they're two points on the same circle. Both counteract the terrible craving about which Lewis Hyde wrote—that need to be nourished by the physical world, a need whose fulfillment is thwarted by the way commodity exchange turns everything into empty calories. When everything tells you there's never enough, secondhand culture says, Look around you. There is.

6

.

BASTARDS OF YOUNG

A FEW years ago, I sat with two of my San Francisco friends in a tiny downtown New York apartment, getting stoned and talking about shoes. Fate and our forming ambitions had pushed us beyond California's dreaming into this colder, harder place; we drew together to preserve the customs and beliefs of home. Our material success depended on modifying our romantic sensibilities to suit status-driven New York. But we weren't letting go easily. Our new jobs—at *The Village Voice* for me, New York University for Rose, a major distributor of independent films for Damien—impressed our parents and provided almost adequate income, not to mention health insurance. Our daily lives resembled those of genuine adults. Yet no role, not "punk" or "slacker" or "poet" or "problem child," had ever felt so contrived.

"Look at my sneakers," Damien said, holding out one Keds-clad foot for examination. At first only making idle drug talk, he soon realized he'd hit upon a metaphor. "Look at my sneakers!" he exclaimed, jumping out of his chair. "Look at me. I dress exactly like I did when I was twelve. And *I love it*!"

Rose and I grinned in recognition. Damien's walking shorts, his beige-and-maroon-striped T-shirt, his droopy sweat socks all had their equivalents in our closets. That very week I'd strolled into an East Village boutique and purchased a children's size-16 polo shirt, in royal blue. Rose favored baby-doll dresses and Mary Jane pumps. Here we were, on the verge of turning thirty, trying our best to replicate the looks our mothers had forced upon us from the racks of Sears in 1976. "That was when my personality first arose," said Damien later, when I asked him about that night—after he insisted that the age he identifies with is five, not twelve. "And so I see myself that way. When I dress that way, it represents me."

When I was a child I sometimes played dress-up, slipping into my mother's shiny cocktail shifts with their strange breast-cups and sticky zippers, just to see what being grown might feel like. Now I don school-girl pleats and baby T-shirts, preparing for parties where high-powered career women wear butterfly barrettes in their hair. Dress-up has become dress-back, and not just in terms of clothes. Slackers have conjured a whole creative world of second childhood drifting into perpetual adolescence. Indie rock stars have compiled their versions of jingles from "Schoolhouse Rock," the series of public service announcements that taught them civics in grade school. Graduate students formed cults around the girls' magazine *Sassy* and teen shows like *Buffy the Vampire Slayer,* looking for the sympathetic voices they felt popular culture hadn't offered them in their own green years. The director Richard Linklater followed his generation-tagging film *Slacker* with 1993's *Dazed and Confused,* a vision of juvenile rowdiness set in the heavy metal seventies and rendered in twilight glow, and in 1996 Todd Solondz made *Welcome to the Dollhouse,* a loving portrait of a pubescent female social outcast. In music, riot grrrls, young women who retooled feminist ideology to fit their own postpunk attitudes, became the darlings of the underground in the early nineties; although some of them were genuinely under legal drinking age, many were in their mid- to late twenties, affecting a younger version of themselves.

A poet who has won awards and dined with the likes of John Ashbery recently presented me with the gift of a Spice Girls Fantasy Ball lollipop. "How did you know Sporty Spice was my favorite?" I asked him, fondly regarding the bug-eyed coquette pictured on the package. "She's every independent woman's favorite," he replied. We both know our appreciation of these kiddie idols does not exactly match the love real thirteen-year-olds feel for them; I'd never scream when Sporty Spice flounced across my TV screen. But that doesn't mean our appreciation was fake, or even entirely ironic. Within the gardens of juvenilia, something thrives that we need; something of ourselves.

My peers were labeled immature before we even reached full adulthood. The "slacker" badge stamped upon our foreheads in our early twenties cemented the belief that growing up was a concept that held no interest for us. In 1986, journalist Susan Littwin coined the phrase "Postponed Generation" to describe "the crisis of this generation of young adults, hovering reluctantly in the passageway to maturity in a world for which they were unprepared." The forty-eight-year-old Littwin characterized the "children of the children of the '60s" as simultaneously spoiled and abandoned, unwilling to accept the responsibilities that a sluggish economy and changing attitudes about family were denying them anyway. Self-appointed Gen X spokespeople like David Leavitt and Bret Easton Ellis confirmed Ms. Littwin's dire assertions, scoring with novels that put a new spin on the time-honored image of decadent youth. By the mid-1990s, the stereotype was set: we were losers, baby, as the twentysomething "manchild" Beck so eloquently put it. Adorable Peter Pan had become the vaguely seedy Wayne and Garth of *Wayne's World*, unable to depart the caves of their parents' basements and get on with their lives.

Young people who had been looking forward to donning their very own business suits and throwing suburban barbecues took umbrage at this portrait. Backlash articles and books like 1994's *Late Bloomers*, by two Brown University grads named David Lipsky and Alexander Abrams, vehemently argued that they were being as adult as they could possibly be. "We want to turn our attention to the smaller questions (what wine, what car, what way to spend the weekend)," Lipsky and Abrams whined. They hoped the economy would pick up and the turmoil caused by feminism on the domestic front would abate, so that they could turn into their parents, as they were supposed to. But not every ostensibly postponed person wants to walk into that box. Some contrarians have serious problems with an image of adulthood based on conformity and status-driven materialism. Adopting youthful costumes and customs gives their rebellion a lighthearted veneer, beneath which a real conflict rages. The explorations that lead bohemians to nurture new value systems usually begin in youth, and the search for alternatives doesn't magically stop after college. In fact, it intensifies as responsibilities grow. The perception of adulthood as the phase when questioning gives way to cool contentment doesn't make sense in an era when no basics, not your dress code nor your family structure nor the shape of your career, are solidly in place. Slackers refuse to act like grown-ups because they believe that to do so would be to lie.

Adulthood's old markers—getting married, becoming a parent, deciding upon a career—can't be read so easily anymore. Many people who don't consider themselves nonconformists are crossing these thresholds later in life or ignoring them altogether. Our culture's current focus on the dark side of conventional family life, from the horror of incest to the hypocrisy of middle-aged men who abandon their wives for younger women, makes "settling down" an unsettling proposition. The same is true in the workplace. Career success today means making quick bucks on the stock exchange and staying alert for the next opportunity rather than nurturing a long relationship with a business community. Our most admired professionals and adult role models, doctors and lawyers, are now scorned for compromising their standards in the service of greed. The sunken virtue of our public leaders isn't even worth remarking on. In our current state of social disarray, proudly displayed family and career success often prove to be trick mirrors, sure signs of lurking corruption.

Bohemian values suggest it may be wiser for some to reject these once respectable paths; responsibility sometimes comes in defying the ideal. An artist may decide to remain childless because she knows that her vocation will prevent her from devoting herself to a family, or an activist may refuse to work for a corporation because she disagrees with its environmental policies. Such decisions involve sacrifice, and their consequences grow the later they come in life. At a certain point, you're not playing around with the future anymore; you're in the thick of things, and what you choose will probably last. I've known people in their midthirties who've left hot careers in the entertainment business and moved to smaller towns to study fiction writing or open thrift stores; their abandonment of secure big money may seem like a postponement, but to them it was the start of doing something significant.

Young parents raising families that don't conform to the usual hierarchies may also be accused of irresponsibility. The haunting image of a three-year-old nearly setting himself on fire while his stoned guardians search for some misplaced hashish in another room, which closes "Slouching Towards Bethlehem," Joan Didion's 1968 essay on the Haight-Ashbury scene, epitomizes the horror with which most people greeted the countercultural notion that children might not need as much protection from the adult world as most parents assume. Yet most bohemian parents don't resemble those careless freaks at all; in fact, the ones I know are frequently more diligent and involved than some who advocate the usual separate spheres for parent and child, then hire babysitters every weekend and plop their kids in front of the TV when they are together. Parents who bring their kids with them everywhere, to parties and sometimes even to work, refuse to "protect" them from a world they're going to encounter soon enough anyway. They make the adult world less of a mystery for kids, and because the patch of it where they live tends to honor adults' impulses to be expressive and playful too, these parents get to have childlike fun with their offspring without being embarrassed. Working hard to balance the need to keep their kids safe and healthy with the desire to let them experience life fully, these bohemian moms and dads challenge themselves every day.

The central tenet of bohemian life—that our everyday choices must be constantly reassessed and renewed—contradicts the assumption that maturity tames doubts and wanderlust. The dominant notion of adulthood is all tied up with the concept of settling: fixing your position in life and then making do with it. Most people naturally resist that compromise; that's why growing up is generally viewed as a necessary evil. Our culture fetishizes youth, making nubile pop stars into sex symbols and plastic surgeons into millionaires, partly because we have never come up with a process of maturing that isn't steeped in soul-constricting concession and denial.

For many bohemians, the main evidence that the grown-up world was a dangerous illusion came from watching their own parents squirm behind the mask. As a child of divorce whose family struggled financially after his stepfather was laid off from a corporate job, Damien learned young to act like a little adult: to take charge of himself and accept life's difficulties. He knows firsthand that children today must learn responsibility, cope with uncertainty, and accept hardship, all supposedly adult tasks. Conversely, to maintain his creative edge, Damien must maintain a sense of spontaneity and a willingness to question the status quo, qualities usually associated with youth. Assigning those traits to a certain life stage never made sense to him. They all play a part in his character, whether he chooses to disguise some of them or not. Putting on the costume of a boy while acting like a man, Damien acts out a metaphorical dialogue between those designated roles.

"I don't think it has anything to do with wanting to be a child forever," Damien said of his self-presentation. He sees that impulse much more in his elders, members of the baby boom generation, the first to gain its identity primarily from its youth. As they grow into an uncomfortable middle age, many baby boomers cling to the magic bullet of youthfulness. Boomer self-help gurus like Gail Sheehy and Tom Peters encourage their readers to resist growing up because callowness will keep them flexible as they strive for status and material success. There's nothing wrong with middle-aged people staying limber, but these adaptive strategies miss the very element that made 1960s youth culture revolutionary: the conviction that if the kids ruled, society would change. The boomer take on sustainable youth, based on keeping your inner child alive to benefit your outer adult, is useful in surviving unstable times. Sometimes it can challenge conventional priorities: Tom Peters suggests that the stymied businessmen who read him could enter the Peace Corps to learn new skills. Ultimately, though, boomer youthfulness is narcissistic, erecting a fountain of youth that is as make-believe as the edifice of adulthood.

"We transformed youth into a lifestyle, a political manifesto, an aesthetic, a religion," wrote the memoirist Richard Rodriguez, reflecting on his countercultural peers. "My generation turned adolescence into a commodity that could be sold worldwide by 45-year-old executives at Nike or Warner Bros. To that extent, we control youth."

The baby boomers' legacy of commodified youthfulness has left unresolved the larger questions about what adulthood should be. "I have something I have to say about the boomers, because I hate them," Damien said. "They've criticized us for not cohering into some kind of movement that was going to change the world. As though they did! We're able to very intimately see what those movements actually meant, how they worked or didn't work or became something else." Damien's anger carries a challenge for our elders to take this younger group of perpetual adolescents more seriously. Perhaps the postponements that critics so often accuse us of are simply signs of our taking the time to consider how we might end up with a real working definition of "adult."

What few people have grasped is that the endless adolescence of Generation X was never meant to be taken literally; it is a kind of ritual, the public interrogation of a myth. On one level, this has meant scrambling and unscrambling the images, scrutinizing vintage and contemporary visions of growing up to get at their changing meanings. We are trying to distill some truth from these stories and signs, to see what it might be like to reach adulthood free of habit, without our suits already picked out.

■

ROCK-AND-ROLL GIRLS (AND BOYS)

The baby boomers did leave behind one major tool to use in this pursuit: the snotty, starry-eyed music called rock. As the first popular art form specifically directed at young people, rock and roll has always been the main channel for their excitement and anxiety. In the 1950s, when it first emerged distinct from the rhythm and blues and country music that inspired it, rock and roll was linked to notions of teenage daring, and often delinquency. From drag-racing soap operas like "Teen Angel," to Chuck Berry's lascivious yearnings for jailbait, to the wrong-side-of-the-lunchroom love affairs recounted by the Shangri-Las, rock and roll spoke for the reckless young heart that ruled itself and risked all.

The rock and roll of the 1950s and early 1960s gave American youth an ardent voice. But what really made the link between youth and rock subversive was the attitude that arrived with the Beatles. The bands of the British Invasion, and Bob Dylan in the States, turned rock's teen dramas into morality plays about adolescent integrity and the price of growing up. "Hope I die before I get old" sounds like a joke now, tossed out by a feckless lad who would one day look back in embarrassment. But in 1965, the Who's "My Generation" severed a contract few thought could be broken. Until that moment, young rockers and their fans generally accepted that their wildness would pass, or at least would stop dominating their lives. Elvis dutifully recorded ballads that would appeal to his mother; Little Richard publicly enacted a psychic battle between his good, woman-loving, churchgoing, "mature" nature and his bad, homosexual, rock-and-rolling side. Other rockers, like Chuck Berry, were already past youth and celebrated it from afar. But the British Invasion bands were young and proud and determined to express exactly who they were. They encouraged kids to look to each other for guidance and to stop viewing their audacious youth as only a phase. For all their elders' denunciations of their funny clothes and floppy haircuts, the British bands took themselves seriously as citizens of the world. Their stance changed the way kids looked at themselves.

The British Invasion sparked this evolution by making rock bohemian. Most 1950s rock artists were working-class kids or journeymen musicians who did not have the time and luxury that have forever linked bohemianism to the middle class. The British Invasion bands included art-school students along with the rough lads. Each major group's spokesperson and artistic focal point—John Lennon, Peter Townshend, Mick Jagger—considered himself an artist, not merely an entertainer. These rockers were pretentious; they had opinions. Soon they were mouthing off about all sorts of things, from politics to religion to drugs. They presented a worldview and a world in which to realize it, and their peers, their fans, took them seriously. Adults had been scared by the likes of Little Richard and Elvis, but those Dionysian figures had their polite Apollonian sides, too, and so it seemed that the threat they represented could be contained. Besides, once those artists' fans jumped on the spouse-kids-and-job track at around twenty-one, they usually let their love of rock drift into nostalgia. As the 1960s sped on, John Lennon and his kind just kept getting older, as did their fans. And they never got polite.

Neither did Bob Dylan, whose old-man voice and grizzled baby face blended youth and wisdom in one figure. Dylan never acted young when he was young, and these days, nearing sixty, he's more of a kid onstage than ever. What Dylan's art stressed about youth was its constant motion. His most famous lines on the subject—"He who is not busy being born is busy dying"; "I was so much older then, I'm younger than that now"—stress rejuvenation through change. Dylan's philosophy of youthfulness strives to find a balance between the wild challenge of teenage rebellion and the substance of wisdom. He became a political icon, even though he rarely sang specifically political songs, because his philosophy was the same one that fired the social movements that took rock as a soundtrack and an inspiration.

Since the 1960s, rockers have cultivated this image of youth as the spirit in motion against the patterns of an unconsidered life. Patti Smith was already thirty-one when she sang, "I'm so young, I'm so goddamn young," at the end of her song "Privilege (Set Me Free)," but she understood that the number on her passport didn't mean she was fibbing. In England, punks scorned "geezers" past the age of twenty-five, pushing classic intergenerational conflicts to the point of war. But in America, where Smith, the Ramones, Debbie Harry, and other punk pioneers were not that goddamn young in the first place, punks started out fully engaged with redefining adulthood. As the first generation of rock-and-roll bohemians to watch many of their elders turn sustainable youth into simple vanity, American punks were the first to see the negative aspects of perpetual adolescence as well as its promises, and to begin seeking a balance between green impudence and mellow resignation.

By the time the Reagan era rolled around, rockers knew that growing older was inevitable, no matter how many pairs of Keds you kept in your closet. The indie scene of the 1980s and 1990s, the very one belittled for adopting boyish clothes and girlie haircuts, is the most upstanding, self-sufficient, and, arguably, mature scene rock has yet produced. Perfecting the do-it-yourself ethic punk had introduced, indie rockers make their own records, book their own clubs, publish their own fanzines, and tour in their own bands. Many indie players associated this autonomy with adolescence, partly because many were high-schoolers when they joined the scene, but also in deference to rock's portable teenage cosmos. Emphasizing the freedom that comes with thinking your own thoughts for the first time, and trying to keep that freshness going as they mature, form communities, and take on obligations, indie rockers strive for a practical version of the 1960s youth ideal.

"We are the sons of no one, bastards of young," sang the Replacements' Paul Westerberg, one of indie rock's boyish heroes. And that's precisely what we are, who have formed our lives from this haphazard culture of noise and tune and style—the daughters and sons of an ideal that was abandoned by its parents. We are striving to do it proud, and being called losers for trying. Fifteen years after Westerberg first sang those words, the bohemians of this generation are in their thirties and early forties, struggling to figure out which aspects of conventional adulthood might be acceptable and which must change. Many have personal styles and pastimes that outsiders would label less than mature, if not downright childish. But they are not children. They are adults of their own making, busy being born.

■

THE 1970s: A BRIEF INTERRUPTION

Before I delve into some stories of this difficult endeavor, I must take one moment to address a recent phenomenon that has puzzled many on-lookers. As the indie rock scene ballooned into mass-marketed alternative culture, an odd development occurred on both the mass and subcultural levels. The 1970s, once the most vilified of decades—especially abhorred by those of us who endured a youth in its clutches—suddenly became a cornucopia for nostalgics. Hipsters started flocking to clubs in platforms and polyester, and soon fashion designers like Anna Sui and Todd Oldham were copping the look. Movies like *Dazed and Confused,* which did have a hard-rockin' soundtrack, led to revivals of *Saturday Night Fever* and *Grease.* Seventies television basically got its own channel, Nick at Nite, and the sitcom I personally despised most as a child, *The Brady Bunch,* received not one but two movie-length revivals. Studio 54 reopened and the Bee Gees made it back onto the charts. Some people even started drinking Fresca again.

There are many reasons why this era, once considered contemptible by bohemians for its near-complete mutation of the radical messages of 1960s rebellion into moneymaking, hedonistic, empty-headed fluff, has now won their fervent interest. One is the millennial urge to make sense of history, the overlooked as well as the commonly celebrated. Members of the indie generation particularly feel compelled to reconsider the cultural junk food forced upon us as kids, now that we've realized that we are, at least in part, what we've eaten. Endless episodes of *The Partridge Family* and the dulcet tones of the creepy brother-sister duo the Carpenters or the bionic Swedish pop group Abba helped make us the alternately fanciful and sarcastic people we are today. So we thought we'd better check out what was going on beneath the brightly colored packaging.

We've found plenty, some of it much richer than we'd expected. It turns out that the 1970s were not as devoid of content as everyone thought. During that shell-shocked time, artists and other cultural producers waded through the aftermath of a revolution, trying to repair what had been botched and salvage what had survived. And a second wave of social insurrectionists had just begun to fight. I don't have to belabor how the sexual liberation movements of the 1970s changed America and established the cornerstone of contemporary bohemia. It's worth noting, however, that stuff once scorned as the tawdriest dilution of countercultural values—disco, which momentarily usurped rock, and television sitcoms like *The Mary Tyler Moore Show*—homed in on the desires of newly independent women and gay men more directly than did most avenues of expression in the 1960s. *The Brady Bunch* and the great *Saturday Night Fever* had serious subtexts, showing the effects of social change on mainstream institutions of the family and masculinity. And if you thought nothing could be mined from the sugar mountain of the Carpenters' music, you obviously haven't seen a bootlegged copy of indie filmmaker Todd Haynes's brilliant (and now off the market because of legal threats from Richard Carpenter) first film, *Superstar: The Karen Carpenter Story,* which employed Barbie dolls to enact the tragedy of the honey-voiced, anorexic sister.

The 1970s revival has also fueled the indie generation's ritual youthfulness. With old-fashioned notions of maturity thrown into chaos by the previous decade's youthquake, the 1970s produced strangely rarefied visions of childhood and adulthood. The Saturday-morning cartoons that dominated kids' view of the world turned young adults, like the college-age characters of *Scooby-Doo* and the rock band Josie and the Pussycats, into cartoons. Other programs, like *H. R. Pufnstuf,* used human actors as well as giant puppets cavorting across neon-colored landscapes, leading kids to imagine huge purple daisies and talking dragons as part of their world. These diverting chimeras turned the mind expansion of the hippie era into kid stuff, and created a vision of childhood as a fantasyland. They were the antidote to the other major narratives offered us, the dramas-in-real-life of our afternoons and evenings. In series like *Family* and *James at 16* and in made-for-TV movies like *Sarah T.: Portrait of a Teenage Alcoholic,* the juvenile-delinquent images of the 1950s were updated for the therapeutic age. If Saturday-morning shows painted childhood as a wonderful comic strip under marshmallow skies, these programs made adolescence a nightmare scenario of negligent parents, predatory pimps, and bad trips. In these two aspects, television portrayed the transition into adulthood as an awakening from a dream into a nightmare.

Adulthood was made even more confusing by the fact that the parents of 1970s kids seemed to want to turn themselves into walking cartoons. The overstated virility and ripe femininity of the era's clothes set the mood: the stereotypical swinging couple wore silky Qiana and ass-flattering pants, the woman revealing her nipples and the man highlighting his body hair and bulge. Icons like Burt Reynolds, the comfortable avatar of the style, and John Travolta, the skinny striver who reached it by force of will, look about as "natural" now as bewigged Elizabethan archdukes. Complemented by the high-technology craze for futuristic furniture and fluorescent lighting, the 1970s vision of sexual maturity now comes off as a synthetic joke with a deeply poignant underside. Revisiting those fashions, sinking into the sexy disquisitions of love doctors Isaac Hayes and Barry White or the castrato erotics of the Bee Gees and the young Michael Jackson, 1970s revivalists can experience a fantasy of adulthood so exaggerated that it can't help but expose the fragility of its fiction—and begin to reveal the more complicated truths beneath the Members Only veneer.

Growing up in the 1970s meant coming to terms with profound failures in the public sphere, from Watergate to the energy crisis, and with the collapse of the youth movements that had for one brief moment promised an alternative. It sometimes seemed that cartoons were the only thing left. "I think that the obsession with the Brady Bunch and Abba is a way for people to connect with their innocence, even though they know it's a joke," said Barry Walters, a connoisseur of such so-called trash. Some cynical practitioners of the 1970s revival never go beyond its cheap plastic veneer, but its savants, like Barry, know jokes are a doorway into the unconscious—a vital patch of self, and society, to explore on the journey to maturity.

■

THE MAGIC KINGDOM

"Every passion borders on the chaotic," wrote Walter Benjamin, "but the collector's passion borders on the chaos of memories." Benjamin, a rare-book collector, described the modern hunter-gatherer as part sage, interpreting arcane messages from the past, and part child, playing with worn things and making them new. "For children can accomplish the renewal of existence in a hundred unfailing ways," Benjamin continued, citing "the whole range of childlike modes of acquisition, from touching things to giving them names." The indie generation's exploration of America's rec-room junk heap works this resurrection. Collecting Barbies, board games, or battered stuffed animals is a whimsical hobby, honoring adults' enduring need to play. But the pastime can take you deeper, to dig out the meanings encoded in the trinkets that help form every child's view.

Most collectors I've met are specialists, obsessed with a particular brand of sneaker or era of cookbook. Barry Walters is different. He gathers playtime itself. He is a thirty-six-year-old music critic who writes regularly for national publications. With dark hair, a mustache, and a smart goatee, he dresses in the natty, understated style of a professional in the arts. He exported his New York accent to San Francisco ten years ago, landing the rent-controlled attic bachelor pad where he's lived ever since. It's lazy to call Barry's home a shrine, so I'll call it a diorama: his collection so effectively makes its own little universe, it could be under glass. Barry has transformed his spacious studio into a Magic Kingdom filled with department-store toys and other artifacts of fun. A mountain of Barbies and Barbie-esque dolls extends toward the ceiling near his couch. His refrigerator is covered with kiddie greeting cards and doctored photos of teen idols. One chair holds a teddy bear collection, the souvenir of a long-ago love affair. Another corner bursts with Barney dolls, and nearby a shelf contains Oscar the Grouch in his trash can and Dolly Parton as a troll. Neatly arranged on various shelves and side tables, Hello Kitty paraphernalia adds a Japanese touch. Fish tchotchkes reflect Barry's preference in pets. A disco lunch box earns an honored spot, as does the first toy Barry bought as an adult, a Pee-wee Herman doll. Mostly, though, stuff comes in multiples, dazzling in its variety. Even his bathroom boasts a New Kids on the Block towel-and-washcloth set and a rubber monster in drag.

As Barry and I sat talking on his green vinyl couch one autumn evening, uncovering the roots of this colorful preoccupation, it soon became clear where it wasn't rooted—in nostalgia for an idyllic youth. "My mother was forty-one when I was born," he said. "My siblings are now in their late forties. Growing up with them was almost like growing up with aunts and uncles. And I was really brought up to be mommy's little man.

"That's a classic psychological term," he continued. "If there is a problem in the family, you become like your mother's husband; she relies on you emotionally. My father was a binge drinker; he would be okay for months at a time, and then I would come home and he would be passed out on the kitchen floor in a puddle of urine. It was terrifying. They were about to legally separate when they had me, and when I was eleven they split up."

The scenario Barry describes sounds like one of those crisis-ridden 1970s *ABC Afterschool Specials*. He quietly adjusted to the disruptions, acquiring a dutiful clearheadedness. Part of his passion for toys stems from a desire to unravel that other television fiction, which these play-things also promote—the one that portrays childhood as strife-free. "I can see through the lies of childhood, because I've known the painful realities of it," he said.

When he was young, Barry had a roomful of toys, gestures of apology from his father, but his playmates were his teenage siblings, who danced him around to *The Ed Sullivan Show*. "Because of my older brother and sister, and my mother, too, I was immediately in love with popular culture," he recalled. "I wanted to look like a Beatle or David Cassidy. That was unusual for a kid." In high school, he started crashing the punk clubs near his upstate New York home. He never had any problem passing for older. The one time he was challenged, a couple of punk angels came to his aid. "It was a Ramones show," he remembered. "I ended up sneaking in the back door, and the Ramones let me in themselves. They just saw this kid who was desperate to get in."

I wasn't surprised to hear that Joey Ramone reached out to a hungry kid like Barry. He undoubtedly remembered the moment he realized he'd never be a proper grown-up, and the way rock saved him from having to force himself into a mold that didn't fit. "For me, the whole pop and rock world presented a form of adulthood that was not a trap," Barry said. As soon as he got a taste of that world, which honored self-expression instead of tight-lipped denial, he couldn't get enough. He moved to New York straight out of high school in 1979, attending Fordham University by day and haunting the clubs by night. Newly out of the closet, he caught the last ebullient moment of post-Stonewall, pre-AIDS gay liberation. But his tastes rarely sent him to the discos. Instead he went for New Wave.

If the polyester costumes of adulthood in the 1970s were uninten-tional parodies, New Wave stars at the turn of the decade deliberately made theater of the era's confusion about youth and maturity. Cyndi

Lauper, with her ball gowns and clownlike, multicolored hair, and Boy George, who looked like some kind of warped china doll, were adults goofing on the notion of rock as immature. Skinny-tie and science-nerd bands like Blondie and Devo did the opposite: they turned the clothes of the bureaucrat and technocrat into disguises, suggesting that beneath their professional outfits, these so-called normals were as out of control as everyone else. David Byrne of Talking Heads, in his ridiculous over-sized suit, epitomized this style, which Barry adopted. He would wear vintage suits and his father's old skinny ties, satirizing a role that he well knew men frequently failed to fulfill.

One performer who made an art of New Wave's twisted dress-up was Paul Reubens, the comedian who became infamous as Pee-wee Herman. It's amazing that *Pee-wee's Playhouse,* the series Reubens created in the mid-1980s, ever made it out of the underground and onto national television. Not only did the show barely hide its homoerotic subtext, it relentlessly satirized the moralistic and condescending approach of most kids' shows, while freeing the id-fueled perversity that lurked behind the messages. Pee-wee himself, in his natty bow tie and cosmetically bright red cheeks, was a creature caught between life stages, Barry's "little man" made comical. The fact that Reubens was banished from his TV playhouse after being caught masturbating in a Florida gay porn theater only endeared him to adult fans like Barry, who saw in his sneaky but always good-hearted episodes the assertion of their own desires, and the suppression of those desires that they'd experienced as kids.

Barry had collected a few toys before buying his Pee-wee Herman doll in 1985, but that purchase cemented the theme of his collection: the exploration of America's warped attempt to force kids into carefully controlled safe zones. "There's a part of me that is fascinated by the sickness in it," he said, holding up his latest acquisition, a Barbie-sized hamster cage. "Look. Barbie can't have normal hamsters; her hamsters have to wear lavender bows. They're not chewing on toilet-roll cardboard, they're in this little pink and blue wonderland."

In such a circumscribed world, there's an inevitable return of the repressed—as in Earring Magic Ken, a doll Mattel inexplicably released in the late 1980s. "What were they thinking?" Barry marveled, pointing to his copy of the rarity. "That's the question on every gay person's lips. Could a Ken be more gay—and, specifically, look like a really nelly hustler? He's wearing a mesh shirt and a Freedom Ring necklace and a purple leather vest!" Earring Magic Ken may have been a bizarre misstep or a sly bit of workplace subversion on the part of an anonymous designer. Barry likes the doll because its existence suggests that our culture's attempts to hide certain realities, especially ones having to do with sex, are bound to backfire.

Repression can explode when lied-to children reach adulthood, manifesting in emotional turmoil. Barry feels that his interest in children's things allow him to enjoy a form of excess less dangerous than the ones that he has seen destroy too many adults. His careful diet, rigorous gym regime, and devotion to therapy illustrate his concerns about keeping his body and soul sound. "Because of my father, I learned firsthand the dangers of addiction," he said. "I've never drunk. I got drunk once. I smoked pot once to try it, I never got high. I sniffed a bottle of Rush [amyl nitrate, the popular 1970s 'disco drug'] once and loved it, and it scared me. My form of ecstasy has always been music and popular culture." Barry's collection presents an alternative to the more dangerous forms of indulgence common in rock circles, like drug addiction, which, Barry was quick to point out, can genuinely stunt one's emotional growth.

Many social outsiders turn to drugs and other forms of destructive behavior because being excluded from the norm is a painful experience, even if your own choices lead you there. There's something wistful about Barry, presiding over his Magic Kingdom, and something willful, too: he and the friends who also collect use their avocations, in part, to make up for what society still denies them. In this enchanted world, they can reflect on their lives and hit upon insights more supposedly normal folks may never reach.

Barry gave up talking to his blood kin years ago, and he doesn't plan to have children. "I don't have a family," he said. "I have lots of friends who are either gay or unmarried. I think someone who is single, or at least childless, has the time to explore who they are, much of which was formed by their childhood. They can revisit things—in a critical way, in a celebratory way. A parent only has the time to revisit those things surreptitiously, through his or her own child."

As I departed his aerie, Barry offered one last comment on his seemingly superficial pastime. "We as a generation are a lot more serious than we're given credit for," he said. "Giving each other toys is a way to share something that we all went through together. I feel like I'm a pretty together adult, and that's partly because I acknowledge the child inside myself."

■

D R E S S I N G   U P   F O R   R E A L

Although few bohemians court their inner child as flamboyantly as Barry does, in public he exhibits only the most subtle signs of playfulness. He'll wear polka-dotted socks or a Hello Kitty watch, but you'd really have to squint to notice these accessories. "I have to present the other side of myself," he said as he talked about his toys. "I wear muted colors and traditional styles—adult styles. I buy a lot of clothes at J. Crew. And I've never been sexually attracted to young or immature people."

Barry is striving to become a good adult, at peace with his past and firmly headed toward the future. He dedicates a corner of his life to a childlike hobby to help him do that. Some of his colleagues would say that his ongoing interest in rock and roll is also childish, but he has turned that adolescent fixation into a respectable career. He has been lucky that way. Many others whose interests don't jibe with the requirements of the adult ideal either make do with the marginal existence of the low-paid slacker, or give up on their teenage dreams. Some, however, tiptoe from one existence to another, turning the childhood game of dress-up into a double life.

Sophie Chamberlin is one such tightrope walker. Sophie is a photographer, publishing her candid shots of rock musicians and regular people in local and national magazines. Her vocation offers few assurances beyond freelance contracts and the satisfactions of the work itself, and Sophie has made the process of selling herself harder by refusing to settle on one style, swinging from hard-edged photojournalism to slick studio photography to avant-garde experiments. Sophie the artist aims for risk; she's stimulated by instability to keep reaching for new views. But Sophie is also a tenured professor at a community college in the East Bay, teaching introductory composition to urban kids and immigrants. That Sophie trusts permanence and longs for it. Unlike many artists, who cultivate less glamorous practical skills once they've reached a certain age and no longer want to scrape, Sophie has always pursued both wildness and convention. She has been juggling her two lives since her mid-twenties, and she's over forty now.

She came to San Francisco after college in Oregon, looking for music and a chance to mess around. "California was the free place where you do the thing you couldn't do elsewhere," she said one afternoon when I dragged her out of her darkroom and up to North Beach for an espresso. "The bad thing, the child thing." For Sophie that meant hanging out in punk clubs like the Mabuhay Gardens and the On Broadway, looking for the rock-star heroes she'd discovered on vinyl as a baby rocker growing up in an industrial town on the Eastern Seaboard. Like Barry, Sophie wanted the opposite of what she saw in her native surroundings—trapped women like her mother, lugging groceries and feeling lost, and the overworked men like her father, with so little joy in their lives. But, having inherited her parents' pragmatism, she embarked on her explorations armed with a just-in-case scenario. In graduate school, she studied film and imagined making art-house masterpieces. She also got a master's degree in composition and started to teach.

"I would be out in the clubs until two and three in the morning, and then I'd put on my teacher uniform and go to class at eight A.M.," she remembered. "It worked out for me somehow. I needed both—anarchy and this totally structured situation."

Her punk friends thought it was funny, this image of Sophie in a navy suit with chalk in her hand. They were outrageous, with mohawks and tattoos; most worked in restaurant kitchens, hidden from the straight world, or in weirdo refuges like record stores. Sophie didn't think that she was more mature than any of her friends, but she did feel different. "It was discussed," she said. "Some people would tease me about my having to get up and go teach. But it never got to me."

At that point, Sophie saw her double life as a temporary thing, making things easier until a flash of inspiration would make her into a famous artist. But like many people pursuing parallel paths, she found her commitment to both deepening. She liked teaching more than you're supposed to dig your day job; working with students engaged her mind and made a tangible mark on the world. After two years at school, a strange set of circumstances drew her deeper in. She and a few other part-timers at the college were teaching classes with writing labs, working more than the allotted amount for uninsured, unpensioned staff. The union that represented them decided to fight this unfair practice and set a legal precedent. By sheer stroke of luck, because she happened to have taken on such a class that term, Sophie found herself in on a union settlement that led to an offer of immediate tenure.

"The only time I ever thought about the future was when I took that tenure-track job," she said. "Suddenly, I had to consider retirement plans. That makes you think, Fuck, I'm gonna die."

Sophie might have resolved her differing impulses at that point by adopting the life of an academic professional and making film a weekend hobby. But her muse threw her a curve one spring when, on a whim, she decided to take a photojournalism class.

"I went to that class and it was like, 'This gives me something to believe in.' It was like religion. I found my tribe," she said, flashing her wide smile. She spent the next summer sitting out on her stoop with her friend Matt, a radio scanner between them and cameras at the ready, waiting for fire alarms.

"We tried to get work by chasing fires," she explained. "If you photographed in the middle of the night, nobody else wanted to work those hours. It was the only way you could get your pictures into the dailies. Matt got his photos onto the front page. He was more aggressive. He's a full-time photojournalist now."

Hanging out with Matt taught Sophie that she wasn't ready to settle on teaching, but neither did she relish the limits practitioners placed around her new preoccupation. Photojournalism thrilled her, but she wanted to tell longer stories through her images, something shooting for the dailies didn't offer. Plus, she was already in her late twenties, older and less willing to do just anything for work than Matt and the other camera cowboys the papers liked to hire. So she carved out a few opportunities, forging ties with a small magazine that would publish her photo essays and hooking up with an annual arts festival that she could document over the years. She didn't really want a job with a newspaper, she told herself. She wasn't willing to let her hard-won passion for photography be diluted by the drudgery of shooting press conferences where nothing happened except the mayor shaking somebody's hand.

A new presence in her life kept her artistic senses honed: a lover whom she'd met in the unlikeliest of places. Donald Tsai had just arrived from Hong Kong when he showed up in one of Sophie's night classes looking to hone his language skills. His English was fairly low-level, but a few after-class conversations revealed that he knew a lot about film. In fact, he'd worked in the movie business back home, before deciding to try his luck as a graphic artist in America. Eventually Sophie acquiesced to his endless offers of after-class coffee, and six months later he moved in with her. Sophie didn't expect this love affair to unspool into yet another double life, but it did. The language barrier made it hard for Donald to establish close ties with Sophie's punk friends. For a long time, she didn't mind this; she loved him, and cherished the small realm they established at home, cooking curries and pasta, renting videos, discussing the meaning of art. "Donald is really creative," she said. "He lives inside his head. Has a little world of his own in there." Having access to that world rejuvenated Sophie.

Donald wanted to get married, but Sophie never could see their compartmentalized love encompassing enough to merit that vow. He moved into his own apartment; for years their relationship was like moonlighting, with each partner going about his or her business during the day and turning toward the other at sundown. After turning thirty-five, though, Sophie began to wonder if she shouldn't wish for a more ordinary love. She tried to integrate Donald into her other social circles, dragging him to the rock shows she photographed and even to a few academic dinner parties. But he didn't like the crowds, and she felt burdened by his presence. Finally, after a decade of wavering, she broke up with him.

Now she was single, and ready to hunt down a regular life. Or so she thought. Her career was still split, which she knew bothered her colleagues in academia and confused her photographer friends. Her old pal Matt kept trying to line her up with regular newspaper gigs until she finally convinced him that she liked not knowing her next assignment. And her department chair at school finally gave up on pushing her toward a higher-paying, more administrative role.

Sophie has accepted that she makes her more conservative workmates uncomfortable. "They don't like that I don't want to play the game," she said. "They know that I have another career, and that certain days I won't work, because of my other career. They see that I don't want to be a full-time professional. That challenges them."

Sophie has resolved that her divided selves can learn from each other—that the artist can take a few tips from the professional about negotiation and self-respect, and the pro can honor the artist's insistence on making room for her vision. "It took a long time for me to take on the identity, that I was a photographer," she reflected. "It was hard for me to charge money for my work, to admit that it was a profession. Because it was a love. It was a gut love. It took many years to go from saying, 'Oh, my God, you're gonna pay me for that?' to 'You are gonna pay me! And it's gonna be like this.' "

Part of her new decisiveness, she says, is inspired by her new man. After breaking with Donald, Sophie was determined to find a guy who would be a proper husband. She met a few who suited her requirements, and she might have settled into a comfortable middle age somewhere in the East Bay suburbs, with a new kid and a career that would make a great hobby, as many of her friends had. Instead, she hooked up with Ian Baxter. Mr. Wrong.

Ian is a twenty-three-year-old bike messenger with a mellow outlook, enhanced by daily marijuana smoking. He has a bleached-blond crew cut and three tattoos on his torso. For fun, he plays bongos in a weekend free-for-all jam session on the steps of U.C.–Berkeley's Sproul Hall. Sophie met him when he posed seminude for a magazine photo spread she shot on "San Francisco's Most Daring Dudes." She didn't expect much beyond a entertaining fling; she ended up with a serious companion.

"Ian may be really young, and certainly there are parts of him that are rebellious," she admitted. "But he's eighty years old in certain ways. He is a very independent thinker, strong in being able to say no. That is the thing that I have been working on. I'm trying to form my own voice. One of the reasons I'm attracted to him is that he's done that.

"That has something to do with your child thing," she continued, homing in on my inquiry into sustainable youth. "One of the luxuries of being a child is integrity. It's really tough when you're older; I think it gets harder. Acceptance is certainly part of maturing, but adulthood in its negative aspect is just swallowing life whole, not sorting it out. Integrity is a gift of youth, and then afterwards you either maintain it or let it go."

Maintain it or let it go—that's been the pushmi-pullyu in Sophie's circuitous quest for maturity since she first woke up after a punk show and put on her navy blue teacher suit. Many bohemians grow into similar manifold lives, choosing snarled complexity over the relief that comes with convincing yourself life can have a solid center. Sophie has come to terms with disorder by now. She and Ian are currently looking for a house for her to buy; he doesn't have the money to go in on it, and she doesn't expect him to last as long as the water heater, but that's okay. Sometimes she wonders if her decision to never really make a decision about her life's purpose has muted the expressions of her potential. But every time she thinks about sticking to one direction, she feels her future narrow. And Sophie never wants to stop loving the thought of the future. She's seen too many grown-ups go through that.

■

THE MOVING SPOTLIGHT

Children learn by example, but there's recently been debate over whether they absorb more from their parents, who exemplify what they could become, or their peers, whose vistas unfold alongside their own. Sophie and Barry were kids who longed to be different from their families, soaking up lessons from them that felt more cautionary than commendable. As teens, when they looked around for people to admire, they began at the source of their comfort and inspiration: rock and roll. Joey Ramone and Patti Smith possessed few virtues in the eyes of their folks, but Sophie and Barry believed that those artists' self-assertions represented the good life. Yet what they sensed in the music and the strutting images that promised so much was only part of the real life of rock and roll. Onstage, musicians may transform themselves within the rhythm's alchemical liquid, but they're only human before and after the show.

Rock stars are our avatars of perpetual adolescence; some have used their power carelessly, even destructively, while others have forged new paths to maturity. But most rock musicians never get to be stars. They may never make it further than their basement rehearsal rooms. Many subsist on the love of a few dedicated fans and the pleasure they get from their work. If they do sign a record contract, they could end up making the same kind of living as a waiter in a not very fancy restaurant, or a record-store manager. They'd get no health insurance, no stability, and certainly less credit in the straight world than the average maître d'. Yet these strugglers continue to live the dream. Inspired by their idols, whether Mick Jagger or Courtney Love or Method Man, to pursue sustainable youth, they occupy a shaky position in their communities, envied for their freedom and eyed warily for their defiance.

E. Blake Davis's tale could belong to many who've chosen this trick-ster life. He never wanted to be anything but a musician, and he's spent years defending that desire. He rose, he fell, he rose again, he took a break, he's surviving. Blake has achieved adult success more than once, in the eyes of his family and peers, only to be plunged back into the role of the eternal adolescent. By now, he's developed a fatalistic calm about his life's grand design.

I bribed Blake with a Thai lunch of crunchy spring rolls and basil chicken so he'd tell me the saga of his ricochets between fame and frustration. He looked a little more worn than the last time I'd seen him, when his band, Papa's Culture, played Central Park Summerstage in New York. Then, he seemed like the reincarnation of Cab Calloway as a chubby white guy—porkpie hat, spiffy resort clothes, a wicked gleam in his slightly buggy brown eyes. After the show, in more casual garb, he was the Blake I'd known since 1990, when I lived in an East Bay apartment a few blocks from the record store where he then worked, a charming jokester with apple cheeks and a grin that sometimes sagged a little under the weight of his ambitions.

At the Thai restaurant, that burden seemed heavier than before, but optimism still gleamed through. Blake had wanted nothing but music his entire life, he told me. The love began when he was a boy in West Hollywood, spending his nights pondering the meaning of Neil Young's album *Rust Never Sleeps*. "Even when you're eleven years old, you listen to 'Ride My Llama' or some other song, it's like he's showing you this hidden world. It might be a long time before you figure out what that world is, but it's great." Hooked into music's beautiful firmament, Blake bounced around from one style to another. He went New Wave, dressing in kimonos and dyeing his hair, and playing guitar in a band that sounded like the Psychedelic Furs. Moving north for college, he started spinning records in the deejay booth of a dive called the Birdcage, refining his skills at toasting, the Jamaican style of rap.

Biding his time with odd jobs and occasional schoolwork, Blake wondered if he would ever find his spot in the rock-and-roll galaxy. He didn't have a great voice, and his guitar playing, while passable, posed no threat to the aces he met kicking around in bands in Oakland. He found indie rock boring but didn't really know how to blend funk and rap to get the sound he wanted. Then he met a guy named Harley White, hanging out at the Birdcage. The two struck up a songwriting friendship and made some demos; Blake sent copies to everyone he knew in the music business—roadies for local rap groups, his old band-mates, music critics (me, for example) who sold their reviewers' copies of albums at the record store, and a guy he knew in L.A. who'd just signed a production deal with Island Records.

"This guy was like a very cool big brother to me and a lot of my friends," Blake said. "He knew the Beastie Boys; he couldn't be in this restaurant without somebody important coming up and saying hi. He took ten bands to Chris Blackwell, [then] the president of Island Records. Blackwell's on the phone all day, and my pal is playing him tapes. I probably got signed because Blackwell wasn't paying attention." Blake affected the English accent of a harried Blackwell. "Who's that young man? Can he do a record cheap? Okay." He smirked. "I got in on the coattails of a Hollywood schmooze guy who happened to be a friend of a friend."

Thus did Papa's Culture become a national act. This thrilling moment only lasted long enough for Blake and Harley to gather up a handful of musicians and record the album. Before they even got to tour, Blake's fancy friend lost his production deal and the project was canned. The grown-up feelings that had surged in Blake while he negotiated the Island contract and then led his new team in the studio dissipated when he realized how easily Papa's Culture could be terminated.

"I thought I was being responsible when I read the first contract," Blake said. "I can read, I thought. I've been to college, and it's a good thing I learned about this contract stuff from reading all those fan magazines when I was ten! Really, I was just a kid and I didn't know what was going on."

It seemed that Blake and Harley weren't growing up to be pop stars after all. The record-store job beckoned. But before he could sign his first returning time sheet, Elektra Records decided to give them another chance.

"A friend of Harley's old band manager who worked for Elektra picked up our contract," Blake explained. "We got really focused. We got ten thousand dollars or something. Of course most of it went to pay off student loans, but we did invest two thousand in rehearsing for a month. Harley's sister Erin joined the band as a singer, my friend Jim signed up on drums. We'd done the album that Elektra had bought with completely different musicians. But this was a hot band."

This incarnation of Papa's Culture did simmer, blending 'round-the-world rhythms and wry melodies into carnival music for a fantasy cruise ship. Erin had a sweet soul wail that complemented Blake's hoarse toasting style, Jim kept a mighty beat, and a sprightly horn section added extra sauce. When I saw them in Central Park, the band rocked the rainy June afternoon. But Elektra did not know how to roll with this Papa's Culture. "The label didn't like the band because it didn't sound like the record," Blake said. "It was more an in-your-face, rockin', groovin' band." Finally ready to conquer the world, Papa's Culture was dropped by its label once again.

At least Blake had managed to impress his dad—the same dad who had made him throw out his Kiss records and denounce rock's evil influence when he got busted in seventh grade for trying to sell fake pot made out of oregano. "When we went on tour, my dad sent me this letter," Blake said. "It said something like, We didn't think you could do it but you did. Like, You've really shown to me that you could make music your life, and you've proven the cynics wrong and I've proud of you. It was intense. Of course, that was a great moment, and then the next month we got dropped."

Despite being denied what finally looked like a career, Blake made sure his dad wouldn't revert to his former opinion, at least not right away. With a great bunch of musicians behind his ideas, he wanted to grab his chance to carve out that space in music's hidden world. He took charge of the band's business, arranging gigs all over Northern California. This, he says, is when he really started feeling like something other than an oversized kid.

"I kick-started the band into being a fierce working band," he said. "We were making money, we were taking control over our own lives, we weren't going to let any corporations tell us we weren't a good band. When you deal with clubs or restaurants, weddings and things, then you feel like you're an adult, you're responsible, you fill out the tax forms and all that."

Papa's Culture achieved local celebrity status. They were selling out the big clubs and getting played on local radio. At a show in Sacramento, Blake met a woman named Brandy, and the encounter turned out to be more than a rock-and-roll one-night stand. The two became a steady item. His life was falling into order. He'd found a way to be a grown man and be himself. "I'd always dressed weird, got up late, stayed up late," he said. "My mom, who had always encouraged me, would say, 'I'm so glad you found a job that lets you sleep in.' " Blake never got cocky about his success, and he didn't go for the high life; he concentrated on keeping Papa's Culture tight and marketable. For a while, it seemed he'd written himself a ticket to adulthood.

But bands, with all those different personalities flying around, rarely stay together very long. His mates' own grown-up choices started leading them away. Half the members went on the road as sidepeople with big-budgeted stars like Sheryl Crow and John Hiatt. Harley decided to cultivate his own projects; soon his sister, Erin, joined him. By 1996, Blake was throwing together makeshift versions of the group just to keep the money coming in. What had been a mission had become a chore.

So he quit. Back to square one. He found new creative partners and started spending hours working on Sunkist, a darker, trippier project, something based on recordings instead of a live show. "I go to the studio four or five days a week. I try to work as hard as I can," he said. Every so often he'll haul out the Papa's Culture concept for a wedding or a club gig, but his attentions are elsewhere. Unfortunately, so is his income.

After making it in the role of the visible, economically viable working musician, Blake is now back to being the sort of working musician who doesn't get paid for his labors. He and Brandy, who got married in the summer of 1997, are borrowing from Blake's mom to get by. He is lucky to have a parent who trusts his talent enough to invest in the fallow period while he's reorganizing his imagination. As for himself, he's philosophical, and ready to take a day job.

"Pizza delivery, I think, is my next move," he confided. "I know that sounds funny, but I think I'm going to do it. It's like the drummer says in that movie *Spinal Tap*: 'I'd like to be a shoe salesman. What size, sir?' I'd like to be a pizza delivery boy. Pepperoni, ma'am?"

A quick chuckle and a familiar grin didn't entirely convince me that Blake was joking. Any other friend who'd ridden a hard goal as far as Blake had would have felt degraded hawking pies, but he had reached a denouement. "I have my life's work," he said. "Most people never find that, honestly. I believe that following it is good for the world."

Having touched success and fought against catastrophe, Blake accepts the artist's role as a free particle in a society that prefers its members fixed. He's found hardship in that position, but also power. The contradictions amuse and enliven him. "This is what it's like to be a musician," he said. "Papa's Culture was working at a wedding this past summer. The bride and groom had invited the musicians to eat; they loved the band and they wanted us to be merry and have fun with them. But the caterers had miscounted the number of guests. So while the band was in line for food, they started commenting, 'Oh, we're running out of food—well, if the band wouldn't eat . . .' A couple of the guys in the band just put their plates down and left. And I realized, that's a centuries-old feud—the musicians' place at a wedding.

"At another wedding this past summer, for a couple I didn't know well, I was playing a duet with another guitarist during the ceremony. The bride came around the corner, and she looked gorgeous. She looked right at me and gave me a little wink. I'm playing and trying not to turn red! Once again, this is a centuries-old relationship, this time played out between the bride and the musician.

"You start to feel like a part of a tradition," he concluded. "You realize that the things that happen at the gig have happened many times before and will happen many times in the future. It's a role." Some people say that being an adult means knowing your place in the world. As slippery as it sometimes seems, Blake knows his.

◼

R A I S I N G   E A C H   O T H E R

Blake has crafted an identity from the myths the culture has thrown at him: circusmaster, jazzbo, life of the party, trickster. But there is a more communal way to grow up within the rock-and-roll world—through the smaller, interlocking spheres of a particular scene, where overarching images matter less than the reference points created among a group of friends. The hardcore punk scene became another family for kids in the late 1970s and early 1980s, and throughout its evolution from a subterranean network to a viable (and, purists think, corrupted) commercial arena, it has served as a guide for people exploring new lifestyles, just as surely as church groups and sororities have for more conventional types.

Lynn Perko and Jone Stebbins are two such punk-bred soul sisters, devoted to the scene's ethic since they played together in a Reno band called the Wrecks in their early teens. Now they are working musicians in a group that has a chance to keep them fully employed, if not make them superstars—a band whose name, Imperial Teen, reflects the sustainable youth that punk idealizes. The name isn't meant to imply some jailbait fetishization, though. On one level it's a joke, since three of the group's four members are in their thirties and well over their days hanging out in club parking lots waiting for somebody else to buy the beer. But "Imperial Teen" also implies a tribute, to that youthful integrity Sophie talked about. The wholeheartedness of youth can be noble; it fills you with the energy to try what scares you by convincing you that your beliefs are worth everything, maybe even your life. The thirtysomething punks in Imperial Teen have held on to that conviction much longer than convenient.

Lynn and Jone have worked hard to stay true to punk since those first basement gigs in Reno. As women in a scene dominated by boys, both made sure to protect themselves. Jone went the route of the double life, going to beauty school and becoming a sought-after stylist; she still occasionally cuts hair at a ritzy Pacific Heights salon. Lynn, who has a hard time imagining anything more satisfying than sweating behind her drum kit, has maintained financial equilibrium by holding on to a waitress job at the same China Basin bar where I first met her in 1987. As lifetime members of the punk club, they patched together comfort from whatever resources presented themselves. It hasn't been easy, but they've succeeded by relying on each other and keeping their priorities straight.

"Punk-rock values are timeless," said Jone. She offered me a list of punk principles: "Integrity, a sense of yourself, not being afraid to challenge authority or to question why. Taking an active part in your life, rather than just being a consumer. Being ready to blaze a different path or try something new. And to feel really strongly, even if you change your opinion."

"We're still punk rockers, but we're not stereotypes," added Lynn. I stifled a smile; this milk-fed Amazon, who in another life would have been an Olympic skier or a forward in the WNBA, never fit anyone's stereotype. When I first saw Lynn play, she was in the great mid-1980s San Francisco band Sister Double Happiness and was already the object of adoration from women on the scene. Few women drummers were visible then, and none drove the beat with as much fervor. To watch Lynn Perko drum is to witness a spiritual and physical transfiguration, a woman fully in touch with her higher power. The sight has inspired more than one woman I know to risk exploring her own.

"It was like being reborn, in a way," Lynn said about going to her first punk show as a teen in Reno, a Seven Seconds concert held in some kid's rec room. She'd always loved the big noise of Led Zeppelin and Pink Floyd, but here was a racket being made by people like herself. That same year, she met Jone and the other girls in the Wrecks, and joined up when their drummer got grounded. The band broke up after high school, but Lynn had found her passion. The physical act of drumming, coupled with the peaceful anarchism preached by the positive wing of hardcore punk, became her sustenance.

She moved to San Francisco and tried out for the Dicks, a hardcore band led by the charismatic Gary Floyd. Lynn was the only girl to show up for the audition, and she got the gig. She ended up staying on the road with the band for two years.

"The road was the worst," she recalled. "Staying in people's living rooms, making a dollar, five dollars a day. I got really burned out. I felt like this was a go-nowhere scene. All these neo-Nazi punks started moving in and ruining it. I didn't want to be involved, because I was still a normal person, in a way. I liked to work out, to eat right. I had a curling iron plugged in backstage, and people were making horrible fun of me!"

By the time the hardcore scene got nasty, Lynn was twenty-four years old. "Some people were getting too fucked up on drugs," she said. "It was just terrible. I didn't want to live my life in a club where people are puking." Her bandmate Gary agreed; the often crass machismo of the hardcore scene no longer worked for him either, as he tried to reconcile his rocker side with his gay lifestyle and growing preoccupation with spirituality. Sister Double Happiness was the vehicle for Gary and Lynn's more adult brand of punk. The band lasted for eight years.

Meanwhile, Jone, who had moved to San Francisco a few years after Lynn, was making her own changes. "I'd been doing the punk thing for ten years," she said. "If you get into music when you get to college, you'll be sick of the bullshit at thirty. But I was already sick of it at twenty-four." Jone immersed herself in learning to style hair, but she kept a finger in the music world, working behind the scenes at local record labels and clubs. Much of the indie-punk network that thrives today is sustained by young people like Jone, who long ago passed through their adolescent rebellion and have turned to the business of keeping the community in touch with itself. These are the entrepreneurs who distribute the music, edit the fanzines that publicize bands, and run the venues that give them a place to play. "I thought punk was a valuable form of communication," she said. "And I had spent so much time doing fanzines and playing in bands and booking clubs that it was a marketable skill."

Contrary to the cliché of punk rockers as a bunch of brew-swilling, needle-popping layabouts, Lynn and Jone embody the scene's enduring work ethic. Operating on the edge of the mainstream, punks and indie rockers have no choice but to tend to their own successes. Their criteria simply differ from the ones that preoccupy most strivers—they're not aiming for a fancy car and a fat 401(k) (although health insurance is one reason many hold down a day job). Adult success, in this scene, isn't just about getting stuff for yourself. It's also about realizing the chance to share what you have with others.

Which doesn't mean that punks don't occasionally imagine a more affluent existence. "Sometimes I just love to get into the car and go out and shop at Target," said Jone. "I can get really into it. You've got a list, and things are checked off, and you feel like you've really done something! I think, God, this is great, I'd love to be a suburban housewife."

"I fantasize about blowing all this off someday and just changing my identity," Lynn admitted. "I think I could do it for a while. But then my skin would start to crawl! I couldn't survive in the suburbs without medication."

The friends agree that their male counterparts don't seem to entertain the same ambivalent attraction to middle-class comforts. Jone speculates that the maternal urge forces women rockers to look beyond the next tour. "You've got to make a home for your baby, if you're gonna have one," she said. "You have to lay the groundwork." Without a boyfriend, she hasn't resolved this part of her life yet, although she says she might hit up a gay pal if the ideal straight guy never comes along. Lynn lives with her mate, Dan, who has nothing to do with the music scene—he's a former European-league basketball player who now works in the state ferry system. They've discussed parenthood, but she remains unsure.

"We talk about it every four months or whatever," she said. "He would totally watch the child if I was away on tour, or his family would. I think I'd be a great mom, but sometimes I just don't know if I can have a child. The absolute inescapability of it all."

Like many people who sidestepped the usual career-family path in their twenties, Lynn and Jone are now having a hard time fitting such agendas into their lives. This isn't because they are selfish or capricious. It's because the conventional roles are still so narrowly dictated that variation sometimes seems impossible. "We could be each other's nannies," Lynn said wistfully, imagining Imperial Teen morphing into a family business. She's seen friends in bands opt for the family way and just vanish, into some other version of life that she rejected long ago. Most people she knows are still like her, waiting a little longer, hoping for some possibility of integration.

"For most people, music is part of their young lives," said Jone. "When you're a certain age, you stop, and you start becoming a mom."

As punk grows older, though, and as more women refuse to abandon the freedom it gave them, other forms of adulthood are surfacing. Lynn and Jone point to these with hope.

"I was hanging out with a friend of mine today who's thirty-three, and she has a twelve-year-old daughter," said Jone. "She's an alternative mom: she's got tattoos, and her own hair salon, and a lemon-yellow Cadillac. Her daughter goes to a really hoity-toity private school. My friend drops her kid off at school on her motorcycle. She goes to Mom Day, and has to relate to all these rich ladies. At first they may be put off, but she commands respect, because she's so okay with where she is."

That's one of the things rock and roll was about in the first place—being okay with where you were, even if it wasn't where your parents or the television said you should be. That openness is what adulthood is necessarily evolving toward. With the old institutions broken down, and no new patterns set yet, the only model that makes sense would honor the realities of the moment as much as it would any fabricated ideas about the future. Sustainable youth aims for that, while rejecting thoughtless immaturity—Lynn turns green when she walks through the Haight and sees costume punks still wearing the fashions, chanting the choruses, and copping the attitude she gave up long ago. She doesn't look for punk on the outside now. It's her internal code. "I still have a little time," she said. "It's not like, if the band doesn't make it, it's all over. Whatever we do, it's us, and that feels good. Anything can or can't happen." Spoken like a real adult.

7

.

SELLING OUT

I T was 1992 when I boarded a United Airlines plane bound for New York City, clutching a one-way ticket. I was leaving home again, this time with far more trepidation than I'd had in my first reckless dash from the familiar. I'd grown painfully attached to the familiar, in fact— and not only to my beloved Bay Area, with its daydream-colored sunlight, and its produce plucked from heaven, and its girls in their thrift-store dresses wandering the streets. I had ties now: a boyfriend I lived with and loved; friends who'd seen me through too many drunken nights and lucid mornings to be anything but family. The night before I left Oakland, I lay on the bare futon that was the only thing not boxed up in our house and wept for hours. I wasn't bluffing. I didn't want to go.

Boarding that plane the next day, I felt as fuzzy as I had six weeks earlier, when Jon Pareles, the chief pop critic of *The New York Times,* rang me up and asked me if I'd be interested in coming east and working for him. The phone call was the bolt from the blue that every writer dreams about, but I politely staved off Jon's professional advances. I had just entered the Ph.D. program at U.C.–Berkeley; my immediate plans revolved around mastering Old English. "No thank you," I said. "I'm previously committed." I hung up and went back to *Sir Gawain and the Green Knight*.

"Ann," my boyfriend Eric called from the living room, "did you just turn down an offer from *The New York Times*?!?" Yes, I said. Within seconds, he was handing me the receiver and demanding that I call Jon Pareles back. "You can't just turn down *The New York Times*," he announced. I could, I protested. It was easy. The one time I'd been in New York I'd been plagued with a colossal sinus headache and an overwhelming sense of my own insignificance. The myths of that metropolis did not intrigue me; I was a West Coast loyalist who liked Nathanael West much more than John Dos Passos, X's *Los Angeles* better than anything by the New York Dolls, and burritos more than pizza. Not to mention ocean sunsets, which I knew I'd die without.

Besides, I reasoned, as a writer I had my audience—the cappuccino sippers, retail clerks, and bike messengers who read my stuff in the local alternative weekly, where I'd worked for five years. I loved the letters they sent and the way they struck up conversations with me at the Paradise Lounge. Being a big fish in a small pond suited me fine. I had no yen for sophisticated cocktail parties where elegant experts posed in their Armani and gossiped about the goings-on at *The New Yorker*. More than that, I had no idea how to write for people who weren't like me, who wouldn't get my offhand references to local bars like the Albion and legends like Don Ed Hardy the tattoo king. I wrote in a language bound by my physical world. Trying anything else, I thought, would cost me my voice.

Eric wasn't having any of that. He'd always thought of things on a different scale, having grown up near New York's centers of cultural power, where bohemians ruled not just their own forts but the overarching institutions that filtered their ideas and customs into the mainstream—the publishing industry; Ivy League academia; the entertainment biz. Eric wanted me to call Jon Pareles back, even though it might mean entrusting our relationship to the gods of long distance, because he believed in the connection between the place where we lived and Out There.

And so I came to confront the eternal bohemian predicament. Would I trespass beyond the little world I'd so eagerly homesteaded? If so, what elements of it could I carry with me, and would they die when exposed to foreign air? Would I be susceptible to the virus of conformity? If it infected me, would I ever be allowed to come back home?

These questions vexed me as I took the phone from Eric and dialed that New York number. Some seed of purpose made me put my apprehensions aside. I was a writer, after all—reaching people was my gift and my calling. My loudmouth ways had lifted me out of teenage-nerd obscurity and connected me to other freaks as I roamed through my twenties. I'd found a comfort zone in bohemia, a place where the weirdos did win. But I never forgot my past as a very uncool kid hearing an Elvis Costello record and tingling at the sound of a voice that reminded me of myself. One reason I write is to reach other kids like that, to give them what counsel and hope I can offer. Another reason is to suggest to the straight world that those kids, and the grown-ups they become, are worth more than it thinks. Pop music had given me a cunning way to promote my views and make a living at the same time. Working at the *Times* would greatly expand my range.

I knew that it would be harder to stake my ground in New York, but this offer had landed in my lap, and it seemed like my duty as a rabble-rouser to take it. So I said yes to Jon. Then everything moved so fast I didn't have time for second thoughts. Before the Northern California winter brought its damp chill to our underheated apartment, I was furnishing a dusty one-bedroom in Brooklyn and trying not to drop lunch crumbs in my lap in the presence of editors who talked about their summers in the Hamptons. I had entered the well-appointed rooms of Upper Bohemia, where the underground's innovations and insights are translated to the larger public.

Despite the enduring romance of the obscure genius, most of the bohemians the general public knows about, from Balzac to Eddie Vedder, eventually land in Upper Bohemia. It is home to the artists whose work consumers actually buy, and to the journalists, gallery owners, theatrical producers, scholars, and small businesspeople who have made such transactions possible. No longer hard up materially, these lucky few face another struggle: to carry the values they developed apart from society into its conformist heart. "There are always those who believe that they can take convention or leave it," wrote Russell Lynes, identifying this caste in 1953. "Those who leave it with a flourish are true Bohemians. It is those who manage to both take it *and* leave it who are the true Upper Bohemians."

Bohemians have always waffled between repulsion and attraction to the bourgeoisie that shares their space like a noisy next-door neighbor. "What gives bohemia its love and rage and creativity is its uneasy embrace with the enemy," the historian Stephen Duncombe once noted. Upper Bohemians play out this drama publicly. They embody the specter of compromise that presses hard upon all of us. As the unofficial conscience of the bourgeoisie, bohemia can never exist entirely apart from the mainstream its denizens claim to abhor. No matter how many inner circles bohemians create, or how sternly they sanction members who exit, there is no truly separate sphere. We are city dwellers, consumers, workers, members of families and neighborhoods and fluid social networks; we still live within the system we want so much to change. Even rebellion demands involvement, with its threat of absorption. As the Clash's Joe Strummer once so eloquently put it, "He who fucks nuns will later join the Church."

Faced with this reality, bohemia's ideologues have come up with a few criteria for judging Upper Bohemians, discerning real sellouts from those tricky figures who cross into the mainstream with integrity. Bob Timm, a ska fan who writes an on-line column about his favorite musical scene, recently laid out some parameters that could apply to any moment in bohemia's history. Selling out, he explained, comes in three varieties. The Abandon Sell-Out involves discarding your lifestyle, and therefore your beliefs, to make money: a ska band turns to pop metal; a Revolutionary Communist Party member takes a job at Archer Prewitt. The Exploit Sell-Out entails going into the mainstream, too, but this time you take your lifestyle or artistic expression with you, and cash in on the subculture in ways that offend other members: a ska band reduces the music's good-time humor to grotesque self-parody, degrading the tradition in order to appeal to ignorant listeners' misunderstandings about it; a pro-sex feminist poses for *Playboy,* turning her progressive take on sexual liberation into old-fashioned self-directed sexism. The Poser Sell-Out applies to those on the other side of the divide, who adopt elements of the bohemian lifestyle because they think it will pay off: a metal band turns to ska the moment it becomes fashionable; a tabloid television producer starts filming segments about Lower East Side squats because they're "edgy." Virtually every tale of bohemian compromise involves some combination of these transgressive acts.

Bohemians fear such temptations because their kinship seems more conditional than that shared within most communities. Bohemians draw together to cultivate a set of shared interests and beliefs. They are not necessarily linked by gender, class, or race—the three markers that, no matter how fluid postmodernists claim they are, are genuinely tough to abandon. An "ex–colored man" (as the writer James Weldon Johnson once named the African-American sellout) can't really shed his race, as many painful tales of passing have proven. But an ex-bohemian can abandon the individual mannerisms and shared beliefs that set him apart. An increased income and a more secure social position, a change in neighborhoods or participation in customs like marriage or child-rearing, all tend to change your worldview. "You'll be yelling for lower taxes pretty soon," said a friend when Eric and I bought our tiny brick row house near downtown Brooklyn. "And you'll be calling the cops on the kids hanging out, playing hip-hop on their boom boxes on the corner."

I haven't disrupted any street parties yet, and I happily pay my property taxes (which, since my neighborhood's not so ritzy, are disturbingly low). But I know what my friend means. If the main function of bohemianism, beneath its shifting pageant of styles and art movements, is to rock society's foundations, then fulfilling even one of that society's expectations can feel like a dangerous concession. Ambivalence and self-delusion mark the great sellouts in literature, from the pompous journalistic hacks in George Gissing's Victorian novel *New Grub Street* to the tragic strivers in the Hollywood horror tales of Nathanael West, Ernest Lehman, Budd Schulberg, and F. Scott Fitzgerald. The biographies of Fitzgerald and other writers who attempted to make a California buck at the cost of their physical or spiritual health lend the fictional tales a sordid patina of reality, and they seem even more pointed as the culture of celebrity grows like a bacterium. When the most popular male talk-show host in America is a libertarian who wears assless pants and the biggest pop star is a deliberately single mom who has repeatedly taken on the Catholic church, living an alternative lifestyle seems more like a smart bit of self-promotion than a righteous venture.

Bohemian enclaves usually blossom in overlooked corners of society, and their relative isolation creates a certain freedom. It's easier to try new things when virtually no one is looking; you don't have to deal with others' judgments or misinterpretations, and the lack of demand for the stuff that interests you keeps costs down. One problem with aiming to be the next Madonna or Howard Stern is the effect such moves have on the shared space of the fringe. Sellouts who export bohemia inevitably bring curious onlookers back in. The art critic Dave Hickey has dubbed these trespassers "looky-loos." Essentially, they're tourists: people who descend on a locale, spend their money on the most marketable native artifacts and customs, and depart without really absorbing the atmosphere. When bohemian centers become tourist destinations, the real work of transforming the basics of love, work, and identity—not to mention the more challenging creative endeavors of artists and seers—is obscured by a spectacle that turns such efforts into routines performed by oddballs who make themselves into jokes.

Many bohemians insist that the worst kind of sellout is the person who participates in such tourist attractions, which elevate style over substance although only substance—our ideas and values and genuine art, not our cool clothes or yummy coffee drinks—stands the test of time. Yet the tourist trade has always helped bohemians survive. The sociologist Caroline F. Ware noted the presence of tour buses in Greenwich Village in the 1920s, carrying out-of-towners eager to peep into its dens of free love and hashish smoking. Tourists similarly invaded Haight-Ashbury after the Summer of Love, and now cruise Capitol Hill in Seattle in search of the ghost of grunge. A modern-day Lot seeking the sinless in these Sodoms would be hard-pressed to find a boutique owner who'd refuse to sell to a looky-loo, or a starving artist who'd pass on lunch paid for by a corporate talent scout.

Pretending that bohemia exists apart from its own commodification is futile. Whether or not we resist buying and selling goods outside our own little circle of pre-approved participants (and no merchant interested in keeping up with her rent is likely to maintain such boundaries for long), we're still partners in the fundamental bourgeois game of trading money for identity. In that game, the chips belong to whoever can afford them: tourists and corporate vultures as well as you and me. This recognition has disillusioned many would-be cultural revolutionaries. But the crisis creates the very challenge that makes bohemia relevant. The goal is to figure out what it means to be a self-styled outsider when there's no outside. Taking this step, which inevitably feels like a compromise, requires a serious adjustment in perspective. It forces us to admit that we are linked to the larger world in ways that we despise as well as those we might accept. Some people can't deal with this knowledge. I've certainly wrestled with it. And while I was trying to make my peace with selling out, one of the bohemias to which I pledge allegiance wrestled with this problem almost to its death.

■

C O R P O R A T E   R O C K   S T I L L   S U C K S

Indie rock was a little world until it became the whole world, briefly; then it collided with the sun and shattered into meteors and ash. There you have my attempt to condense the saga of modern-day bohemia's biggest sellout act (or subversion, for any optimists still out there) into a cautionary bedtime story for the little rebels coming up now. Over the past five years, such retellings, more violently cast, have often reduced this fruitful, cataclysmic era to a sob story. Hopelessness makes things simple. Consider this statement by Tom Frank, indie ideologue and editor of *The Baffler,* published in his journal during the rise of so-called "alternative culture":

"Our culture has been hijacked without a single cry of outrage," he wrote. "However we may fantasize about Madonna's challenging of 'oppressive tonal hierarchies,' however we may drool over Pearl Jam's rebel anger, there is, quite simply, almost no dissent from the great cultural project of corporate America, no voice to challenge television's overpowering din."

Frank followed this grim description of entrapment with the hint that an alternative-by-a-different-name does exist, maintained by a cadre of contrarian culture-makers (of which, of course, he is a shining star). "We inhabit an entirely different world, intend entirely different outcomes," he confided. "They [the corporate colonists] seek fresh cultural fuel so that the machinery of stupidity may run incessantly; we cry out from under that machine's wheels. They manufacture lifestyle; we live lives."

What was this glamorous cabal, setting the night ablaze with its alien campfires, detectable only by those with senses pure enough? Not a gang of political renegades on par with Rosa Luxemburg or Che Guevara, but a shaggy crew of guitar players, 'zine writers, college-radio deejays, record-label runners, club promoters, and other inhabitants of what one festival organizer dubbed the International Pop Underground. This loose but exclusive network started forming in the early 1980s, when the first youthful fans of American punk rock decided to start a bunch of bands and make music for each other. Those kids became the luminaries of a pantheon that didn't register on the Top 40, and they established the avenues through which its missionaries selectively converted new recruits. They were the members of Hüsker Dü, the Replacements, Black Flag, the Meat Puppets, Fugazi, Babes in Toyland, and eventually Nirvana; they ran labels like Twin/Tone, SST, Homestead, and Sub Pop, and edited 'zines like *Conflict* and *Maximumrockandroll*. In the shadow of a rock world dedicated to megastars and one-hit wonders, indie rock made a noble, vitalizing move. It burrowed under, and in the dark, it grew.

Indie could thrive as an insurgent outgrowth of the rock-and-roll marketplace because of opportunities within the very consumer culture many of its leaders scorned. The rise of niche marketing has allowed corporations to fool consumers into thinking mass-produced goods are designed with their individual tastes in mind, but it's also given new life to entrepreneurs, who no longer have to build a better mousetrap; instead, they simply come up with snares for groups no bigwigs have targeted yet. Indie was the perfect mousetrap for college-aged rock fans in the early 1980s, when mainstream music wallowed in an identity crisis. The alternative to anonymous pop was something warm, amateurish and local, something you did yourself—indeed, "DIY," short for "do it yourself," became one of the scene's slogans. Its heroes, like Paul Westerberg and the guys in R.E.M., were ordinary-sized, their musical skills powerful but rough, and their audiences built gradually from a hometown core. As the indie chronicler Gina Arnold once wrote, fans could imagine having a beer with them after the show, and then go have one.

Indie was not the only oppositional music culture to arise during the 1980s. Hip-hop, which began cooking on playgrounds and street corners in New York right around the time the first indie musicians were learning the chords to their favorite Velvet Underground songs, has actually had a far greater impact, both as a popular cultural force and as a business profiting its artists. Selling out is a topic of discussion within hip-hop, too, echoing the historic African-American argument about assimilation. Yet the common exclusion of African Americans from both the nation's marketplace and its cultural conversation makes entering the mainstream a generally positive thing for these artists and entrepreneurs. For the most part, they want to reach as many people as they can, and they're happy to embrace upward mobility by expanding their own companies, often with the assistance of corporate labels. While "keeping it real" remains a mantra among hip-hop artists, few see any contradictions in augmenting that reality with the material comforts afforded by a hefty paycheck.

The ethos of indie, on the other hand, perpetuated foreboding about such success. This fear was a twofold reaction: to the banality of the era's commercial rock acts, with their bleached hair and good-time hits, which indie kids considered shallow; and to what fame had done to the rock heroes of the previous generation. Janis Joplin, Jimi Hendrix, and Jim Morrison all fought demons that would have dogged them even if they'd never made the charts, but fame exacerbated their self-destructive tendencies. To indie rockers, these boomer icons were both victims and embodiments of the counterculture's arrogance. Felled by sexism, racism, or poisonous machismo, Janis, Jimi, and Jim were swallowed, like the revolution their music helped inspire, by the very forces they opposed.

With these visions of deadly indulgence in their minds, indie rockers mistrusted rock stardom from the beginning. Yet (and this fact is rarely discussed in romantic descriptions like Tom Frank's) that didn't stop most of its heroes from trying to sell out anyway. The Replacements and Hüsker Dü both entered into major-label deals that soon proved disastrous; their horror stories became fodder for antimajor purists. But it shouldn't be overlooked that they did try. R.E.M., one of indie's most beloved bands, began its career on I.R.S., an independent label very different from basement start-ups like Twin/Tone, home to both Hüsker Dü and the 'Mats. Owned by Miles Copeland, the brother of Police drummer Stewart, I.R.S. was a really big indie—or a brand-new major, depending on your point of view. While the members of R.E.M. preserved their scruffy anti–rock star personae even after they moved to the undeniably corporate Warner Bros. in 1988, they never really resisted the push toward mass popularity. They believed in themselves more strongly than they did in the indie myth.

The mainstreaming moves of such bands added up throughout the 1980s, as the corporate-tourist take on indie rock, later known as "alternative," grew in tandem with the real thing. The extent to which big business did ignore indie gave it room to grow unhindered by marketing plans and image consultants, and its acolytes fondly recall the feeling of superiority that came with knowing your favorite band was better than the stuff on the charts. Yet the mass media always lurked at the door. Many indie rockers railed against the corporate rock machine, but others took it on and began revitalizing it. Small inroads suggested new prospects. Modern-rock radio, the first alternative imitation of college stations, was formatted as early as 1982. *Spin* magazine, which eventually became the number one alternative rock magazine, first hit the newsstands in 1985. MTV debuted its alternative-flavored program *120 Minutes* that same year, with Peter Zaremba, singer for the underground garage band the Fleshtones, as the host.

By the time Seattle's Sub Pop Records reimagined indie independence near the end of the decade, it had become not just any old myth, but an origin myth, a story that created a world. Sub Pop's founder, Bruce Pavitt, believed passionately in that legend's moral lesson about doing things yourself. He began his career selling compilation tapes of strange, fantastic music from all over the world. When he decided to upgrade this kitchen project and make it a real label, he followed indie's model of thinking locally and focused on the burgeoning Seattle rock scene. He found a partner in Jonathan Poneman, a college-radio deejay and secret Ozzy Osbourne fan; the two set forth in search of artists that would make Seattle seem like the source of something big. Soon they found Soundgarden, a band with a baby rock god named Chris Cornell for a lead singer and an experimentalist named Kim Thayil on guitar. They also signed Mudhoney, led by Mark Arm, who in his previous band, Green River, had forged a détente between Seattle's punk crowd and the metalheads in the suburbs. Then they hooked up with Nirvana, destined to become punk's Beatles. These bands combined the raw candor of punk with the resolve of classic rock. They wanted their noise to dent the souls of everyone who heard it.

"When I joined Bruce at Sub Pop, he was very much a DIY traditionalist," Jonathan Poneman told me years later. "The thing that I brought in was a belief, naive as it may have been, that these bands should be huge! Popular music is a vehicle for a lot of different ideas and values. When I saw Soundgarden I just went, Holy shit! I thought that maybe if we could get the music out there and people will listen, we could change things."

Rock and roll had already changed the American social landscape more than once, when Elvis shook and rattled, and during the counter-

culture's days of rage and hope. Indie had a more targeted effect. It operated as a reform movement, fighting the bloat of the music industry
by reviving the values that had made rock so powerful in the first
place—its democratic, even anarchistic spirit, and its iconoclasm—and
restoring the conduits for those values, like independent radio stations,
mom-and-pop record stores, and local nightclubs. But most indie idealists were so invested in staying small that they forswore the attempt to
gain much influence. Pavitt and Poneman jumped the fence, emphasizing the commercial potential of their artists in marketing campaigns that
poached the language and graphics of big-time corporate rock and roll:
Mudhoney's sound evoked phrases like *Superfuzz Bigmuff,* Soundgarden, *Screaming Life.*

When Sub Pop first enacted Jon and Bruce's plan to make indie massive, Rich Jensen was living in Olympia, a college town an hour down
the highway from Seattle where Kurt Cobain first learned the rules of
indie. Jensen's group house hosted the record-release party for *Sub Pop
100,* the label's first big vinyl compilation. "On the spine of the record it
said, 'Sub Pop, an international media conglomerate based in the Pacific
Northwest,' " Rich recalled with a grin. He remembers the thrill of
small things, like the discovery of Sub Pop fans in Germany or Aus-
tralia. "Just the idea of finding each other was exciting," he said.

By the time Rich joined the company as business manager in 1991,
Sub Pop had erected its mythical identity. "We put out Girl Trouble and
Beat Happening records, and it was every bit as exciting," Jon said of
the smaller-selling artists who remain integral to the lore of that golden
period. "Green River, Soundgarden, Nirvana, all these bands had this
power, particularly in the context of the times. But then, because we
started getting flak, Bruce and I both fed off that. As if we were big
moguls, this huge Machiavellian thing. We totally played with that. You
have no choice but to play with it."

"We deal with myth and magic," Rich chimed in. "Certain poses
were made at the beginning of Sub Pop, and the world embraced it.
There was a mixture of planning and being able to go along with the
flow. It was a rare opportunity." In the label's glory years, Sub Pop
didn't so much court the mainstream as toss it a challenge, asserting that
this music represented the only stream that mattered and was powerful
enough to dominate the music world without needing to change course.
The label's poses proved more powerful than its returns, and overexten-

sion caused a financial emergency at the beginning of the 1990s. Yet the risk that Sub Pop took in flaunting the power of punk had made the Northwest rock's ground zero, and precipitated a shift toward the underground, a shift most of the indie world's residents never expected.

As Sub Pop grew, key indie players elsewhere were also moving toward a bigger audience. R.E.M. jumped to Warner Bros. in 1988, and Sonic Youth, the New York art-rock band whose members theorized punk better than anyone since the Sex Pistols and Malcolm McLaren, agreed to a deal with the major label DGC in 1990. Their presence, and their assurance that going corporate hadn't compromised their art, helped persuade Nirvana to leave Sub Pop for DGC the next year. Nirvana's Kurt Cobain was an old-time believer in indie independence, who admired Sonic Youth for succeeding at staying true to themselves. His choice to leave Sub Pop helped the label, getting it out of its financial hole when the exposure DGC offered filtered back to increase sales of Nirvana's Sub Pop catalog. He probably expected to deal with his new role in the corporate marketplace slowly and conscientiously, as his labelmates and role models had.

But Cobain didn't get to nurse his value system during a gradual rise. *Nevermind,* Nirvana's first album for DGC, made him a star as big as those dead sixties legends, and sent the myth of indie independence into major crisis mode. Nirvana's multiplatinum sales convinced the giant music corporations to sign any passing punk with a loud guitar and a bad attitude. An ugly word, "grunge," became common vernacular for what most indie kids kept calling punk. Fashion designers debuted grunge lines; teens in malls started getting temporary tattoos. Nirvana just kept selling records, and Sub Pop's other big bands made the jump one by one, until finally the label itself signed a distribution deal with a major. Other groups from the Seattle scene who'd never recorded for indie labels, from Alice in Chains to Pearl Jam, became rock stars, too. Each success story signaled a dip in indie's autonomy, and its credibility.

The scene's informal historians now describe this influx of mainstream interest and corporate money as if it were the Black Plague. The virus was soon named "alternative rock," a term invented by marketers to include not only the artists who'd come up from underground, but any lame group that could imitate the stance. These days, with everything from rehashed swing to Christian metal being sold as "alternative," it can be hard to remember that mainstream rock really did get much better after *Nevermind* went platinum. "Before Nirvana broke, there was a great feeling that we were the Other, and we knew we were better than the big guys," said Craig Marks, who was *Spin*'s music editor throughout this era. "Then for a while, in the early 1990s, the best stuff was actually really, really popular. It was a boon to everybody that the band that sold the most for a while was unimpeachably good."

The standard that Nirvana set not only enriched the moment, it remedied historical injustices. Kurt Cobain sought to educate his fans about the bands that had inspired him, increasing interest in undeservedly forgotten groups like the feminist Raincoats and the gloriously chaotic Germs. Other overlooked greats, like Alex Chilton, and irreverent newcomers, like Pavement, found themselves reaching unexpectedly swelling audiences. The adventurous spirit that infused rock then hasn't been purged by the onslaught of artless alternative clones—if it had, the true avant-gardist Beck wouldn't be a pop star, nor would the purist veterans the Beastie Boys, nor the audacious Courtney Love.

Inspired by indie's anarchist patina, some corners of the music industry also reconsidered its social influence. Benefit albums such as *Born to Choose,* compiled by Craig Marks on Rykodisc, and the Rock for Choice concerts conceived by music journalist Sue Cummings and the all-female band L7 made concrete the feminist politics many indie artists espoused. A new generation of daughters-of-feminists formed bands, and although the most radical among them—the riot grrrls of Olympia, Washington, and Washington, D.C.—vehemently rejected mainstream support, the many women who did infiltrate the mainstream through the alternative window corrected rock and roll's gender balance. By the time alternative became a marketing niche, that important shift was permanent: while rock-radio programming rules had once restricted women to one song an hour, now entire formats were dedicated to them, and mixed-gender bands became commonplace. Gay men and lesbians, who had never had more than a tiny toehold in any rock subculture—including indie—also entered as the scene expanded.

In the long run, alternative's effect on indie was as complex as any other process of cultural transformation. Some things were lost; some important changes took hold. Some people benefited unfairly; others got the credit they'd always been due. The zeitgeist shifted for a while, then shifted back, yet the moment's influence remained. We'd still be debating its benefits and faults no matter how events had unfolded. But in

April 1994, a disaster struck that made levelheaded assessments seem almost obscene.

That month, Kurt Cobain stuck a shotgun in his mouth and proved once and for all that being a rock star was killing him. He left a suicide note suggesting that his triumph had been nothing but a fake, that reaching out beyond his little tribe had destroyed him and it both. Even though his widow, Courtney Love, screamed "Fuck you!" at his ghost when she read portions of that note during a Seattle memorial service, Cobain's message survived her protests. Kurt Cobain killed the myth of indie independence as surely as he killed himself.

When Kurt Cobain appeared on the cover of the countercultural signpost–turned–corporate rock organ *Rolling Stone* in 1992, he wore a white T-shirt upon which he'd scrawled, "Corporate Magazines Still Suck." His defiant presence made it seem possible that the indie spirit of resistance might survive its own assimilation. Cobain's death refuted that gesture. The reactions were extreme and visceral. *Maximumrockandroll,* the long-running 'zine published by the renowned arbiter of punk integrity Tim Yohannan, printed a cover photo of an unidentifiable face with a gun in its mouth; the caption was a remark by Nirvana's producer, Steve Albini: "Some of your friends are already this fucked." Gossips blamed Courtney Love for Cobain's suicide, claiming her lust for fame had pushed her husband over the edge. That such talk was cruelly disrespectful of their dead comrade and his widow didn't bother the indie rockers who participated in it. Soon their disdain spread to the living, as Bay Area youths organized boycotts of the band Green Day, which released its first major label album just months after Cobain's death. Cries of "sellout" reached a truly out-of-control pitch when the former Dead Kennedys singer and anticensorship activist Jello Biafra was severely beaten at the punk fort 924 Gilman Street, for some breach of integrity—although it's still unclear what Biafra, who remains as true to indie principles as anyone, did wrong.

A bomb had hit this bohemia, and suddenly it seemed pointless to deal with the culture at large except through protest, deflection, or retreat. Perhaps the saddest result of Cobain's suicide was its effect on those uncool kids who'd picked up *Nevermind* at some chain record store and discovered a route to a better life. Craig Marks watched the tragedy's aftermath from the perspective of those fans, *Spin*'s readers. "Everybody accuses that generation of being cynical. I don't think it was true. But it became true when Kurt killed himself," he said. "It still has a much underestimated aftereffect. To get everybody believing in this person fairly deeply, and then to have that person bail out, is like having Dad leave home. It's really fucking with your family. Our readers didn't really know what to make of it. Mostly they felt extremely angry, at Kurt and at the whole process that had built him up. We were all sort of implicated in that."

The cynicism that descended on the music scene after Cobain died made it hard to feel the widened sense of possibility that is one of rock's great gifts. "However you shared a Nirvana song, whether you saw them in concert or heard it on the radio, that was a real relationship," said Craig. "Only those who'd never witnessed kids discovering this music could dismiss it. I think Kurt bailing on the scene really did fuck with kids' heads. How could it not?"

I'm not interested in laying blame for Kurt Cobain's demise. He was a great artist and a very troubled man who lost sight of his own value—though Nirvana's fans never did—under the pressure of having to perform as both salesperson and commodity. Having fallen in love with indie rock when it was in the shadows, Cobain never trusted what caught the spotlight. Then, suddenly, there he stood. He couldn't stand it, for many reasons: the health problems that had plagued him from childhood, and that life on the road exacerbated; the drugs he became addicted to, trying to still his pain; the manic-depression that showed itself in the erratic pulse of his songs. Repulsion at the moneymaking machinery of the pop industry was another reason. Still another was his fear, reinforced by the scorn he earned from indie purists before his death, that he had committed that most grievous bohemian offense, letting the tourists in.

But those who mourn the loss of indie's Eden, whether they see Cobain as its traitor or its martyr, weep for an illusion. There is no real outside; there is only negotiation. True, there was a time when an unplanned alliance of overlooked boys and girls demanded rights to rock and roll's here and now, walked away from the cardboard substitute being sold to them, and made their own roar. "The unheard music," the band X called it in one song: indie kids used that sound as a blueprint to construct a lucid dream. Their other America—just one of many that contradict America's airbrushed ideals—has survived its own surfacing. The self-governing entrepreneurial networks that indie established en-

dure, now making their inroads on the Internet as well as on college radio and by word of mouth. Small labels still distribute their anthems
and intimacies; 'zine writers still go to the copy shop and run off their
manifestos. A willfully elusive avant-garde has emerged, making music
that strives to slip beyond the prepackaged definitions of the commercial "alternative" world.

As those indie denizens journey outward, others tangle with the
mainstream. Their efforts can be massive and heavily organized, like the
all-star stadium concerts the Beastie Boys have organized to promote a
free Tibet, or more spontaneous, as when the veteran British punk band
Chumbawamba used the fame gained by a surprise major-label hit to
get the word out on national television about the case of death row inmate and political radical Mumia Abu-Jamal. If there is no outside, then
perhaps the best use for the myth of indie independence is the way it
helps people remember their principles in the face of compromise. Admitting your desire to affect the mainstream might not be as glamorous
as the punk dream of ripping down the system, or as comforting as the
indie fantasy of constructing a realm totally our own. It may even be
sold out. But I think it can make a difference, on a human scale.

M y   S o l d - O u t   L i f e

As I write these hopeful words, the devil on my shoulder spits, punk-
rock style, in my ear. I know that some will tell me I'm being willfully
naive to placate my own conscience. After all, there is no better example
of a sellout than me. I work for the biggest newspaper in the country—
when I'm not publishing celebrity profiles in those slimy music glossies
that still suck, according to St. Kurt. I did not use the money I've made
to start my own little record label; I bought a house, albeit a really narrow one without a rental unit, on a respectable if rather plain block
near downtown Brooklyn. My partner in this purchase is a straight
white male with whom I've had a monogamous relationship for the past
decade, and we have participated in the state-sanctioned heteronorma-
tive institution of matrimony. I spend many of my formerly wild nights
sitting with my husband in our mortgaged living room, watching television. Sometimes, as we watch, we eat pizza, with sausage. For all you
righteous vegans out there, that's meat.

One glance at my expensive haircut would make it clear to any purist that my principles, nurtured in the lovely spiritual greenhouse of the Bay Area, have collapsed. They gave way the minute I stepped off that plane into mean-spirited New York, where the smell of money and status overwhelms the senses like napalm every morning. The instant I started getting real dough for my writing, the second I abandoned my loyal community of alternative-weekly readers for the faceless subway skimmers who clutch *The New York Times,* I trashed the moral fiber I'd built up over so many years of hard labor in the boot camp of bohemia. How long was it before I bought my first pair of hundred-dollar shoes? Before I sipped my first glass of overpriced wine at a bar where models hovered? Or started listening eagerly to gossip about powerful people I didn't know, in hopes that one day all this useless knowledge would grant me access to the truly moneyed and influential? Did I really think I could resist the temptation of moral emptiness, like some boho Joan of Arc staying true amid treachery? What a fool.

If only the story of my corruption were that simple. I wish I could have sold out when I landed in Manhattan at twenty-seven years old, acquiring fame and a hefty stock portfolio along the way. Then at least I'd have an innocent self I could try to resurrect, if I were to renounce my rotten ways. But my secret shame as a habitué of modern-day bohemia is that I sold out from the beginning.

It started when the corporate-tourist version of rock and roll sucked me in, before I even knew the real one existed. I had no older siblings, and my parents had last boogied during the swing era; there was no way I could tell the difference between the two albums, purchased at Kmart, that initiated me into a life of passionate listening. One was *Maybe Tomorrow,* by the Jackson Five—a teenybopper group, it's true, but one with a lot of credibility thanks to little Michael's genuine talent and their groovy association with Motown Records and the fabulous Miss Diana Ross. The other was the self-titled debut by the Osmonds. Nothing could have been less cool than that group of Clearasil-covered Mormons, who specialized in whitebread ripoffs of the songs Michael and his brothers did for real. I simply didn't know that choosing my favorite Jackson (Marlon) and singing along with "Honey Chile" offered incipient liberation, while selecting my favorite Osmond (Jay—at least I liked the underdogs) and dancing to "One Bad Apple" made me a conformist and a dupe. The Jacksons were my ticket into bohemia, the Osmonds the signal that I should be escorted out. I've made that round trip so many times it became my life.

In high school I learned that the rock-and-roll bohemia I'd found on the radio wasn't open to everyone. I cherished my arty-girlness, suffered derision from jocks and stoners because of it, and still believe that it was a genuine attempt to challenge the norm. But the presence of a lone figure in the Blanchet High School halls constantly threatened my self-esteem. Jim Barnes, the only punk at our school, wore black leather and ripped jeans, had spiky hair, and listened to bands like the Damned. Every day he scared me and made me feel stupid, although we never exchanged so much as five sentences in four years. I didn't think he would beat me up, the way the stoner kids occasionally tried to do, or make snide remarks, like the jocks. His silence proved far more damaging. I was New Wave, you see, a polka-dot-wearing representative of punk's feminine, commercial side. Never mind that I hung out in the same dives Jim did, just on different nights, or that our outlaw experiences meant we shared more with each other than either of us did with the three hundred other students in our school. Jim Barnes saw me as a sellout, and I knew it. His tacit disapproval slammed the door to bohemia's inner circle in my face.

I've come to understand that the punk–New Wave distinction exemplifies an important complication within the bohemian sellout debate. In musical youth markets, pop is generally aimed at girls, while rock belongs to boys. New Wave was punk's version of pop, dominated by female and distinctly unmacho artists such as Blondie's Debbie Harry and the twerps in Devo. Throughout the history of mainstream encroachment on bohemian scenes, the emergence of female interest in a form, be it jazz, Beat poetry, countercultural rock, hip-hop, or electronica, often signals, to insiders, that subculture's corruption. I didn't see the inherent sexism in Jim Barnes's attitude toward me, and I doubt that he did, either. Had we ever talked, we would have discovered that we loved the Clash equally. But the codes of our respective camps didn't allow for such dialogue. He wouldn't stoop to approach me. Just as important, I wouldn't dare to reach out toward him. At that young age, accepting my identity as a sellout kept me from exploring the more radical aspects of punk culture. Some flaw in me, I figured, meant I'd never deserve its secrets.

And so my life proceeded, like a pendulum. Intense identification with the hidden and the misfit gave way whenever someone or something made me feel as if I'd never be weird enough. In college, I applied my fears of selling out to my obsession with becoming an important writer. Nights, I'd drink beer with my poet pals and wax grandiose about how we were going to change the world with our gutter verse; days, I'd show up, hungover, at my college newspaper offices and crank out record reviews. Writing about bands was what I loved to do, and I was good at it—good enough that I'd landed a gig with the local music paper, the *Rocket*, while still in high school. But I knew that reviewing music wasn't "real" writing, the way poetry was. Tainted by money, understandable to almost anyone, journalism was a sold-out form. Tortured by the knowledge that I had a gift for the kind of writing that true literary revolutionaries wouldn't even settle for, but getting ever better assignments from the *Rocket*, I finally skipped town. I was convinced that San Francisco, its streets dyed with poets' blood, would purify me.

Of course I was wrong. The job I landed at Planet Records put me directly in harm's way, since any group of music heads always includes at least one scribe. Sure enough, a sweet and geeky clerk who wrote for a local rag soon noticed the poems I banged out nightly at the office typewriter—many of them were based on Elvis Presley songs—and suggested I call his editor. I hesitated, but not for too long. My attempts to immerse myself in the world of letters were going badly anyway. Literature's most elitist substratum, language poetry, was all the rage at San Francisco State University. The boys I swooned for could spout Derrida paragraphs like Dylan lyrics, and sniffed at any poem that was vaguely comprehensible to any reader minus a linguistics degree. Unsurprisingly, only one girl in our little wine-drinking clique, a steely blonde who acted butch but was really femme, qualified for their sincere lust and intellectual respect. I hung around those boys for a long time, hoping somebody would like my poems, which constantly displayed sellout tendencies like pretty imagery and direct emotional expression. Eventually, the boys refused to publish any of my creative work in *Ink*, the journal I had helped found. They liked my interview with Kathy Acker, though. I remember sitting in the hallway at Fulton Street after one of them told me they'd rejected my work, stunned silent, utterly desolate. Right there, I decided that if fate made me a sellout, I couldn't fight it. I never wrote another line of poetry again.

The nagging sense of illegitimacy stayed with me as I inadvertently honed my craft at the *SF Weekly*. Finally I decided that if I couldn't be a creative genius myself, I could at least devote myself to the holy pursuit of literary scholarship. I signed up for the graduate program in English at U.C.–Berkeley. Academic discourse enraptured me, but journalism still paid my rent. Finally, after one too many conversations about the effects of impenetrable "discourse" on the politics of the left, I realized that journalism did something more. It allowed me to actually communicate with people like my old Fulton Street flatmates, none of whom could give a rat's ass about Jacques Lacan. At the very moment I should have been memorizing academia's knotty lingo, I realized that selling out its elitist rules meant joining a much larger social dialogue.

Certain academics were beginning to voice similar sentiments, and supplementing their vitae with journalistic publications. I looked to them for inspiration. But I spent more time with the rock criticism of Greil Marcus, Robert Christgau, Lester Bangs, Simon Frith, and Ellen Willis, which taught me that writing about music was really just a way of writing about the world—a bastard way, it's true, but there were possibilities in that very border identity. Rock criticism is a genre disrespected by just about everyone, considered trivial by "serious" critics of high art and literature, who think it's lowbrow, and shunned by the anti-intellectual wing of the rock world, who think it's pretentious. Rock criticism offers its practitioners the freedoms of the fugitive, who travels between worlds and chooses among their rules. Realizing this, I felt pride, for the first time, in the kind of writing that had chosen me.

Embracing selling out didn't do my academic career any good. Eventually I got that call from Jon Pareles. Off I went, my suitcases stuffed with posters from San Francisco punk shows and my dog-eared copy of Greil Marcus's *Lipstick Traces*, to invade Upper Bohemia without letting it conquer me. Although I strained to adjust to the formal and clear-minded style favored by the Paper of Record, I enjoyed the much greater impact my work had. But in four months, I was back in the arms of what I thought was a more genuine bohemia. At first I sneaked around: on occasional days off from writing *Times* reviews, I'd go down to *The Village Voice* and hang with the music editor, Joe Levy, who was so cool that he got personal phone calls from the Beastie Boys, and who'd been my mentor on the first few really serious pieces of rock criticism I'd published, right in his pages. I was a *Voice* wannabe. When a job opened up for a features editor just a few cubicles away from Joe, I jumped.

Apparently, the few people in the New York publishing world who noticed my move were shocked. Why would anyone leave the great Gray Lady for a shaggy downtown muckraker past its prime? Well, I wanted do right by the bohemia that had raised me. Alternative newsweeklies were the winged messengers of modern-day bohemia, and the *Voice* was their U.S.S. *Enterprise*. It represented the closest thing bohemia had to an official culture—and if officialdom seems anathema in this world, the stylistically freewheeling, unabashedly left-biased, highly personal prose that *Voice* writers perfected made their presumptions of authority okay. The *Voice* stars were my unbought heroes. They still are.

It only took a few months slumping in my chair at the same frustrating staff meetings they attended to realize that the sacrosanct community brought alive in their articles did not correspond with reality. In my three years as a *Voice* editor, I witnessed a protracted war—not unlike the one raging in my own head—between creativity and commerce, protecting your own principles and cracking the dominant culture's windshield. Despite the efforts of the writers and editors who kept alive what integrity the institution maintained, the *Voice* was a moneymaking mechanism at heart. Its publishers, tending the bottom line, made sure that when a question of compromise arose—whether in relation to advertising space versus editorial, issues of distribution, or worker-employee relationships—the *Voice* sold out nearly every time.

Working there wiped out any lingering illusions about the wisdom of rooting a personal value system in a single social institution. My fellow staffers and I often joked that the *Voice* was a dysfunctional family. The metaphor is one I've heard thrown around at many nonprofit organizations and alternative businesses, where a deep attachment to your work is often expected to substitute for reasonable pay, hours, public recognition, and benefits. But the "family" part of the *Voice*—the intense camaraderie, the shared creed, the sense of a deeper purpose—wasn't actually the problem. *That* was the fact that we weren't a family, but participants in a business, thrown into the usual battles between employees and management, affected by the drive for profit and the need to keep competition at bay. There is no outside. I've spoken to friends who've worked at indie record labels, in art-movie houses, even for social service organizations whose government funding never totally freed them from the pressures of the free market that surrounded them, and their disenchantment echoes mine.

After three years, I quit the *Voice*. Actually, I took a leave, to write this book and "freelance," which is that thing writers do when they're seeking a new mission. It took me over two years to admit I wasn't coming back. I could hardly bear giving up my fantasy of a little slice of America outside the norm, where success and selling out didn't have to be eternally linked. Leaving our little *Enterprise*, I began to see that every margin I'd entered, from the Seattle art-punk scene to the circle of language poets, from graduate school to the East Village, has its own way of failing that dream. Each clique sets standards establishing true outsider status, and arrives at its identity through heated dialogue with that despised guiding force. Only the most isolated rebels escape regular contact with the forces—bosses, neighbors, and less "enlightened" friends and family members—that perpetuate the conventions they despise. Those who want to affect the frameworks they think need fixing must take the chance of engaging with them.

Rebellion and compromise are complementary actions in developing an independent worldview, just as running and stretching develop an athlete's body. One makes you strong and the other makes you flexible. The poets and the punks who refuse to stretch often end up cramped, giving up hope and the human desire for contact with strangers. Eventually, they sell out, too, by accepting the dominant view that they can't dent the larger scheme of things. Meanwhile, some of the sellouts they've scorned do get soft and lose sight of their origins. Others, though, stay vigilant, pushing toward a finish that nobody can predict. That's where I'm headed, I hope, chased by a sellout past that I'm learning to be proud of.

■

SOME SPIES

These Olympic metaphors dignify the choices made by Upper Bohemians, but don't specify what they're working toward. The specifics, as always, are confusing and contradictory. Most social critics would not place activities like getting rock bands to sign major-label contracts, or marketing blue nail polish to teenagers, or persuading a men's magazine to publish an article about sex workers that's more insightful than exploitive, high on the scale of social significance. In fact, some argue that the outlandish styles Upper Bohemians propagate are pale substitutes for substantial opposition to the power structures that order our lives. Triumphs of taste mean nothing, according to this view, because everything is reduced to product in the end. Occupied with the symbolic realm, bohemians today fool themselves into thinking their actions make a difference, when in fact they only amount to diversions that ultimately reinforce the way things are.

I've already made clear how much I disagree with this argument. The signs and symbols through which we express our identities and personal beliefs—from the hairstyles we wear to the slang we use, the music that moves us, and even the deities we worship—form the daily vernacular of our lives. The changes I've discussed in this book regarding the family, sexuality, maturity, and many other "personal" subjects all take place in the juncture between symbolically revealed beliefs and material circumstance. These matters all fall under the rubric of values; taste is a more difficult sphere to gauge. Yet I don't think it's an accident that both new values and new tastes historically emerge from bohemia. Defining taste can be a frivolous pursuit, if its acolytes choose to treat it as such; it can also entail recognizing the ways modes of expression, from popular music to leisure wear, influence more serious aspects of public life. Sometimes the impact is obvious: when protest songs topped the charts during the Vietnam War, they helped galvanize the fury of a generation. Sometimes the impact is more subtle; it takes hindsight to recognize how shifting skirt lengths relate to the unfolding story of women's liberation. The step between wearing a miniskirt and being a feminist is a perilous one, and such style choices can have multifarious, even opposing, meanings. This complexity doesn't undermine the place of taste in our efforts to define ourselves and forge communities.

Most Upper Bohemians work in fields that shape the public's taste— the music and film industries, fine arts museums and institutions, book and magazine publishing, the content end of cyberspace, fashion. Some downplay the worth of their contributions, saying they're just about fun. Others, though, keep in mind the uses people make of the culture they consume, and push to influence the messages put forth by a pop song or a miniskirt. These Upper Bohemians gamble; they compromise, trying to guard their values against the demands of a marketplace whose

power they can't deny. They tap the power of the corporate-tourist machines that can either drain bohemian values of their power, or advance
them as society's new rules.

Barbara O'Dair is one Upper Bohemian devoted to these delicate
conversions. Like me, she began her media career in the alternative press
after falling for poetry in college. (Unlike me, she's kept up her versify-
ing, recently publishing a chapbook with two friends.) Barbara's first
postgraduate gig set a course for a radical life: she coedited the groundbreaking anthology, *Caught Looking: Feminism, Pornography and Cen-
sorship,* which makes the case for erotic freedom in no uncertain terms.
Subsequently she's gone down alleys her liberal friends would consider
far riskier. She's worked at the *Orange County Register,* the most important newspaper in what she calls "the most conservative county in the
world, except maybe in Iran." She's also served as editor-in-chief of the
celebrity glossy *US.* Until recently, she was the executive editor of *Details,* a New York–based men's magazine engaged in a circulation battle
that has it upping the number of seminaked supermodels pictured in
each issue. It's a job that demands a strong stomach and a total mastery
of office politics.

Barbara entered the inner circles of popular media the way a spy-
movie heroine infiltrates a foreign embassy. Her friend Holly George-
Warren arrived more haphazardly. Holly started her career in New York
as a waitress and a punk-rock musician, hanging out in the East Village
in the late 1970s with underground types like the filmmaker Richard
Kern and scene queens Ann Magnuson and Wendy Wild. With Wild,
she formed Das Fürlines, perhaps the only all-female punk band that
ever played polkas. She wrote for various groovy 'zines and wrote a
book called *Musicians in Tune: Seventy-five Contemporary Musicians
Discuss the Creative Process.* Freelancing gigs at *Rolling Stone* turned
into regular work in the early 1990s, when she was appointed the editor
of a newly revitalized Rolling Stone Press. That's where Holly met Barbara; the two collaborated in editing the anthology *The Rolling Stone
Book of Women in Rock: Trouble Girls.*

Like Barbara, Holly became a new mother late in her thirties. Barbara lives in New Jersey with her partner, Frank Gadler, but they remain
unmarried. Holly tied the knot with Robert, a musician eight years her
junior, ten years ago. With their powerful careers and radical feminist
politics, these women are quintessential 1990s-style Upper Bohemians.

I've collaborated with both of them on different projects, including *Trouble Girls,* but until I got them together one night for a long talk at a café across the street from Holly's rent-stabilized East Village apartment, I didn't know the whole story of how they'd "arrived."

Growing up at the tail end of the 1960s, Holly initially thought she'd make her mark in politics. She grew up as "the lone weirdo" in a tiny town in North Carolina, and bolted for Chapel Hill as soon as she was old enough. Reality soon awakened her from her radical reverie. "I was going to go to law school and save the world," she said. "One night, a famous radical lawyer came to speak on campus, and I went to see him with my roommate. She was asking all these questions, and afterward he invited us to stop by his hotel room to 'continue our political discussion.' " Holly scoffed. "We got there, and he opened the door wearing nothing but a towel. Pot smoke came wafting out of the room. We started talking, and sure enough, he eventually asked us to spend the night. I said, 'Bye! My friend stayed. The next morning this limo drives up to our hippie house and lets her out. What was really sick was, his wife had just had a baby."

Factors other than the piggishness of a left-leaning Don Juan turned Holly away from political activism. With the counterculture looming like a nosy older sibling and their own causes doused like so many drowned fires, campus insurgents in the 1970s had a hard time maintaining their pride. "Every cause I supported lost!" exclaimed Holly. "The ERA, the [campaign against the] death penalty. All the way down to a two-hundred-year-old oak tree we were trying to save. I was a vegetarian then, and it got chopped down to build a steakhouse.

"Then Patti Smith played on campus, and I said, Fuck that shit. I'm going to move to New York City and be a punk rocker and hang out on the scene."

Holly arrived in Manhattan feeling nihilistic. She started waiting tables; she wanted nothing more from life than good tips and loud, fast music. "I had no career goals," she recalled. "But a friend from Chapel Hill was working at this baby magazine, and they needed someone to read unsolicited manuscripts. So I started doing that." An industrious worker despite her dark philosophies, Holly was eventually promoted to a full-time editorial job. She turned her new workplace into a slacker refuge: she hired her bandmates in Das Fürlines and other pals, and after hours they put the magazine's resources to use making flyers, book-

ing tours, and generally giving sustenance to their punk-rock aspira-
tions. After five years of workplace subversion, the parenting mag was
sold to a big corporation and Holly quit.

"I'd decided I really wanted to be a writer," she said. "By that point
I'd gotten tired of playing in bands. I'd met Robert; Wendy was dying of
cancer. I decided to really focus and work hard." She lived a flexible life
for another five years, writing, editing, and hanging out. A couple of her
freelance projects involved *Rolling Stone,* and an editor there, Anthony
DeCurtis, encouraged Holly to try writing for the magazine.

"*Rolling Stone* was a mainstream magazine, and I was punk rock,"
she said. "It seemed very tainted to me. But I really liked Anthony, and
the first record review I wrote for him was of a Nick Cave album. I
thought, Cool! I was getting to write about stuff that I liked that I considered 'outsider.' Most of the artists I was writing about were really
happy to get into *Rolling Stone.*"

Holly wasn't looking to get more professional, but circumstances in-
tervened. "Out of the blue, they started up Rolling Stone Press again
full-time, and offered me the editor's job," she said. "I had to soul-
search to decide. To me it was selling out. I didn't know if I wanted to
be part of the corporate thing." She finally decided to approach the job
as if it were a waitress gig. "I said, I'll try it; if I don't like it, I'll just
quit. Or they'll fire me." She did like it, more than she expected, especially when she managed to do books on punk rock, Kurt Cobain, and
the Beats alongside the celebrity picture books that pay most of the bills.

Holly's leap to mainstream success may sound unusually serendipi-
tous, but in fact rap sheets like hers aren't that rare in Upper Bohemia.
Some culture-industry insiders are calculating sharks who claw their
way to the top on broken promises. But it's just as common to find people who stumbled into their careers while running after some ruling passion. Holly's long-lasting unwillingness to admit to herself that she
actually had a career is common, too. As I saw at Planet Records, bohemian workers often feel that caring about income will somehow taint
them. The history of the popular arts overflows with examples of
cheaply bought support, especially from women, who traditionally
haven't been educated to stick up for themselves financially. "I still
think I'm getting underpaid for what I do," Holly said. "I'm trying to be
more aggressive about that. It's one of the negatives of the boho
lifestyle—I've never been really driven by money."

For Barbara, disillusionment was the price of the realization that money mattered. The child of an upper-middle-class Westchester family that faced financial crisis when her parents divorced, she dropped out of Princeton to chase the punk-rock train to the East Village in the mid-1970s. Her first magazine job was at the marijuana users' monthly handbook, *High Times*. "It felt like working at *Good Housekeeping* to me," she said of the clash between her punk attitude and the publication's hippie vibe. "When I was there they wanted to become the *Rolling Stone* of the eighties, which is why I took the job. But it didn't work. They had to go back to centerfolds of giant pot plants to satisfy their core readers." Barbara moved on, and eventually landed what she thought would be her dream job, at *The Village Voice*.

"I had all these utopian notions of community and like-minded kin-dred spirit–hood, but they just completely dissolved in the everyday world of putting out that newspaper," she said. "I thought everybody who walked through those doors had a heightened political conscious-ness, and I was just blown away when that was not the case. Particu-larly on gender issues. And the union was bullshit."

Barbara eventually learned that she was getting paid less than male employees of her rank. Discovering the serious limits of this bohemian community forced Barbara to rethink her priorities. She filed a sex dis-crimination case, and when it failed, started a women's caucus that still survives at the paper. But finally, she decided to wage her battles else-where.

"After I had the wool pulled from my eyes about the alternative press, I decided the most important thing was to win on all fronts," she said. "I wanted to do what I could within my job, but I also needed to gain a significant level of power, and be able to take care of my family. I felt totally, one hundred percent responsible for my life, and that was much more compelling, ultimately, than any false idea of community."

When I was younger, I would have scoffed at Barbara's liberal-femi-nist privileging of money and power over countercultural rabble-rous-ing. But her success (and my own alternative-press experience) compels me to consider her viewpoint. At the various conservative or apolitical publications where she's worked since the *Voice*, she has infused her work with her radical views. Her chameleon identity, as she calls it, has furthered more than her own bank account.

Her most intense challenge came right after she left the *Voice*, when she took the job in Orange County. "I felt like I'd pulled off this wild feat, where I was just Barbara O'Dair, girl reporter, and they knew nothing about my life," she said. "I got a little red Honda, had my little house in Long Beach. It was like a fantasy, like I was living an alternative existence. That was the true alternative!"

She went to California in the late 1980s, the very moment when Jesse Helms and his archconservative cronies launched their attack on radical art. Right-wing Orange County was the last place a feminist would want to be. But freedom lurks in strange places. "The *Register* is actually a libertarian newspaper, so on all social and cultural issues, like anticensorship, they were fine. There were a lot of ironies like that. The music critic there was only interested in Australian pop. So I got to cover all the rap shows. I was writing about Niggaz With Attitude in Anaheim! It was wild."

Barbara left the *Register* after a year, returning to New York to pursue a marriage that eventually failed. She worked at *Entertainment Weekly* for a while, polishing her glossy-magazine skills. Then another one of the bohemian beacons of her youth cast its light on her. She took a job as deputy music editor at *Rolling Stone*. Barbara was thrilled to be a part of the central chronicle of rock-and-roll America. Still, she proceeded with caution.

"I'd stopped trying to have my workplace represent my identity," she said. "The work itself represents me, but that kind of overidentification with one's occupation, I refuse it. I just cut the cord. And it was a very profound cut for me."

When the hopes she'd brought to the *Rolling Stone* job didn't pan out, Barbara was prepared. "I couldn't see any future there at all, because of the environment, the culture," she said, referring to her observation that nearly all of the top editors at the magazine have been male. "I was the deputy music editor, and I couldn't see them making me the music editor, or the editor-in-chief. It wasn't out of the question, but the odds were slim." Instead of despairing, she aimed to accomplish all she could. Her biggest goal became the women-in-rock book.

"I thought, Before I get out, I have to do this book," she said. "This was something important that I'd always wanted to do, and I knew I could do it there." Before the project could really get going, however, Barbara was nudged—not out, as she'd expected, but down the hall, to the editor's office at sister publication *US*. At first she was devastated to be leaving, but she soon found she preferred her assignment at the women-oriented celebrity rag. "I was able to be myself and come into my own," she said. "I had much more power."

She used this new authority to work an ingenious trick. Treating *US* as if it were *Rolling Stone,* she tested the limits of grocery-store-rack celebrity journalism. She brought in better writers, expanded the coverage to include in-depth reporting on the entertainment industry, and slipped in plenty of innovative artists alongside the sitcom stars that were the magazine's staple. She managed this subterfuge for three years, longer than most editors survive in the cutthroat, trend-defined world of glossy magazines. But the brass at Wenner Enterprises knew that more standard supermarket fare would sell better, and the pressure to conform grew too great. Barbara walked away with her spirit intact. In the meantime, she and Holly managed to finish their book.

At *Details,* a magazine known more for photos of hot babes than for cutting-edge feminist discourse, Barbara had a new set of quagmires to negotiate. She recently chose to move on. Like most bohemians, she started her life aspiring to grandness, arrogantly hoping that her convictions were powerful enough to burst through the wall of the mainstream and inflict permanent damage. Now she acts more carefully, but those convictions remain. Like Holly, like me, she thinks it's silly to abandon hope, but wise to look for that hope in unexpected places.

"I don't feel that I've ever really changed my orientation," Barbara said. "I did stop looking for the world to give it to me. I withdrew a little bit, and got practical. Some people are so alienated that they can't enter another world. But my identity is something I get from myself, and I carry it around with me."

S A Y I N G   Y E S

If Holly and Barbara still feel stung when purists call them sellouts, at least they can take comfort in knowing they belong to an illustrious line. The journey from the edge to the center of the professional world is the classic bohemian adventure, retold in lurid detail by every generation. Its heroes, and its villains, shape the culture we all consume. But there's another version of this tale, unfolding not in the great halls of commerce but in the domestic sphere. Changing values in bohemia and beyond have made selling out a private matter, too, especially regarding the primary relationship in many people's lives.

I'm talking about the institution that Simone de Beauvoir once called "a surviving relic of dead ways of life," and that Frank Sinatra sang about as "the tender trap." Marriage—it's the other thing you can do, besides getting a regular job, to persuade your parents and the state that you've grown up. Most straight people walk that aisle at some point in their lives; historically, this includes bohemians, despite the key role sexual experimentation has always played in the unconventional life. Rampant womanizers and mama's boys, suffragettes and flappers have all given the institution a spin, though many disregarded the rule of monogamy. In the dark days of the closet, more than a few homosexuals also wed. Sometimes, as in the case of the writer Lytton Strachey and the painter Leonora Carrington, these "fake" marriages were quite passionate. No matter how far freethinkers bent the confines of matrimony and or how many demanded its eradication, marriage remained a normal part of bohemian life.

But for all that does not change within bohemia, the mood surrounding matrimony has. It's changed everywhere, what with the rise in divorce, the increased attention paid to domestic violence, and the changing image of single people, from pathetic lonely hearts to independent types who make sex and love just one part of an active existence. "You never dreamed of your wedding, even as a little girl?" my old friend Constance asked incredulously one night when we were dissecting our attitudes about the subject. "Well, neither did I," she admitted after a half-second's thought. I wasn't surprised. Growing up during the sea change of feminism, we'd been well prepared by popular culture to explode the marriage myth. We watched *The Mary Tyler Moore Show* and *That Girl* for lessons in becoming a glamorous single gal, and learned from *Kramer vs. Kramer* how dangerous legal ties could be. Constance did suffer a brief, delusional engagement to a bank clerk when she was twenty, a phase she remembers as an out-of-body experience. I never even strayed close to that petal-strewn path, because by the time I'd left my teens, I'd found an arsenal of arguments against it in my women's studies classes.

Women's liberationists had long been suspicious of the institution of marriage, but the fierce ex-hippie chicks who renewed the feminist movement in the 1970s attacked it at full throttle. Feminism was wild back then, as in-your-face as rock and roll. One spectacle those outlaw libbers staged was a 1969 attack on the New York City Marriage License Bureau. Five women stormed in and charged the office's officials with fraud, distributing pamphlets to waiting brides that detailed how marriage legally allowed for rape and indentured servitude, stripping women of sexual freedom, the right to travel, and compensation for their domestic labor. Ti-Grace Atkinson, one of the protest's leaders, declared all married women hostages, warning that "the price of clinging to the enemy is your life."

Such rants betrayed intolerance, but their fire impressed me more than the gloppy spun-sugar illusions that weighed down every family wedding I'd been dragged to as a kid. I wasn't sure I had a right to such dreams, anyway. They belonged to the sorority sisters who dated thick-necked future Boeing executives and ran at the sight of the leather-jacketed boys I always wanted to drag back to my dorm room. I never saw an image of a bride who looked remotely like me; brides were thin, demure, unblemished alpha females. I couldn't imagine being so placidly perfect, even for a day. Nor could any of my friends.

Especially my gay friends, who were legally barred from even trying. By the time I met my first serious boyfriend, marriage was no longer forcing most women into servitude; Atkinson and her sisters hadn't eradicated it, but they did further its evolution from a form of male ownership to a promise, at least, of partnership. Fundamentalists of all kinds still demand that wives defer to their husbands, and conventional ceremonies, religious or secular, still reduce brides to fragile damsels and puff up grooms as conquering knights. But the marriage laws have been changed for the better, and most of the couples I know write their own vows and treat each other as equals. Now the problem with marriage isn't so much what it asks of heterosexual women as what it denies to homosexual women and men both.

Inspired by and in league with feminism, gay activists since Stonewall have argued for free and equal partnerships undefined by gender roles. It makes sense that gays and lesbians would fear the further intrusion of the state into their bedrooms, considering its record of punishing them for sodomy, taking away their children because of their supposed perversions, and denying them access to their lifelong companions in moments of mortal crisis. In light of these exclusions, the white glare of the wedding industry takes on an Aryan sheen, as if asserting straight people's superiority to justify brutal inhumanity. In the 1990s, though, some gay activists began arguing for legalization of gay marriage as a civil rights move. Noting that the legalization of interracial marriage was a crucial gain for black civil rights in the 1960s, leading thinkers advocated making this issue central in the fight to make gays and lesbians full citizens.

The dispute continues, with radical queers calling marriage stumpers sellouts as the advocates take the matter to the courts. In May 1993, the Supreme Court of the State of Hawaii responded to a case brought by three same-sex couples arguing their right to marry according to the precedent set in *Loving v. Virginia,* the 1967 decision that found bars to interracial marriage unconstitutional. The court found in the couples' favor, horrifying conservatives. By 1996, though, right-wingers had mobilized, proposing the Defense of Marriage Act, which defined marriage as a union between male and female and thus made Hawaii's accomplishment irrelevant. Vitriol flew as right-wingers raised the specter of queer open marriage, incest, and even legal unions with dogs in speeches as hateful as the racist diatribes that had greeted blacks during the 1950s and 1960s. The bill passed by overwhelming majorities in both the House and the Senate. President Clinton, forgetting his gay and lesbian constituency, signed it into law in seclusion one September midnight.

Gay and straight progressives alike witnessed these developments with sinking hearts. Those who believed that the right to marry would afford gays and lesbians more dignity and freedom—not to mention access to partners' health benefits and the assurance that they would not be banished from lovers' hospital rooms or funerals—felt themselves pushed out of the democratic conversation. Those who thought marriage itself was the problem recognized that the Defense of Marriage Act not only forbade homosexual participation, it reasserted the superiority of legally bound couples. More than ever, marriage seemed like an unnatural act, its privileges reinforcing a hierarchy that denigrated single people, alternative families, and couples who chose not to bend to convention and the state.

Yet the pull of convention is strong when it comes to matters of the heart. The same myth of romance that smothers frank talk about sex upholds this institution, even where you'd expect it to wither. Most bohemians express some hesitation about matrimony, but end up wed.

They just wait much longer, and when they do succumb, they spend a good deal of energy—often within their self-designed ceremonies—trying to make sense of their decision. "Another tree falls in the forest," says one resolutely single friend whenever a long-attached couple marries. The pair blushes, mumbling about relatives and health insurance, the bride insisting that she won't be wearing white.

Actually, the last time my friend made that crack, she was talking about me.

Eric and I recently celebrated our tenth anniversary. We've been through five homes, three or four career changes, two years of long-distance romance, various episodes of serious doubt and passionate resolution—all the stuff that could easily make up the first decade of a modern marriage. Why not have a party to toast all we've been through? It would mitigate the pressures our families had started to exert, reward all the pals who'd seen us through bad times and good, and get us a nice new set of flatware. It might also provide a way for us to make clear to the more traditional folks in our lives what we think really matters about long-term love.

When I watch my women friends stand up and marry their men, I don't see dainty flowers about to vanish into suburban kitchens. I see Jill, a Harvard professor who married her lover and academic colleague, Larry, to cement their commitment during a time when their tenure tracks diverged by thousands of miles. And Susan, whose fast-track career in marketing fulfilled her ambitions while allowing Jesse take time to finish his Ph.D. And Katherine, who would start directing her first feature film nine months after giving birth to her daughter, Caroline, leaving Brian to be primary caretaker while she worked fourteen-hour days. These women are anything but hostages.

I also know many gay couples who staged their own rituals, insisting on their right to the tradition. The "alternative wedding," gay or straight, has become de rigueur in bohemia. Everybody twists the form some, the extent of the contortions depending on the participants' level of discomfort with convention and stomach for theatrics. These new ceremonies may seem like elaborate rationalizations to some, but if there's anything to the old idea that you can tell the nature of a marriage by the tone of a wedding, then their variations are more than just show.

Most bohemians have their favorite "crazy wedding" story. Mine was provided by my cousin Greg, a classical musician and practicing

anarchist who lives in downtown Seattle. He pledged his troth to Kate,
a high-spirited nurse who's his match in everyday unorthodoxy. They
had a Halloween costume wedding at a mountain lodge with a troll
motif, which required even the most buttoned-down guests to don
clown suits and animal disguises and sing along with Elvis Presley's
"Can't Help Falling In Love." Greg appeared as Elvis, in flowing side-
burns and cape; Kate conjured the bride from her favorite musical,
Brigadoon. Her maid of honor wore the costume of a French domestic
straight out of a porn movie, and Greg's groomsman doused himself in
gold paint in hopes of evoking Louis XIV, who was called "the Best
Man" in his day. Their minister was a "Monister," wearing a set of
black cardboard wings that made her look like one of the monkeys
from *The Wizard of Oz*. The liturgy consisted of testimonies from
pals, a Gregory Corso poem, and a passage from *The Little Prince*. My
mother fretted that the whole shebang would give my uncle Bill, Greg's
dad, a heart attack, but he made it through with his clown hat on, and
despite a freak snowstorm that rendered the hot tub unusable, everybody had a fine old time.

By having a wedding, and not just a big anarchistic party, Greg and
Kate demanded entry to a powerful club; by reconfiguring their ritual,
they modified the rules of membership. Their ceremony stretched the
rites of wedlock to accommodate wider notions of love and union than
could fit in a rented limousine. It saluted their tight-knit family of
friends, and made clear to blood relatives that those bonds matter to
them as much as the ones they'd inherited. It also exalted them, in all
their weirdness, instead of forcing them into costumes representing social roles they'll never fit. A conventional marriage always seems to be
a deal with society: you grant us legitimacy and we'll fulfill the
monogamous, materialist, procreative functions that maintain sexual
and emotional order in the land. The real commitment standard weddings honor isn't between two people, or even among the family and
friends who share in it. It's a pledge to a set of stereotypes that don't
even apply to most people's real lives any more, but which inevitably
affect the expectations and subsequent actions of those who accept
them.

Greg and Kate got married in the spirit of party crashers, changing
the very tone of the institution by messing with its etiquette. They did
their damnedest to make marriage assimilate to them and not the other

way around. This switch isn't an easy one; talking to various friends who've attempted it, I heard many tales of bitter fights and tenuous deals. "You feel like you should compromise, because it's easier," admitted Constance. "I didn't feel strongly enough to fight that hard, to alienate people who were important to me. It's usually an individual who does it to you."

Constance was alluding to a hard fact I've come to accept: hegemony is your mom and dad. Political rhetoric can be formidable, but a strong-willed person can resist hectoring from the likes of Pat Robertson. And although advertising has a way of seeping into our dreams, a little alertness can combat the slick persuasions of the Crate & Barrel catalog. But Mom and Dad are a different matter. You may have spent a lifetime in disagreement, the yelling matches of your teen years fading into resigned sighs exchanged over the phone. You may very well have given up on fulfilling their wishes. But given the choice, most dissenting kids want to put the fight aside at some point and just coexist. Even the biggest flaming radicals and queers I know still go home for Thanksgiving if they can. Sometimes everybody comes to tears; sometimes it works out okay. But they go.

If selling out in the work world involves admitting that we all live within the structures of late capitalism, selling out in the personal sphere usually means acknowledging that our chosen families don't eradicate our biological ones. That doesn't mean you have to agree with the folks, just attend to them. Constance, whose dad had died when she was twenty-one, knew her mom wanted to walk her down the aisle. She wanted to give her that. It was up to Constance and Ivan to figure out what kind of aisle it would be.

Constance made her own pink wedding gown, along with pantsuits for her bridesmaid, her mother, and her female minister, and sashes for the groom and groomsmen. Ivan baked the cake—a landscape painting in butter and flour, representing his grandmother's house and land, where the wedding was held. A workmate of Constance's did the flowers; Ivan's band members brought their own sheet music for the processional and the reception. Ivan even made the rubber stamp of two cartoon cupids that decorated their invitations and the matchbooks they handed out as souvenirs.

"We had the money to do it the other way," Constance said. "But we wanted to do everything we possibly could ourselves." Constance and

Ivan pretty much live on their own resources, making their own clothes, doing their own home improvements, creating their own forms of entertainment. It's an indie-rock approach to life, and they applied it to their wedding. Even their minister was a pal from high-school days, sanctioned by one of those start-your-own-ministry coupons from *Rolling Stone*.

Going the indie route took a lot of work, but it gave Constance and Ivan artistic control over the biggest party they'll ever throw, and, more profoundly, over the portrait the wedding made of their relationship. Their celebration wasn't word-heavy—the ceremony itself lasted about twenty minutes—but it spoke eloquently through graceful, home-shaped details. "It's an opportunity for you to totally express who you are as a couple," Constance concluded. "For people who have standard weddings, it shows who they are. They are conformists. Princess for a day, big church wedding, the limo, the deejay." She grinned. "We had a polka band."

If Constance and Ivan represent the careful reinvention of the wedding ritual, the other inveterately unwed couple in my life, who've been together longer than the fifteen years I've known them, lent poetry to the casual approach. It's impossible to elope in public, but in a sense, that's what Christopher Mascis and Stephanie Kurtz did. After thirteen years together, they announced in March 1996 that they would marry seven weeks later. Like Constance and Ivan, they'd pondered taking the plunge for years, but never bothered. Then Chris's father had a minor heart attack. "On the plane down from Seattle to Reno it became pretty clear to me that, Hey, this is the time to get married and start a family, because life is a transitory thing," said Chris.

The date they chose would be the anniversary they'd always observed. Invitations were hastily issued; they reserved an Italian restaurant in the shadow of the Kingdome, where their beloved Mariners play baseball. The wedding party was easily assembled—just Chris's dad as best man and Stephanie's sister as maid of honor. For music, they made sure their boom box had batteries and cued up Pavarotti singing "Nessun Dorma." After a moment of silence at 7:05 P.M.—the starting time of Mariners evening games—the pair took their places near an overflowing antipasto plate and said their vows in front of yet another buddy empowered by the Universal Life Church. The quick ceremony was followed by dinner and a hour of spontaneous toasting from all corners of the room, and then Chris and Steph invited a whole crew back to their honeymoon suite, where everybody ordered drinks from room service and vied for the chocolates on the pillow.

"I do wish I'd written down what I wanted to say, because I totally muffed it," Stephanie said about the ceremony.

"It was a Marx quote, right?" asked Chris.

"It's this really great quote from Marx, yeah, where he's saying how much he loves his wife because he's been with her so long, he knows where every wrinkle came from," she said. "You have so much history with someone that you have marked each other. Not just, I put a ring on your hand, or I hit you with a frying pan and you've got this big dent on your head. But you've marked each other in so many different ways."

Chris and Stephanie's ritual felt like part of an ongoing relationship, instead of an imposed point of origin. The toasts, which dominated the evening, allowed old comrades and family members to reminisce about all the time we'd spent together, with this couple the solid unit around which we often revolved. When I met Chris and Steph, they lived in a little rented house across the street from me near the edge of the University District. She was five years older than my eighteen years, he three; in my green view, they were an old married couple. As time passed, they remained a constant in my life. It would have been strange if they'd conformed to the outdated pipe dream of the virgin and her noble consort that today's white weddings still promote.

"I wanted to get married in a white dress, but goof on it," said Stephanie. "So I made one out of rice paper. I tried it on so many times it self-destructed. I actually took it with me to the wedding, thinking maybe I'll have the guts to crawl into this thing that's falling apart." Instead, she opted for something she felt comfortable in. "I also had this other dress that makes me look really cute," she explained. "It's very dark blue. Some people thought I was getting married in black, like, Oh, she's making such a statement. But no, it was just my favorite dress."

By being spontaneous, and putting first the things they would have wanted anyway—good food instead of fussy catering, comfortable clothes instead of starchy formal wear—Chris and Stephanie integrated their wedding into their daily lives. "So many of the weddings I'd been to had been about anything but the people's love for each other," Chris said. "I'd seen all the politics, the bridesmaids standing there in these horrible dresses, the girls going on diets and all this shit.

There's all this stuff that surrounds weddings that's not about the most important thing."

When I asked them about that thing—the reason to get married at all—Chris and Stephanie mentioned the desire that the baby they'd have a year later be fully accepted as part of their families, and the wish to express their love in public, both reasons I'd often heard before. But Chris also mentioned something I hadn't thought about. He got married, he said, because it was the only honest thing to do.

"The nice thing about not being married is that you have the sense that you can do anything," he recalled. "But then, you're in your mid-thirties, and you think, I can do anything, and for the last however many years, this is what I've done with it. I was finally happy to give up my bachelor impulses, because being single didn't mean anything to me."

I brought up the fact that plenty of married people have affairs; I didn't see why he thought marriage would take away those "bachelor impulses."

"The fact is, I was in a relationship for thirteen years where I supposedly could have acted on those feelings, because we hadn't said we wouldn't. And I didn't," he answered. "I didn't even come close. Being independent in that way was no longer a particularly interesting fiction to carry out."

Marriage offers those who believe in it the chance to tell the story that they feel best represents their relationship; this is exactly what gay people who embrace the ritual say they want. One such crusader is Dan Savage, the social critic behind the syndicated sex column "Savage Love." Dan and his boyfriend, Terry, adopted a baby boy in the spring of 1997. Dan wanted to mark their new status as a family with nuptials. Terry wasn't so sure. Their ongoing argument, which I checked in on before baby D.J. had arrived, sounded a lot like the one inside my own head, complicated by the fact that Dan and Terry can't legally participate in a traditional wedding.

"I think it embraces our oppression to say marriage is not a gay institution," Dan explained. "It's like saying law or medicine is a male profession because women were excluded from it. It's not a gay institution because they don't let us get married, not because there's something inherently heterosexual about marriage."

"You sound like Andrea Dworkin," Terry huffed, invoking the fun-

damentalist feminist who strikes fear in the hearts of the open-minded.
" 'Embracing our oppression'! He's afraid if we don't say we're getting
married, our parents won't take us as seriously. But we're not gaining
anything by doing it. Straight people gain whoever's insurance is better,
and other legal rights."

Dan and Terry are blessed with supportive families, but they both remain acutely aware of their exclusion from what the larger society's definition of a union. "The problem with being gay is that you can never just
take your lover's hand walking down the street," said Dan. "So if I do
grab his hand, how much of it is my wanting to, and how much is wanting to make a point that I should be able to? With the wedding, part of me
wants to make everyone I'm related to jump through a very big hoop."

I understand that desire; whenever Eric and I imagined our wedding,
we came up with myriad impish details that would horrify our parents,
aunts, and uncles. But in Terry's hesitation, I sense the familiar feeling
that trying to purify this loaded ritual is just too much work. Once, I
was earnestly discussing my ideas with a lesbian friend who is quite opposed to marriage, relating all the different ways we felt our ceremony
could critique the institution. I went on and on until she interrupted me:
"It is going to be fun, too, right?"

It can be hard to get to the part of marriage worth celebrating. "I
would love to have a wedding," said Terry. "I would love to have something where everybody had to accept who we were and what we were
doing, that we were a couple, that we love each other, that we want to
create a family. I just don't want to go through *that wedding thing.*"

Dan has seen "that wedding thing" in action; he's a Universal Life
Minister (the bohemian enthusiasm for this obscure sect seems to be evidence that *it*'s the real threat the Christian Coalition should be worried
about), and for a while he married people one night a week at a local
nightclub. "I've married people who I didn't think should be sitting near
each other on a bus," he said. "People would come in with all the legal
paperwork, couples who'd only known each other three months. It was
so disgusting. I don't do it anymore. I just couldn't."

Dan thinks that homosexuals are actually more likely to take marriage seriously than most straights, precisely because they have nothing
tangible to gain. "I think it has more meaning that way, because it's a
completely symbolic thing. Gay people don't get married for stupid reasons," he said.

It was just an offhand phrase, but it hit me. I didn't want to get married for stupid reasons. My concerns weren't about what might happen between me and Eric. I wondered what getting married would change between us as partners and the world at large. I feared the inertia that makes so many people give up their own ideas in favor of the easiest thing, and the pull of other people's preconceptions. Jonathan Richman once wrote a song about how much he hates the word "wife"; it makes him think about mowing the lawn. I wasn't sure any redefinition could completely skirt all that history—or, given the time-honored function of ritual, that it even should.

At the same time, I began wondering about my assumptions regarding the few friends I had who'd married young. Were they really the sellouts I thought they were? When my old San Francisco State chum Cassandra married Dennis in a little Swedenborgian church in Pacific Heights, she surprised her most unflappable friends. Getting married at twenty-six was definitely weird behavior in our circles. Even weirder was the fact that after she and Dennis wed, Cassandra basically stopped holding a job. I'd never asked Cassandra why she'd made these decisions; she's one of those people whose convictions are so strong that you rarely think to challenge them. But now I needed to know how she'd handled taking on the most conventional of feminine roles when everyone around her was trying a different freaky lifestyle. What I learned from talking to her and Dennis was that sometimes nonconformity happens where you least expect it.

"I used to call myself a housewife all the time." She laughed. "It drove people crazy! They'd be so offended. I took this Ancient Greek class a long time ago, and I didn't want to take it for a grade because it was so fucking hard, and this was for kicks for me. I said, I'm taking the housewife class. The women in there turned around and gave me the dirtiest looks, like I'd just said something really evil."

Don't think Cassandra is pursuing some Tupperware-party version of the Feminine Mystique. Like many a bohemian before her, she doesn't see much point in laboring over things she doesn't care about, and her passions—poetry and windsurfing, and the admittedly domestic pursuits of cooking and keeping her husband company—don't garner a salary. "What I want to do with my life is not something I will ever get paid for doing," she explained. "I have a really rich intellectual life. When I think about what I would have to do to make money, like get a fucking forty-hour-a-week job, are you insane? I've never been in a situation where I had to do it. And I never will."

Cassandra went from being a single slacker girl, cobbling together enough cash to pursue her passions, to being married to someone who wanted to enable her to continue those pursuits. She was lucky, really. Dennis wasn't looking for a trophy wife or a housekeeper; he was a slacker, too, working lucrative shipyard jobs for a few months so he could take the next several off. "There's plenty to go around, and I don't even have to work all the time," he said. "I was in the same mode as Cassandra—take as much time off as possible. It's more about hanging out and being together than working your butt off all the time for something you don't need. Why go beyond what you need?"

In order to concentrate on the pleasures of their relationship as it was, Cassandra and Dennis rejected the aspects of middle-class marriage that involved upward mobility. They've never had much money, but they don't miss the extras. Their situation was bliss. Then a workplace accident landed Dennis in the hospital and on the permanent disabled list.

You can't see Dennis's injury; he's still a strapping man, muscular and lean, with the glow of health. But when a piece of heavy machinery propelled him off a girder into the water one summer night five years ago, his spine was permanently maimed. He was confined to his bed for months, and although he regained basic mobility it became clear that he'd never be returning to the shipyard. Suddenly, the dynamic shifted in his and Cassandra's marriage. Their friends wondered how they would endure it.

"I did recognize that nothing was going to be the same," said Cassandra. "Physical activity was how our whole relationship had started. The first thing Dennis did when we began dating was buy me a wetsuit, and we started body-boarding every day. Now I go windsurfing by myself."

"It was rough for me, because I had never been dependent on anyone," said Dennis. "It still is hard to adjust to the fact that she does all the physical work now. I'm the guy who pushes the cart in the grocery store, and she picks up all the groceries."

If Dennis and Cassandra's bond had really been formed along traditional gender lines, this crisis would have sunk them. It is a tribute to the strength and adaptability of their relationship that now, five years after the injury, they have fully settled into their new rhythm. Retrained to do computer programming, Dennis works a desk job. The pair bicycle together, an activity Dennis can handle, and when Cassandra goes windsurfing with her sister and brother-in-law, Dennis comes along and watches their kids. "I do the baby-sitting. I enjoy it," he said.

"Dennis is one of the most nurturing guys I've ever met," Cassandra added.

Although his injury cost them a good chunk of their income, Cassandra still doesn't work full-time. She has used her freedom to pursue a graduate degree, and now she can teach nights, a moneymaking activity she actually enjoys. But both she and Dennis are happy to defy the modern requirements of the two-career family. "When the shit hits the fan, I get a job and make money," she said. "But as soon as things aren't dire, that's it. Right after the accident, we were freaked out, like, How are we going to survive? We went on an austerity program, beans and rice. But we've been able to figure out how to just scale back. We even save money now. I don't know how we do it."

With the arrival of a son who is now nearly two, Dennis and Cassandra have entered a new phase of their arrangement. Cassandra knows all the best thrift stores for baby clothes, and Dennis cares for the child while she is in class. Any notion I had that their relationship was traditional faded from my mind as they talked about their parenting style. The divisions of power between husband and wife couldn't be more fluid.

"You adjust," said Dennis. "The relationship was always strong, but coping with all these things that you don't even know are gonna happen makes it really interesting. The way you go about your life together becomes a whole different thing."

My friends' remarks reminded me that the truth in every relationship emerges during that unpredictable excursion, governed by providence and devotion, not legalities. Talking with them helped alleviate my fear of getting squashed by the weight of matrimonial tradition as Eric and I inched nervously toward connubial union. Our first step was a secret one: on our ninth anniversary, a year before publicly acknowledging it, we slipped into Brooklyn's Borough Hall and obtained a marriage certificate. We got legally hitched with zero fanfare, for two reasons: to separate that aspect of marriage, endured strictly out of love for our parents, from the renegade ceremony we wanted to stage; and to prove, by living for twelve months with it hidden in a drawer, that a piece of paper really wouldn't change our relationship. That last test was partly for our own benefit. We both strongly suspected we'd feel exactly the same after the judge pronounced us man and wife, but as everyone who felt otherwise loved to tell us, there was only one way to know for sure. To guarantee that our experiment would remain covert, we chose a colleague whom we liked, but didn't see much socially, to be our witness; we knew that if even one close friend or family member knew our trick, it would eventually get out. The three of us met on Court Street at the beginning of the lunch hour and parted ways, the deed accomplished, twenty minutes later. Eric hopped a subway to work, and I treated myself to a Frappuccino.

Soon, both of us basically forgot what we'd done. We kept arguing about whether we should get married, and the tension increased over the months, as it became clear just how much a big bash costs in New York City. Both sets of parents offered to foot much of the bill, which we gladly accepted, mainly because we still felt we were going through this for their sake. Eventually, we secured a loft space in Queens for the night of March 27, chose a menu of Thai food and Seattle-style salmon, made fluorescent yellow invitations at the copy shop, and persuaded our neighbor, the power-pop king Marshall Crenshaw, to lead the band. Each difficult detail gradually fell into place. Yet we still felt uneasy. We had long, teary arguments about the worth of all this effort and considered calling the whole thing off. But doing so would have been the worst capitulation of all, because then we'd only be legally married, tied in the one way we scorned.

Then one evening we found the means to make a much-needed leap in perspective. I'd been trawling the Internet in search of wedding traditions that didn't make me queasy, and had presented Eric with notes that resembled a nightmarish "It's a Small, Wedded World." Indian flower-petal rituals, Scottish foot washing, ancient Israeli crowns—it was all very lively and educational but utterly disconnected from our experience. As he read my list, Eric showered me with pained looks. Then he noticed one ceremony he thought he could stand. Called "handfasting," it was neither Jewish, his family faith, nor Catholic. There was some dispute over whether it was even historically authentic, which made it all the more appealing.

According to legend, the rite originated in medieval times, when rural couples sometimes had trouble finding a priest or other officiant. They

would marry themselves, in the presence of fellow villagers, who asked
them four questions: "Do you have the means to support yourselves and
to provide for your worldly needs?" "Do you love, and like, one another?" "Do you share your thoughts and ideas, burdens and dreams?"
And the one we really liked: "Do you have the will to argue if you must,
to air your problems, then stand together against adversity?" Once these
queries were answered satisfactorily by the couple, their hands were
bound together by a cord and they were considered married for whatever span of time they agreed upon.

Handfasting is now mostly celebrated by neopagans who like its
Arthurian tinge. We didn't plan to cast any sacred circles, but we appreciated the way the four questions made room for a lot of talking, just as
the children's questions do at a really good seder. The tradition's disre-
gard for an official blessing also suited us. Months earlier we had decided that our friends and fellow writers Robert Christgau and Carola
Dibbell, who are husband and wife, would be our officiants. The way
we stretched the handfasting ritual, they became more like hosts, intro-
ducing us and the group of intimates we chose to help formalize our
bond. We decided that each of our parents would ask one question, to
be answered by a friend or a couple of friends. Then we would speak to
each other, and after that more friends and family members would fasten our hands together with the ceremonial cord. The service would
conclude with a rousing group rendition of "I'm Sticking with You," by
the Velvet Underground, accompanied by my cousin Greg (he of the
Halloween wedding) on the ukulele.

The handfasting ritual gave us a way to make our wedding a celebration of the many communities, some intersecting and others oblivious to
one another, that had long nourished our partnership. The friends we
asked to participate, from high-school buddies to our closest neighbors
in Brooklyn, had entered our lives at different junctures. They ran the
gamut of identity from a single gay man to a long-married straight couple, but that was happy coincidence. We chose people who we felt could
fulfill the requirements of the ceremony, which was to explain why we
deserved to call ourselves married, citing evidence from our everyday
lives. We wanted a chance to testify to that ourselves, not only for the
benefit of the doubtful traditionalists who had pushed us to go legal for
so long, but for each other, because it's easy to take things for granted
when they remain unsaid.

The designated speakers all got nervous as the day approached, and for a few guilty moments I wondered if we were asking too much of them. It was definitely more than the bouquet- and ring-holding required of most attendants. But I also knew that only this intermingling of voices would be able to express the truth about a lot of time and love.

I wore orange that night, a dress designed by my childhood friend Nora Carria. Eric chose an *Interview with the Vampire* look, augmented by blue hair and his green basketball sneakers. Bob and Carola, speaking together, spilled our secret legal status at the ritual's beginning; we heard the crowd gasp, then explode with laughter. Then we entered and had our wedding kiss, and the talking began. Our friends were more eloquent than we'd hoped, and I don't say that simply because they were lavishing us with praise, although the ego boost was certainly enjoyable. What mattered was that we all spoke about the commonplace things we'd shared—the chaotic piles of compact discs and books that fill our writers' house, the times getting lost on the Brooklyn-Queens Expressway, the long days working and the weekends relaxing. And, yes, the maddening, fruitful arguments. I couldn't stop from crying, just like a bride, as I heard Eric's and my life so richly commemorated. Then it was time for the handfasting itself. Nicola Ginzler, who'd arranged our meeting a decade before, was the first to fetter our wrists—an appropriate role for a dominatrix, as she wryly noted. Our parents followed her, as did Eric's eighty-seven-year-old grandmother Cele, Eric's cousin Neil and his partner David, my brother Patrick, Eric's sister Amy, their spouses, and assorted friends. As each loved one touched us and offered kind words, the friends' chorus began "I'm Sticking with You," and even guests who'd never heard of Lou Reed gamely joined in.

One other brilliant idea helped us fulfill our audacious wedding dreams, and I'm happy to boast that it was mine. As we started to plan the ceremony, I found myself preoccupied with questions of propriety coming at me from all sides. Mothers, fathers, siblings, friends, and casual acquaintances all had their say about some little detail that even a wild wedding shouldn't violate. I needed to think of some way to make sure that everyone would drop these assumptions and show up with an open agenda. I'd never live down a direct imitation of Greg and Kate's costume wedding, but I had learned from attending that event that the clothes make the partygoer. So I came up with the idea of festive dress. "A little black whatever is not festive, it is conventional and safe," I wrote in the instructions that accompanied our invitations. "There are plenty of times when it's good to feel safe, but we hope you will come to our party and feel adventurous. Consider this your chance to get into a carnival mood, return to the childlike spirit of play and grasp for the glamour of the rock star and the drag queen."

Some guests grumbled at my demands, others quietly panicked. But when the time came, they all came through. My Wisconsin relatives wore hats shaped like giant Swiss cheese wedges. Our friend Barry donned a bear suit. Stephanie fulfilled a lifelong fantasy of dressing up as a wedding cake, which also served as compensation for the fact that we served only pie. One gay man and one straight man came in drag. There were guys in dashikis, women dressed as belly dancers, glammed-out rockers, turban wearers, and many, many shoulders swathed in feather boas. The costumes harmonized with the room, which a team of pals had decorated with Gerber daisies, plastic toys, piñatas, candy, bunny candles, and holiday lights shaped like electric guitars. In this topsy-turvy environment, wearing their crazy costumes, our guests couldn't help but shed their expectations. The trickster spirit overtook them and they were more open than they might have been to our more serious attacks on wedding tradition.

And so we wed, in our own way. The adventure did make me feel different about my bond with Eric, for about two weeks. Being in the spotlight gave us both a rosy glow. But when it faded, and things went back to normal, I realized that I still didn't know what to expect from the future. I know Eric very well and trust him with my life. I felt that way before March 27, 1999, when we threw our party, and before April Fool's Day 1998, when we formally said, "I do." But if there's one thing I know about love, it's that your preconceptions won't survive it. So now that I'm a so-called wife, go ahead and ask me for advice. All I can offer is what my friends who shared their wedding stories taught me before: that the secret of a good marriage, legal or otherwise, is in giving up the urge to pin love down.

■

GARDENING AT NIGHT

Selling out is usually imagined as a departure, whether the step Out There involves leaving the margins of the work world for your profession's centers of power, or reverting to a more conventional lifestyle after the nonconformist outlands prove too lonesome. But the tourist interest in bohemia also makes selling out a source of controversy within all but its most sequestered enclaves. In fact, the most visible bohemian sellouts are the merchants and administrators who run every American city's hip shops and up-and-coming arts organizations. For bohemia to play a vital role in urban life, its devotees must claim space in the physical world, space in which to find the goods they need to work their private experiments, and then gather to debate its philosophies, flaunt its styles, and enact its spectacles.

I left Seattle in 1984 in search of such an environment. My hometown bohemia was ragged and sleepy then. I found what I craved in San Francisco, where bohemia perpetually renews itself. Yet, had I been more patient, I could have participated in one of the most exciting urban renewals in recent history, in the same nowhere bohemia I fled. There are many big reasons for Seattle's bohemian boom. The rise of Microsoft made a lot of young, creative people wealthy and hungry for a local marketplace. Overcrowding in major cities like Los Angeles drove many people to the Pacific Northwest, looking for a little space and cleaner air. Developments in international trade have made the West Coast a new center of power and given the Northwest a cosmopolitan sheen. All of this contributed to a thriving middle class, which naturally needed a bohemian underside.

Ambition has made Seattle's younger bohemians model citizens in today's alternative America. The music scene, which still draws new garage bands and fans to the city every year despite hard rock's declining popularity, is only one aspect of Seattle's influence. It is now home to the most successful graphic-novel press in the country, Fantagraphics, which relocated from Boston in the early 1990s; the cartoonists who first started publishing in the *Rocket* when I wrote for that paper, among them Lynda Barry and Matt Groening, are the modern-day standard-bearers of that popular art. Seattle also spawned the *Stranger,* an irreverent alternative weekly founded in the mid-1990s by a bunch of Wisconsin expatriates that now rules the cutting edge of alternative weekly journalism. Beyond these major success stories, the many boutiques, live-music venues, microbreweries, cafés, and indie record stores that occupy Seattle neighborhoods like Belltown and Capitol Hill have established a style that now rivals San Francisco's in defining contemporary bohemianism. Seattle bohemia is more punk and queer than its hippie and Beat predecessors, and more pragmatic. Its landmarks are laundromat-cafés, a punk-rock pizza place, and a chain of barbershops–cum–tattoo parlors. The general feeling is one of growing beauty from rubble. "The kids came here to find their utopia," Sub Pop's Rich Jensen once told me, "and it didn't exist. So they built it."

One of those kids who's grown into his success is Robert "Lou" Torregrossa, the manager and co-owner of the Speakeasy. Lou moved to Seattle after college in New England, looking for a sympathetic environment where he could sort out his future. He started hanging with a crowd of aspiring artists and reluctant professionals who organized casual events in warehouse spaces most weekends. Eventually, five people—a playwright, an architect, an attorney, a jack-of-all-trades, and Lou—banded together to found Belltown's first cybercafé.

The cybercafé—a public eating house equipped with computer monitors and Internet connections—may turn out to be no more than a blip on the bohemian landscape. The concept emerged in the mid-1990s, when interest in the World Wide Web exceeded the number of people with Internet accounts. Cybercafés opened in most major cities and enjoyed a moment of trendiness. They're on the way out now, since most people have decided they'd rather surf at home, presumably because it's easier to shop and masturbate, two main Internet-connected activities, there. But whether or not cybercafés last, the Speakeasy stands as an apt metaphor for bohemia's current, constant state of flux. The "cyber" part evokes bohemia as an inward reality, shared by spreading ideas and beliefs rather than spectacles. The "café" part serves the undying need for face-to-face encounters that can surprise and stimulate, and ways to display the physical signs of belonging to this tribe.

The Speakeasy seems to span an eon of bohemia. Its faded furniture and dusty wood floors suggest the greasy wine bars where Théophile Gautier gathered with his friends, but the cement walls and high ceilings reveal that this room was once a warehouse, one of the new urban territories punk and indie has claimed. Computer terminals are perched in a circle near the coffee bar, offering admission to the virtual world that has become a refuge for dissidents of all kinds. For ten dollars a month, the Speakeasy will rent you an electronic post-office box, which offers e-mail and the chance to use newsgroups and roam the World Wide Web. Connections to terminals in seven other locales allow subscribers to boot up in their own neighborhoods. More and more people are purchasing their own gateways to this realm, but half of America's population still lives computer-free. Lou and his Speakeasy partners are justified in viewing themselves as enablers of free speech and education.

"They called cafés 'penny universities' back in England," Lou said. "People would come and discuss literature and philosophy and revolution. The French Revolution started in a café; stock markets actually started in a café in Turkey. They have always been a place where information gets exchanged, and the Internet is just an accoutrement to that.

"The whole idea of just having a public space is really disappearing," he continued. "Starbucks is not a public space. Their philosophy is to get the customer in and out within three minutes. They have a facade of having a café, but if you go into a Starbucks they're generally pretty cold. As much as they try to assume the flavor of whatever town you happen to be in, it really doesn't work, because you know it's Starbucks. It's a retail front for selling coffee, and more important, coffee cups and accessories. It's a branding thing—they create a certain notion of, Oh, I'm getting my coffee from a coffeehouse."

To many, Starbucks, the coffee-bar chain that originated in Seattle and now seems to be on every street corner in urban America, exemplifies the emptying out of bohemian iconography by the corporate machine. Lou has harsh words for that company—yet he also admits that he approached management to see if they'd be interested in putting some Speakeasy terminals in local franchises. (In a typical co-opting move, Starbucks declined, but later installed its own terminals, backed by the computer giant Intel.) When asked if he'd ever consider turning the Speakeasy's café concept into a chain, he admits he doesn't know. "Would I do it for a million dollars? Maybe, maybe not. If it meant having a summer abroad and getting paid, I might be convinced."

The café denizen in Lou disdains Starbucks for sterilizing a vital milieu, and for brewing coffee that's overroasted and bitter. But the businessman can't help but admire the nonthreatening environments the chain has created, perfect for tourists who want bohemian product without bohemian unpredictability.

"You walk into a Starbucks, and it feels good. It smells like coffee. And you know you're going to get your latte in two minutes. You walk into the Speakeasy, and you're going to be in a line. You have to deal with cigarette smoke and weird people. I personally prefer that. But if

I'm a temp worker who's got to be at my desk at nine o'clock in the morning, I might not."

The Speakeasy, with its creaky chairs, old sofas, cheap coffee, and diverse clientele, represents an aspect of bohemia worth preserving. But it's hardly a static space. Actually, it's always being invaded. Lou welcomes any stray temp workers who might happen in, and his partners have made sure to organize events that attract locals. Activists come for meetings and to programs like the forum "Elexion 96," which highlighted twentysomethings' political concerns. Arty types show up for poetry readings and experimental-film series. Movers and shakers in the high-tech world stop by for lunch or to take meetings. Computer nerds and travelers pop in to read their e-mail on the café's terminals.

Sometimes, though, the crowd at the Speakeasy isn't so good for business. A sizable chunk of the café's clientele is truly marginal—unwashed types who wouldn't last five minutes in a Starbucks. Dealing with them made Lou realize he's not always as high-minded as he'd like to be. "It's changed my thinking a lot about open, free access," he admitted. "We provide a free service; anyone can use these terminals. What's happened is that we've created this geek ghetto. All these guys who used to hang out at the library playing virtual-reality games are here now, and they're stinking up the place, drinking water. People structure their lives around not dealing with those kinds of people. If there's a homeless guy snickering at the screen, they don't really want to see that. On the other hand, we don't want to put timers on the terminals and start charging for them."

Facing the problems that have always haunted bohemia's proprietors—rowdy, poor customers with little money, some of whom may be geniuses but all of whom definitely scare off proper customers—Lou lives by a system of give-and-take. The easiest thing for him to do would be to close the café and become just another computer-industry entrepreneur, picking up his latte at the closest Starbucks on the way to his virtual office. But he believes that the florid heart of bohemia needs an earthly body to keep it beating, and that gathering places like the Speakeasy still serve that need best. So where does he land between Starbucks and the halfway house? It's a perpetual balancing act.

"I just don't buy this 'selling out' concept," he said. "I definitely have a product to sell that I want people to buy. My survival depends on it. Three years ago, I probably would not be talking this way. But now I

see why people in corporate America do. It's just articulating meanings
that you have to deal with. Words like 'product,' 'service,' 'value-
added,' and 'integrated marketing' have crept into my vocabulary.
There's no tension for me participating in the capitalist system because I
am no different than anybody else in this country. Whether they think
they're participating or not, they are.

"The tension occurs for me if I were to, say, be a cell-phone salesman,
or a car salesman, or any of those typically-picked-on-for-good-reason
professions. They are selling a product or service mostly with money in
mind, and there's no other reason behind it. I don't know what's going
to happen in the information industry; I could look at where it's going
and have some ideas, but it would change by next year. One thing,
though: I'm very interested in maintaining the space. The café's going to
be around for a while."

T H I S   I S   W H E R E   I   B E L O N G

Selling out sneaks up on you. Or you on it. You're inching along, taking
one logical step after another at work or in your relationships, and suddenly you find yourself all decked out in the trappings of the mainstream. Casual decisions add up until you're no longer sure whose
expectations you're fulfilling. You start to see the human side of people
you once despised on principle. You face many of the same problems
they do: a wish for security, a fear of irrelevance, a building sense that
your huge dreams don't matter as much as your everyday obligations.
What makes you better any more? What did you believe that made you
ever think you could distinguish yourself?

These questions drain the strength of too many dreamers as they
move toward a despair that they call waking up to reality. The regenera-
tive nature of bohemia, which keeps the underground speeding just
ahead of the mainstream it reflects, better preserves our culture than it
does the individuals who make it. Mastering the run-and-stretch rhythm
of survival as a sellout is very difficult, especially since few bohemians
speak up from the middle of this experience. Most of the ideas that have
guided us over the years, and especially recently, have come dressed in
that old spectacular edginess, even if their originators aren't quite so vir-
tuously rebellious in real life. True purists serve a purpose—they are the

guard that has protected bohemia throughout its various incarnations, witnessing its perennial death and resurrection and nurturing it through its fallow periods. But I am tired of the constant search for traitors. We are all Judases, because we all live in the bigger world that cradles and threatens our own.

These days, it's hard to recall how thrilling it can be to see how far those who leave the shelter of their bohemias can go. We have fallen back, toward the dark side of the cycle of breakthrough, negotiation, and exile. Corporate rock still sucks, and gay people still get bashed for holding hands on the street. The plentiful evidence that bohemian values have affected the mainstream—creating new frameworks for institutions like the family and the workplace, giving people different ways to deal with the consumer culture that engulfs them, opening up the cultural conversation about sex and drugs, and refiguring adulthood to better suit the actual shapes of people's lives—is often overlooked. Sometimes it feels as if we've been waiting to let the gloom wash over us, and mourn a utopia we could never bring ourselves to believe in.

In the face of this torpor, I want to propose a radical move. It's one I see people taking in their own lives all the time, one I've chronicled here in stories that are as private as they are exemplary. I suggest that bohemians embrace selling out—if selling out means moving out, into the culture at large, to risk being misunderstood by the mainstream, and to share our views with those perceived enemies who we expect will undermine us. Instead of despairing, let's see what we can accomplish. Pockets of our far-flung tribe have done this: queers have forged links between culture and politics; punks have built an independent economy. Now is the moment to look beyond the different particulars of our identities and see what we have in common. There are plenty of areas to explore, ones I haven't even touched on: the interracial bonds being created in the subcultures surrounding electronic dance music, for example, or the spiritual life of a generation that mixes Judaism with Zen. For too long we have united only within a culture of rebellion. What we need to refuse is the negativity that comes from always defining ourselves against a society we can't help but live within. It's time to stand up for what we are.

Because the shadow of the counterculture still looms, an example of how movements can be left unfinished and then corrupted, I know many people will regard my call to arms as facile. I readily admit that we can't count on a revolution, and I don't think we should anticipate a near future that looks drastically different from the confusion we live in now. That's why I've offered stories that would otherwise have gone by unnoticed—personal epiphanies and battles still raging, meaningless if you think only in terms of an impossible revolution, but crucial to the incremental process through which society actually changes. I advocate the advice of a common postcounterculture bumper sticker: "Think globally, act locally." The bohemian diaspora, as the critic C. Carr once called it, moves on all fronts. Whatever impact this bohemian epoch has had on the centers of power, it's undeniably affected at least one neighborhood in your town. You might even live there. And if you don't, if you still think bohemians are crazy throwbacks to an era when freedom seemed easier to grasp, look hard at yourself. You might find that in some corner of your wishful soul, you are weird like us.

ABOUT THE AUTHOR

Ann Powers, coeditor with Evelyn McDonnell of *Rock She Wrote: Women Write About Rock, Pop, and Rap,* has been writing about pop music for *The New York Times* since 1992. She was a senior editor for *The Village Voice* and an editor and writer for the *SF Weekly,* and her work has appeared in almost every major music publication, including *Spin, Rolling Stone,* and *Vibe.* Powers lives with her partner, Eric Weisbard, in Brooklyn, New York.